New Longman Literature

The Duchess of Malfi

John Webster

Volume Editor: Monica Kendall

Series Editor: John O'Connor

PEARSON

Longman

Edinburgh Gate
Harlow, Essex

Pearson Education Limited
Edinburgh Gate
Harlow
Essex
CM20 2JE
England and Associated Companies throughout the World

First published 2004

ISBN 978-0-582-81779-1

Acknowledgements
We are grateful to the following for permission to reproduce copyright
material:
Manchester University Press for the melodic bars from the 'Madmen's
Song' from the 'Revels Plays' edition of *The Duchess of Malfi* by John
Webster edited by John Russell Brown 1974 and Penguin Group (UK) for
the extract from the poem 'Ode 1.22 Integer vitae scelerisque purus...'
published in *The Complete Odes and Epodes with the Centennial Hymn*
by Horace translated by W.G. Shepherd © Penguin Classics 1983,
translation © W.G. Shepherd 1983.

We are grateful to the following for permission to reproduce photographs
and other copyright material:
Donald Cooper pages 20, 28, 90, 154, 178, 196; Fotomas Index page 229;
John Frost Historical Newspaper Service page 100; Guildhall Library,
Corporation of London page v; Ivan Kyncl/ArenaPAL pages 1, 48, 124,
134, 144, 170, 184, 222; Marilyn Kingwell/ArenaPAL page 92; John
Tramper/Shakespeare's Globe page 232; John Vere Brown/Theatre
Museum pages 66, 164.

Monica Kendall would like to thank the following directors and actors
involved in *The Duchess of Malfi* for illuminating conversations and their
time: Lorcan Cranitch (Bosola in the 2003 National Theatre production);
Philip Franks (director of the 1995 Greenwich/Wyndham's Theatres
production); Will Keen (Ferdinand in the 2003 National Theatre
production); and Phyllida Lloyd (director of the 2003 National Theatre
production).

Front cover: Donald Cooper/Photostage
Janet McTeer as the Duchess in the 2003
National Theatre production

Contents

Introduction

This book in the *New Longman Literature* series has been designed to meet the varied and complex needs of students who are making the transition from GCSE to AS level and then on to A level itself. Each feature – the *notes, commentaries, critical extracts* and *background information* – will help you to meet the new **Assessment Objectives** at both AS and A2 levels.

The textual notes

These in-depth notes, freshly written with the new-style examinations in mind, provide understandable explanations which are easily located on the page:
- **notes** are placed opposite the text with clear line references
- **explanations** of more complex words are given in context and help is provided with key imagery and historical references
- a **critical commentary**, which accompanies the textual notes, raises important critical and performance issues.

Background

There are detailed sections which help you to understand the relationship between this play and others, as well as the cultural and historical contexts in which it was written. You will find sections on:
- the **date** of the play, its **sources**, and where it was first performed
- Webster's life and career
- key dates
- **playhouses** connected with this play
- other relevant **plays** of the period
- the **social and historical background** to this particular play.

Critical context

In your exam you will be required to express your own opinions, taking into account other readers' interpretations. This mini **critical anthology** provides you with extracts from the key critical works on the play in question, from the earliest essays to the most recent studies. There is also a suggested **Further reading** list with brief explanations of what each title is about.

Performance

A unique feature of this book are the exclusive **interviews** with four professional directors and actors who have recently worked on this play: at the National Theatre and on tour (2003), directed by Phyllida Lloyd, with Janet McTeer as the Duchess; and at Greenwich and Wyndham's Theatres, London (1995), directed by Philip Franks, with Juliet Stevenson as the Duchess. There are also many references to the production by Cheek by Jowl which was also at the Wyndham's Theatre, London and on tour (1995–6), directed by Declan Donnellan, with Anastasia Hille as the Duchess. There is also a description of the **performance history** of the play.

Note

This edition of the text of *The Duchess of Malfi* is largely based on the edition by Brian Gibbons (New Mermaids, A&C Black, 4th edition, 2001). Note that in the 1623 quarto, the printer placed entrances and exits all together at the beginning of each scene; later editors have placed them at appropriate places during each scene; theatrical productions make their own decisions on when an actor enters or exits.

Part of the map attributed to Ralph Agas c. 1562, one of the few maps that show the Blackfriars friary (1); (2) Middle Temple; (3) St Sepulchre's Church and Newgate prison; (4) the Webster coachmaking business and childhood home; (5) Smithfield market and St Bartholomew's hospital; (6) site of Red Bull theatre; (7) Barber-Surgeons' Hall (see page 236); (8) St Paul's Cathedral

Date and first performances

'*The Tragedy of the Dutchesse of Malfy*' by John Webster was first performed in 1613 or 1614. We know this because of the names of the actors that unusually accompanied the first printing of the play in 1623: William Ostler, who first played Antonio, is known to have died on 12 December 1614.

The title page of the first printing of the play in 1623 in 'quarto' (a cheap pocket-size edition) states that the tragedy was 'Presented privatly, at the Black-Friers; and publiquely at the Globe, By the Kings Maiesties Seruants'. The type for 'the Black-Friers' is much larger, therefore it must have opened at the smaller indoor theatre, the Blackfriars, leased by the King's Men, and was later also performed at the outdoor Globe. The Blackfriars theatre was on the far western side of the City of London, between the city wall and the Thames. According to the title page the play had to be cut for performance, but the published version was: 'The perfect and exact Coppy, with diverse things Printed, that the length of the Play would not beare in the Presentment.' It is possible that different cuts were made to suit the two very different theatres.

There are no contemporary plans or drawings of the Blackfriars; the sixteenth-century map on page v shows its location. The photograph is of the reconstructed Globe which was built in the 1990s, on the south bank of the Thames, near the site of the original Globe. It shows a performance of *The Tempest*, written by Shakespeare only about two years before *The Duchess*, and probably also performed at both theatres.

The reconstructed Globe

Characters in the play

THE DUCHESS OF MALFI
FERDINAND, DUKE OF CALABRIA, *her twin brother*
THE CARDINAL, *her elder brother*

BOSOLA, *spy employed by Ferdinand, later Provisor of the Horse to the Duchess*

ANTONIO BOLOGNA, *Master of the Household to the Duchess, later her secret husband*
DELIO, *his friend, based at Ferdinand/the Cardinal's court*

CARIOLA, *waiting woman to the Duchess*
JULIA, *wife of Castruchio, later mistress of the Cardinal*

CASTRUCHIO, *old man, husband of Julia*
SILVIO
RODERIGO
GRISOLAN
}
courtiers to the Duchess and Cardinal

OLD LADY, *a midwife*
COUNT MALATESTE
MARQUIS OF PESCARA
TWO PILGRIMS
DOCTOR

Servants, officers, children of the Duchess and Antonio, attendants, churchmen, guards, madmen, executioners, echo

The play is set in Italy in the early sixteenth century: Acts 1–4 take place in Malfi (Amalfi), in Rome and the pilgrimage shrine of Loretto; Act 5 is set in Milan.

Antonio and the Duchess (Charles Edwards and Janet McTeer) marry, as Cariola (Sally Rogers) watches: 1.1.480–493 (National Theatre, 2003)

1.1 *The location is the presence chamber of the Duchess at Malfi (Amalfi) near Naples, Italy, in 1504. Delio greets his friend Antonio, master of the household, who praises the French court*

1 **your country** the Kingdom of Naples

3 **formal** in outward appearance *(i.e. Antonio himself has not changed)*

habit clothes

5–22 **In...foresee** *This is a traditional, ideal picture of the state governed by a rational prince with the aid of learned and truthful counsellors. Webster took much of it from* The Image of Governance *(1541) by Sir Thomas Elyot.*

5 **reduce** restore; bring back (from error)

state the ruling class

7 **quits** rids

7–9 **quits...persons** *This may not be a topical reference to the French court but instead what Webster wanted to happen at the English court, which contained obsequious yes-men and was run by King James's favourite, Robert Carr (see page 234).*

8 **sycophants** (1) slanderers; (2) parasites

9–10 **which...heaven** *i.e.* the King respectfully (**sweetly**) regards the work he has done

on making the court a better place as God's work rather than his own

12–13 **whence...drops** from which there should flow pure, precious drops of water *(i.e. the courtiers should be free from corruption)*

13 **in general** (1) in all respects; (2) to everyone

13–14 **but...head** but if it happens that a malignant person poisons the fountain *(i.e. the court)* near the source of the water *(i.e. the king)*

17 **provident council** wise counsellors

freely frankly

23 **gall** (1) a bitter secretion of the liver: bile *(so someone who is bitter)*; (2) a person or thing that harasses or annoys; (3) a sore produced by rubbing

railing use of abusive language *(with the idea of changing the person you rail at)*

24 **piety** religiousness; devoutness

27 **envious** malicious

29 **I...still** *Bosola's first line is echoed in the last scene (5.5.5–8).*

Antonio

2 In Webster's source, Antonio was a gentleman of Naples and Master of Household to Frederick, King of Naples. In 1501 the French and Spanish invaded and expelled the King. Antonio followed him into exile. The King of Spain then ruled Naples through a viceroy.

4–22 The speech is dramatic irony. Not only will Antonio himself destroy the *fixed order*, but as an adviser to a prince (the Duchess) he fails in his duty to *inform them*. The imagery of 'seeing' and 'blindness' is significant at the end of this scene (1.1.413–417).

Ideas and interpretations

11–22 'In the context of the Jacobean court, at the height of James's extravagance, this is an extremely contemporary political intervention, and we should remember that James I did not call a parliament from 1610 to 1621 except in 1614, the year of *The Duchess*...[the play's] warning of the corruption which flows from the existence of power, is made central to the vision of the play as a whole' (R S White).

Bosola

22–23 There is dramatic irony in the way Webster has finished Antonio's speech at a half line completed by the mention of Bosola. The stress in Bosola is on the first syllable. He is the *court-gall*, the court satirist, the malcontent – a character who appears frequently in plays of this period.

Act 1

Scene 1

Enter ANTONIO and DELIO.

DELIO You are welcome to your country, dear Antonio;
You have been long in France, and you return
A very formal Frenchman in your habit.
How do you like the French court?

ANTONIO   I admire it:
In seeking to reduce both state and people   5
To a fixed order, their judicious king
Begins at home, quits first his royal palace
Of flatt'ring sycophants, of dissolute
And infamous persons – which he sweetly terms
His Master's masterpiece, the work of heaven –   10
Consid'ring duly that a prince's court
Is like a common fountain, whence should flow
Pure silver drops in general, but if't chance
Some cursed example poison't near the head,
Death and diseases through the whole land spread.   15
And what is't makes this blessed government
But a most provident council, who dare freely
Inform him the corruption of the times?
Though some o'th'court hold it presumption
To instruct princes what they ought to do,   20
It is a noble duty to inform them
What they ought to foresee. Here comes Bosola,

Enter BOSOLA.

The only court-gall; yet I observe his railing
Is not for simple love of piety,
Indeed he rails at those things which he wants,   25
Would be as lecherous, covetous, or proud,
Bloody, or envious, as any man,
If he had means to be so. Here's the Cardinal.

Enter CARDINAL.

BOSOLA I do haunt you still.

CARDINAL   So.

1.1   *Bosola reminds the Cardinal that he served in the galleys after his last job for him, but the Cardinal ignores him and Bosola complains to Antonio and Delio*

31–32   **Miserable...it** *i.e. nowadays, there is no reward for doing well*

31   **only...reward** the only reward

34   **galleys** large sailing vessels with banks of oars *(used by all powerful Mediterranean states; the rowers were often slaves or convicted criminals, who might spend all their lives at the oars; see lines 72–76 and 221–222)*

35–37   **I...mantle** *sarcastic: 'Bosola gives mock dignity to poverty and hardship' (John Russell Brown).*

37   **mantle** sleeveless cloak *(worn by ancient Romans and by some dignitaries in the Roman Catholic Church)*

38   **blackbirds...weather** *perhaps from Bishop Joseph Hall's* Epistles *(1611) which describe men who have 'grown wealthy with war, like those fowls which fatten with hard weather'; Bosola may also be dressed in black*

39   **dog days** (1) a time of unhealthy hot weather in August/September, when the sun is near the dog-star Sirius *(contrasting with* **hard weather***)*; (2) a contemptuous reference to the 'dogs' of the court *('dog' is a term of abuse in the Bible and Shakespeare etc.)*

42–44   **I...them** *adapted from the* Essays *by the French writer Michel de Montaigne (1533–92), translated into English in 1603*

43   **arrant knaves** notorious rogues *(with pun on the variant spelling 'errant' = travelling)*

51   **standing** stagnant

52–53   **crows...caterpillars** *often applied to people who use or prey on others (***pies** *= magpies)*

54   **panders** (1) go-betweens in illicit love affairs; (2) those who help others commit evil acts

55   **horse-leech** blood-sucker *(these worms were used to draw blood from people)*

57   **dependences** depending on someone else; subjection *(with wordplay on the hanging horse-leech)*

59   **Tantalus** *mythological Greek king punished in Hades: plunged up to his chin in a river he was always thirsty since the water receded whenever he tried to drink; and always hungry since above him hung fruit from a tree that he could not reach; proverbial figure of someone always hopeful and always disappointed*

62   **service...hazards** *wordplay:* (1) from the game of real tennis (see note to 5.4.54–55): the **service** side of the net, and the **hazard** side of the net; (2) 'to hazard' was also, literally: to put to the risk of being lost in a game of chance *(an apt verb here in connection with* **limbs in a battle** *– the verb was taken from the noun 'hazard', a game of luck at dice with arbitrary rules)*

64   **geometry** *to 'hang by geometry' was a proverbial phrase; there is also a comparison between* **geometry** *= a pair of compasses, and a man on* **crutches** *(line 68)*

supportation (1) physical support *(for his limbs)*; (2) means of living

---

Performance

John Lowin was the first Bosola in 1613/14. He was in his late thirties and had already played Falstaff in Shakespeare's *Henry IV* plays and the title character in Ben Jonson's play *Volpone*. The first Cardinal was Henry Condell, a leading actor with the King's Men. He and his colleague John Heminges famously later gathered together Shakespeare's plays for publication in 1623, known today as the First Folio.

4

BOSOLA	I have done you
	Better service than to be slighted thus. 30
	Miserable age, where only the reward
	Of doing well is the doing of it.

CARDINAL You enforce your merit too much.

BOSOLA I fell into the galleys in your service, where for
two years together I wore two towels instead of a 35
shirt, with a knot on the shoulder, after the fashion
of a Roman mantle. Slighted thus? I will thrive
some way: blackbirds fatten best in hard weather,
why not I, in these dog days?

CARDINAL Would you could become honest. 40

BOSOLA With all your divinity, do but direct me the way
to it. I have known many travel far for it, and yet
return as arrant knaves as they went forth, because
they carried themselves always along with them.

Exit CARDINAL.

Are you gone? Some fellows, they say, are 45
possessed with the devil, but this great fellow
were able to possess the greatest devil and make
him worse.

ANTONIO He hath denied thee some suit?

BOSOLA He and his brother are like plum trees that grow 50
crooked over standing pools: they are rich, and
o'erladen with fruit, but none but crows, pies and
caterpillars feed on them. Could I be one of their
flatt'ring panders, I would hang on their ears like
a horse-leech till I were full, and then drop off. 55
I pray leave me. Who would rely upon these
miserable dependences, in expectation to be
advanced tomorrow? What creature ever fed worse
than hoping Tantalus? Nor ever died any man
more fearfully than he that hoped for a pardon? 60
There are rewards for hawks and dogs when they
have done us service, but for a soldier that hazards
his limbs in a battle, nothing but a kind of
geometry is his last supportation.

66 **pair of slings** cloth (or leather straps) suspended around the neck to support two broken arms

67–68 **swing...crutches** *continuing the idea of the soldier returned from war with broken or missing limbs, going from one hospital to another in the vain hope of getting treatment*

72 **seven...galleys** *see lines 34–37*

74 **suborned it** procured the murder by secret means

75–76 **Gaston...Naples** *Gaston de Foix (1489–1512) was, however, too young in 1501*

78 **melancholy** *believed to be a mental disease caused by too much 'black bile', or a pose affected by some who were unhappy at their lack of advancement*

80–82 **If...action** if it's true what people say, that too much sleep impairs the essential part of a person (just as rust corrodes metal), then it follows that inactivity

82 **want of action** (1) unemployment; (2) lack of military action *(see also 93–94, and Bosola's commitment to* **action** *at 4.2.373 and 5.5.10)*

83 **black malcontents** *The word 'malcontent' was coined in the sixteenth century to describe people who were dissatisfied with society; those with melancholy tended to wear black clothes (like Hamlet).*

close rearing being reared in secret *(those who were melancholy tended to keep apart from other people)*

84 **do...wearing** they do damage because (1) *(moths)* the clothes haven't been worn; (2) *(malcontents)* they haven't been employed

85 **presence** presence chamber: the public room near a monarch's private rooms *(the 1623 quarto, and some modern editions of the play, start a new scene here)*

89 **Calabrian** *Calabria is the mountainous region in the south of Italy.*

90 **took the ring** *Taking 'the ring' had replaced the more dangerous jousting. It was a sport where horse riders competed to carry a suspended ring away on their lance. Thus it is also a sexual metaphor.*

Bosola

76–77 Antonio's comment on Bosola being *neglected* is perceptive: see 4.2.327 and 5.5.87, and also note to 3.2.288. 'In examining Bosola's "neglect", Webster offers us the first tragic figure whose isolation is formulated in terms of employment by another' (Frank Whigham).

76–84 Antonio seems to be contradicting what he said about Bosola earlier (22–28), but perhaps Delio's information that Bosola had spent *seven years in the galleys* changes Antonio's view of the man. In the 2003 National Theatre production, Delio suddenly realised (*I knew this fellow...*: 72) that he had heard about Bosola before. But Antonio's speech is also an example of dramatic irony, since Bosola's *goodness* will be poisoned by employment (spying on the Duchess) not unemployment *(want of action)*.

Language

90 *ring*: Ferdinand's first line is heavy with dramatic irony, as shown when the Duchess later uses her wedding ring to help Antonio's eyesight and to marry him (1.1.408–419); the ring is forced off by the Cardinal in the dumbshow (3.4.35–36), and given by Ferdinand to the Duchess on a dead man's hand (4.1.43–49). It is also the term used for the cord by which Cariola is strangled (4.2.248). The word also has sexual undertones.

| DELIO | Geometry? | 65 |

BOSOLA   Ay, to hang in a fair pair of slings, take his latter
swing in the world upon an honourable pair of
crutches, from hospital to hospital. Fare ye well sir;
and yet do not you scorn us, for places in the court
are but like beds in the hospital, where this man's   70
head lies at that man's foot, and so lower, and lower.

Exit BOSOLA.

DELIO   I knew this fellow seven years in the galleys
For a notorious murder, and 'twas thought
The Cardinal suborned it. He was released
By the French general, Gaston de Foix,   75
When he recovered Naples.

ANTONIO   'Tis great pity
He should be thus neglected, I have heard
He's very valiant. This foul melancholy
Will poison all his goodness, for, I'll tell you,
If too immoderate sleep be truly said   80
To be an inward rust unto the soul,
It then doth follow, want of action
Breeds all black malcontents, and their close
     rearing,
Like moths in cloth, do hurt for want of wearing.

Enter CASTRUCHIO, SILVIO, RODERIGO and GRISOLAN.

DELIO   The presence 'gins to fill. You promised me   85
To make me the partaker of the natures
Of some of your great courtiers.

ANTONIO   The Lord Cardinal's
And other strangers, that are now in court,
I shall. Here comes the great Calabrian Duke.

Enter FERDINAND.

| FERDINAND | Who took the ring oft'nest? | 90 |

| SILVIO | Antonio Bologna, my lord. |

Antonio is awarded the prize as winner of the horse-riding competition. Ferdinand passes the time with courtly conversation

93 **jewel** *sexual wordplay, as with* **ring** *(see note to line 90): it can stand for virginity; married chastity; sexual organs*

94 **sportive** (1) of the nature of amorous sport; chivalric entertainment; (2) not serious; light

fall to action (1) *more sexual wordplay;* (2) *actual warfare*

95–107 *probably from Painter's* Palace of Pleasure *(see page 237)*

97 **gravity** seriousness

104 **office** function; business

108 **thy wife** Julia *(this is the first mention of the character regarded by some as the foil to the Duchess; Julia appears in 2.4 and Act 5)*

fighting *wordplay:* (1) fighting in war; (2) sexual encounters

110 **broke** made; related

113 **children of Ismael** Arabs *(Ishmael was the son of Abraham and the Egyptian Hagar; see the Bible, Genesis 21.9–21. This may be a printer's error for 'Israel' – in the Old Testament the children of Israel are often referred to as living in tents.)*

in tents *wordplay:* (1) canvas shelters; (2) surgical dressings; (3) intentions

116–118 **drawn...put up** *obvious sexual 'double entendres', particularly directed against Castruchio as a cuckold (see note below)*

120 **Spanish jennet** small, light horse often used in sport *(King James was given a jennet of which he was very proud. Knowing how much James demanded flattery, the Earl of Suffolk advised a friend to admire the jennet extravagantly, and tell the King that the horse 'is worthy to be bestridden by Alexander; that his eyes are fire...and a few more such fancies'.)*

Ferdinand in performance

The part of Ferdinand was created by Richard Burbage, renowned for his portrayals of Hamlet and King Lear – characters who also go mad. Burbage was also the first to play Othello, and his audiences must have been vividly aware of the parallels between *Othello* and *The Duchess* (see page 239).

Ideas and interpretations

93–107 'Military heroism is evoked only in brief allusions and associated with the Cardinal, Ferdinand, and their savage, discontented henchman Bosola' (Mary Beth Rose) (e.g. see 3.3 and 3.4). She describes the tournament which Antonio won (90–93) as a 'nostalgic' exercise, 'staged by servant courtiers for the amusement of their betters' and says 'Webster is dramatising an anachronistic neofeudal regime in the process of decline' [i.e. it's a regime based on out-of-date, medieval feudalism – in which the relationship between nobles and their subjects was based on service, not money]. She adds that the play shows a 'crisis of the aristocracy'.

Castruchio

114–118 The name of this old lord, Julia's husband, suggests he is impotent ('castrated'). It seems well known to the court that he is a cuckold; in the 2003 National Theatre production Ferdinand (Will Keen) here held up two fingers behind Castruchio's head (to indicate the 'horns' of the cuckold) for the other courtiers to laugh at. After his second, and last, appearance in 2.1 he follows Julia to Rome, where his sexual inadequacy is again made fun of – this time by Delio (2.4.53–56). He is the stock type of old man with a young, unfaithful, wife.

FERDINAND   Our sister Duchess' great master of her household?
Give him the jewel. When shall we leave this
sportive action and fall to action indeed?

CASTRUCHIO   Methinks, my lord, you should not desire   95
to go to war in person.

FERDINAND   Now for some gravity. Why, my lord?

CASTRUCHIO   It is fitting a soldier arise to be a prince,
but not necessary a prince descend to be a captain.

FERDINAND   No?   100

CASTRUCHIO   No, my lord, he were far better do it by a deputy.

FERDINAND   Why should he not as well sleep, or eat, by a
deputy? This might take idle, offensive, and base
office from him, whereas the other deprives
him of honour.   105

CASTRUCHIO   Believe my experience: that realm is never long in
quiet where the ruler is a soldier.

FERDINAND   Thou told'st me thy wife could not endure fighting.

CASTRUCHIO   True, my lord.

FERDINAND   And of a jest she broke of a captain she met full of   110
wounds – I have forgot it.

CASTRUCHIO   She told him, my lord, he was a pitiful fellow to
lie like the children of Ismael, all in tents.

FERDINAND   Why, there's a wit were able to undo all the
surgeons of the city: for although gallants   115
should quarrel, and had drawn their weapons, and
were ready to go to it, yet her persuasions would
make them put up.

CASTRUCHIO   That she would, my lord.

FERDINAND   How do you like my Spanish jennet?   120

RODERIGO   He is all fire.

122 **Pliny** *The Roman writer Pliny (AD 23–79; he is often called 'the Elder' because his nephew was also a writer) wrote thirty-seven books* On Natural History, *translated in 1601. He wrote that Portuguese mares conceive by the west wind 'instead of natural seed...and bring forth foals as swift as the wind'.*

123–124 **ballass'd...quicksilver** *wordplay: ballasted with mercury (a heavy material – ballast – like gravel was placed in ships to stop them capsizing; the horse is instead loaded with a precious, living –* **quick** *– material that itself runs quickly)*

125 **reels...tilt** *wordplay: (1) the ballast rights the tilt; (2) staggers back when riding in a tiltyard; (3) bawdy meaning: copulate (Roderigo and Grisolan may be laughing at the bawdy meaning)*

128 **touchwood** wood that catches fire easily

128–129 **take fire...fire** *This fire metaphor suggests (1) that his courtiers should not think or act independently; (2) that he can destroy them.*

129–130 **laugh when...witty** laugh only when I laugh even if the subject is very funny

132 **silly** (1) unsophisticated; (2) feeble-minded; imbecile *(this meaning connects logically to Ferdinand's next line)*

134–135 **fool...faces** *Monarchs and aristocrats kept fools in their households (Charles I's fool Muckle John was probably the last court fool in England); presumably Castruchio's fool is a mute.*

136 **my lady** Julia

142–143 **out of compass** (1) immoderately; (2) *wordplay on* **mathematical instrument**

143 **Milan** *about 400 miles north of Amalfi*

144 **Silvio** *He appears only once more, in 3.3 (in Rome).*

149 **Grecian horse** Trojan horse *(the huge wooden horse which the Greeks tricked the Trojans into believing was an offering to Minerva but was instead filled with armed men)*

Ferdinand

126–130 *Why do you laugh?:* This contrasts with Antonio's description of the ideal courtiers to a prince (16–22): Ferdinand wants them to be merely sycophants. Also, 'If Ferdinand silences bawdy laughter and yet speaks bawdily himself, his sexual awareness will seem the more private and dangerous to an audience' (John Russell Brown).

Performance

Directors often cut and rearrange the start of the play. In the 2003 National Theatre production, directed by Phyllida Lloyd, it began with Ferdinand and the court applauding Antonio as the winner of *the ring* (90) and the Duchess presenting him with a trophy. After Ferdinand (Will Keen) chillingly demanded *Why do you laugh?* (127), that scene froze, and Delio was warmly welcomed by Antonio (1–4). Delio then spoke the lines (some cut) admiring the French king (see page 255). In the 1995 Cheek by Jowl production directed by Declan Donnellan, Antonio (Matthew Macfadyen) climbed on stage and helped raise the curtain to reveal all the characters, motionless, the floor patterned like a chessboard. He walked round them until greeted by Delio. After Antonio's *I admire It* (4), Bosola rushed over to the Cardinal; the rest of Antonio's speech was cut.

FERDINAND   I am of Pliny's opinion, I think he was begot by
             the wind, he runs as if he were ballass'd with
             quicksilver.

SILVIO   True, my lord, he reels from the tilt often.   125

RODERIGO and GRISOLAN   Ha, ha, ha!

FERDINAND   Why do you laugh? Methinks you that are courtiers
             should be my touchwood, take fire when I give
             fire, that is, laugh when I laugh, were the subject
             never so witty.   130

CASTRUCHIO   True, my lord, I myself have heard a very good jest
             and have scorned to seem to have so silly a wit as
             to understand it.

FERDINAND   But I can laugh at your fool, my lord.

CASTRUCHIO   He cannot speak, you know, but he makes faces,   135
             my lady cannot abide him.

FERDINAND   No?

CASTRUCHIO   Nor endure to be in merry company, for she says
             too much laughing and too much company fills
             her too full of the wrinkle.   140

FERDINAND   I would then have a mathematical instrument
             made for her face, that she might not laugh out of
             compass. I shall shortly visit you at Milan,
             Lord Silvio.

SILVIO   Your grace shall arrive most welcome.   145

FERDINAND   You are a good horseman, Antonio; you have
             excellent riders in France: what do you think of
             good horsemanship?

ANTONIO   Nobly, my lord; as out of the Grecian horse issued
             many famous princes, so, out of brave   150
             horsemanship arise the first sparks of growing
             resolution that raise the mind to noble action.

FERDINAND   You have bespoke it worthily.

The widowed Duchess enters with her brother the Cardinal. Antonio describes the brothers to Delio

s.d. **Enter...CARIOLA** *The stress is on the second syllable.*

Enter....JULIA *She says nothing so in most productions she doesn't appear until Act 2; some editions have her entering after line 84, but references to her make it even odder that she doesn't speak.*

155 **come about** turned round *(presumably the brothers are returning to Rome by sea – about 100 miles north of Amalfi)*

159 **temper** temperament; character

brave fine; sociable

160 **Will...tennis** *Huge wagers were sometimes placed on games of real tennis (see also 5.4.54–55).*

crowns *in Britain, silver coins worth five shillings (25p)*

161 **single combats** duels

162 **flashes** *either* showy behaviour, *or* transient displays

163 **for form** outwardly

164 **melancholy churchman** religious hypocrite

164–165 **The spring...toads** *i.e. he looks like a good, wholesome man, but in reality he is loathsome*

spring fountain; stream; pool

165 **engend'ring** breeding *(with idea also of hatching evil plans)*

toads *applied to anyone or anything loathsome, repulsive, ugly (see Shakespeare's* Troilus and Cressida *2.3 where Ajax says: 'I do hate a proud man, as I do hate the engend'ring of toads.')*

166 **jealous** suspicious; mistrustful

167 **Hercules** *This mythical Greek hero had to undertake twelve superhuman tasks.*

168 **panders, intelligencers** go-betweens *(in sexual matters);* spies

169 **political** scheming; cunning

should would

174 **Some...done** *Perhaps Antonio means that the 'good' was in bribing so excessively that he, fortunately, did not become Pope.*

179–180 **If he...fashion** *i.e. if he laughed genuinely then pigs might fly*

180 **In quality** in character

181–182 **speaks...ears** *'does not say what he thinks, and pays no regard when asked for favours' (John Russell Brown)*

Cardinal and Ferdinand

162–164, 177–178 The brothers are like actors: their outer selves are not the same as their inner selves.

Enter CARDINAL, DUCHESS, CARIOLA, JULIA and attendants.

SILVIO	Your brother the Lord Cardinal, and sister Duchess.
CARDINAL	Are the galleys come about? 155
GRISOLAN	They are, my lord.
FERDINAND	Here's the Lord Silvio is come to take his leave.
DELIO	(*Aside to ANTONIO*) Now sir, your promise: what's

DELIO (*Aside to ANTONIO*) Now sir, your promise: what's
         that Cardinal? *character*   *sociable.*
      I mean his temper? They say he's a brave fellow,
      betting made Will play his five thousand crowns at tennis, dance, 160
      Court ladies, and one that hath fought single
         combats. *Duels*

ANTONIO Some such flashes superficially hang on him,
      for form, but observe his inward character: he is a
      melancholy churchman. The spring in his face is
      nothing but the engend'ring of toads. Where he is 165
      jealous of any man he lays worse plots for them
      than ever was imposed on Hercules, for he strews in
      his way flatterers, panders, intelligencers, atheists,
      and a thousand such political monsters. He should
      have been Pope, but instead of coming to it by the 170
      primitive decency of the Church, he did bestow
      bribes, so largely, and so impudently, as if he
      would have carried it away without heaven's
      knowledge. Some good he hath done.

DELIO You have given too much of him. What's his   175
      brother?

ANTONIO The Duke there? A most perverse and turbulent
         nature;
      What appears in him mirth is merely outside.
      If he laugh heartily, it is to laugh
      All honesty out of fashion.

DELIO   Twins?

ANTONIO   In quality.   180
      He speaks with others' tongues, and hears men's
         suits

1.1   *Antonio describes the Duchess, with obvious admiration, to his friend Delio*

182   **o'th'bench** on the (judge's) bench

184   **by information** merely by accusation

186–188   **foul...him** *This image of Ferdinand as a spider, his web as a prison, prefigures Act 4; the feeding image is echoed by the Duchess in her last words: 4.2.236.*

189   **shrewd turns** cunning tricks; malicious deeds

192   **oracles** divine revelations

194   **devil** *This word occurs frequently in the play in connection with Ferdinand and the Cardinal (e.g. 1.1.45–48; 5.5.49).*

196   **medals** *Commemorative medals were often issued of rulers.*

197   **figure** shape; mould

temper *wordplay:* (1) temperament; character; (2) *continuing with the 'casting' image:* degree of hardness or resilience in steel

201–202   **She held...her** *perhaps:* (you wish) that she thought less that talking a lot was such a worthless thing, than you thought it spiritually purifying to listen to her

201   **vainglory** excessive pride in what one does

204   **galliard** a quick, lively dance

205   **palsy** paralysis

207   **continence** abstaining from sex; chastity *(with wordplay on* **countenance***)*

208   **lascivious and vain** lustful and useless

209–211   **Her days...shrifts** *i.e. she is so virtuous that even when she is asleep she belongs to heaven more than other women who have just been to confession (in the Roman Catholic Church* **shrift** = confession to a priest, or the priest himself*)*

212–213   **Let...in her** *i.e. women should model themselves on her*

213   **Fie** *quite a strong word to express disapproval, reproach or even disgust at what someone has just said*

214   **wire-drawer** *literally:* someone who stretches metal to make wire; *figuratively:* someone who spins something out excessively *(i.e. Antonio has gone over the top with his praise)*

commendations (1) praises; (2) *ominously:* a Church office commending the souls of the dead to God *(Delio of course would not consciously mean this; see note to 217)*

215   **case** close *(see 3.2.138)*

217   **She stains...to come** *see note below* (**stains** = puts in the shade)

Language

217   This line is repeated by Webster in his funeral poem on Prince Henry (see page 233): 'Young, grave Maecenas of the noble arts, / Whose beams shall break forth from thy noble tomb, / Stain the time past, and light the time to come!' (Maecenas was the famous patron of the poets Virgil and Horace in Rome in the first century AD). It thus ominously links Antonio's comment to an epitaph on death, which Webster's audience may have been familiar with, but it also more positively beckons to some life beyond death – see 5.3.43–44. 'Antonio's eulogy of the Duchess supplies what will amount to a prophetic motto for the Echo scene' (Michael Neill). It is also of note that there are a number of references that Webster 'borrowed' which were originally applied to men, but used by Webster to refer to a woman, the Duchess.

With others' ears: will seem to sleep o'th'bench
Only to entrap offenders in their answers;
Dooms men to death, by information,
Rewards, by hearsay.

DELIO   Then the law to him   185
Is like a foul black cobweb to a spider,
He makes it his dwelling, and a prison
To entangle those shall feed him.

ANTONIO   Most true:
. He ne'er pays debts, unless they be shrewd turns,
And those he will confess that he doth owe.   190
Last: for his brother there, the Cardinal,
They that do flatter him most say oracles
Hang at his lips, and verily I believe them,
For the devil speaks in them;
But for their sister, the right noble Duchess,   195
You never fixed your eye on three fair medals
Cast in one figure, of so different temper.
For her discourse, it is so full of rapture
You only will begin then to be sorry
When she doth end her speech, and wish, in
      wonder,   200
She held it less vainglory to talk much
Than you penance, to hear her. Whilst she speaks,
She throws upon a man so sweet a look,
That it were able raise one to a galliard
That lay in a dead palsy, and to dote   205
On that sweet countenance; but in that look
There speaketh so divine a continence
As cuts off all lascivious and vain hope.
Her days are practised in such noble virtue
That sure her nights, nay more, her very sleeps,   210
Are more in heaven than other ladies' shrifts.
Let all sweet ladies break their flatt'ring glasses
And dress themselves in her.

DELIO   Fie, Antonio,
You play the wire-drawer with her commendations.

ANTONIO   I'll case the picture up, only thus much: 215
All her particular worth grows to this sum,
She stains the time past, lights the time to come.

1.1 *Antonio is asked to attend the Duchess in half an hour; Ferdinand asks his sister to give a court appointment to Bosola; the Cardinal tells Ferdinand that he should use Bosola as an informer on their sister*

218 **gallery** *The long hall that was a new feature in wealthy Elizabethan and Jacobean houses was used for exercise and to hang paintings in – it developed into the modern art gallery.*

220 **suit** petition

223 **h'is** he is

224 **provisorship...horse** *The office of provisor (supervisor) or Master of the Horse was a very prestigious position at court. King James's favourite, Robert Carr, was known to be trying to get this post in 1613.*

225 **Commends...him** recommends and promotes him

227 **Do us commend** send our greetings

228 **leaguer** military camp

229 **caroches** horse-drawn coaches *(Webster's family were coachmakers – see page 228; it was very fashionable to own or hire a coach – which caused traffic jams, more noise and dung, and even road rage!)*

230–231 **entertain...intelligence** hire Bosola as a spy

231 **I would...in't** *i.e. the Cardinal doesn't want to be seen to have any dealings with Bosola*

233 **court our furtherance** seek advancement from me

Duchess

220 The Duchess's first entrance is at 154; she doesn't speak until 220, and departs at 229. After Antonio's speeches in praise of her (195–213, 215–217), perhaps Webster wanted the audience to first have a tantalising glimpse of her. She is never given a personal name: 'Her private person is suppressed in her public role; we never meet Giovanna d'Aragona' (Muriel Bradbrook).

221–225 'To some sections of Malfi society, it seems that moral considerations are irrelevant...the Duchess does not demur at accepting a servant who has been in the galleys' (Martin Wiggins).

Duchess in performance

The first actor to play the Duchess was a teenage boy – it was not until after the restoration of the monarchy in 1660 that women began to appear on the English stage. The first printing of the play in 1623 gives us a name – Richard Sharpe; it is the first ever listing of actors in a published play. Little is known of him, and he may have played the role in the 1620s and not in 1613/14. Note that also there are very few plays in this period named solely after a woman. 'The gender dissonance [i.e. the sexual conflict] between the play's title role and the name of the actor who performed it [first] is all the more striking because the tragic protagonist here is a woman' (Dympna Callaghan).

Ideas and interpretations

230–231 'Webster introduces here the motif of hidden corruption that is to pervade the play' (Hereward T Price).

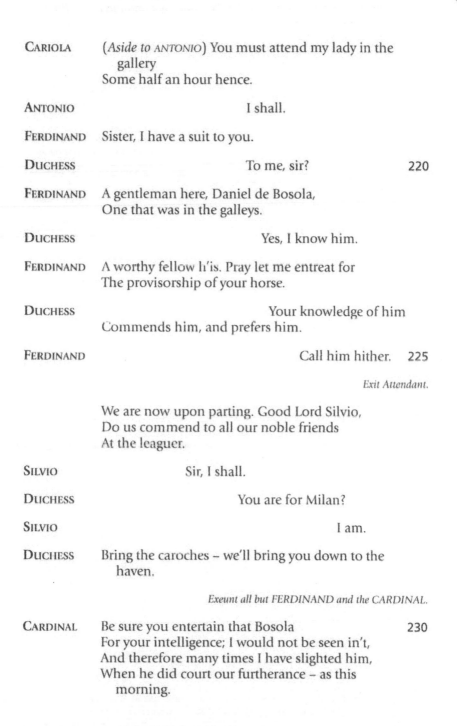

CARIOLA   (*Aside to* ANTONIO) You must attend my lady in the
         gallery
     Some half an hour hence.

ANTONIO   I shall.

FERDINAND   Sister, I have a suit to you.

DUCHESS   To me, sir?   220

FERDINAND   A gentleman here, Daniel de Bosola,
     One that was in the galleys.

DUCHESS   Yes, I know him.

FERDINAND   A worthy fellow h'is. Pray let me entreat for
     The provisorship of your horse.

DUCHESS   Your knowledge of him
     Commends him, and prefers him.

FERDINAND   Call him hither.   225

                            Exit Attendant.

     We are now upon parting. Good Lord Silvio,
     Do us commend to all our noble friends
     At the leaguer.

SILVIO   Sir, I shall.

DUCHESS   You are for Milan?

SILVIO   I am.

DUCHESS   Bring the caroches – we'll bring you down to the
     haven.

         Exeunt all but FERDINAND and the CARDINAL.

CARDINAL   Be sure you entertain that Bosola   230
     For your intelligence; I would not be seen in't,
     And therefore many times I have slighted him,
     When he did court our furtherance – as this
         morning.

Ferdinand suggests to his brother that Antonio would make a better informer than Bosola, but the Cardinal says Antonio is too honest. Ferdinand gives Bosola gold

237 **lured** *a metaphor from falconry: a hawk is recalled to the falconer by means of a lure (e.g. a bait); see note below*

240 **oblique character** asymmetrical feature *(possibly suggesting Bosola is ugly); and/or* sign of mental or moral perversity

241 **suspect** imagine something undesirable in a person

physiognomy the art of judging a person's character or destiny from the features of the face

242–243 **There's...urine** *i.e.* neither studying a person's face nor a sick person's urine will tell you anything about them *(see page 236)*

242 **credit** confidence; authority

244 **cozens** cheats; deceives

246 **take their times** take their time *(before trusting someone)*; choose when to act

247 **Distrust...deceived** *proverbial: 'he who trusts not is not deceived'*

251 **the next way** at the earliest opportunity

253–254 **Never rained...them** *Bosola refers to the myth of Danae and Jupiter (see note to 2.2.19–22); Jupiter was the king of the gods, whose weapon was thunder.*

Bosola

According to Frank Whigham, Webster links Bosola 'to the social problem of the veteran soldier, a stranger in his own land, dismissed from desert as well as from service. Then as now this figure was unprovided for' (see lines 29–39, 61–68, and note to 76–77). This may explain why he is the *court-gall* (23). (Lines 232–233 show that he has been pursuing the Cardinal for some time.)

Ideas and interpretations

237 Bosola's use of the word *lured* indicates that Ferdinand will control him just as the Cardinal later says he will control Julia (see note to 2.4.27–36). Both brothers are seen as hunters.

248 Ferdinand likens a great man to a cedar tree, which Bosola also does at 3.2.260: but there Bosola adds the image of the great man's counsellor/statesman – the spring – who helps nourish the great man/the cedar; Bosola hopes to be that nourishing servant but is neglected. This links up to the idea of the *provident council* that Antonio says rulers need (1.1.16–18), but which both Ferdinand, and King James, have dispensed with.

Language

247 There are many lines based on proverbs in this play. Hereward T Price comments: 'Elizabethan critics regarded them as an ornament of style, readers delighted in them, and poets would try to give pleasure by interweaving proverbs or reminiscences of proverbs into their work. Many figures that appear to be brilliant inventions turn out on inspection to be old proverbs', and he gives as an example 4.2.136–138: *Thou sleep'st...cat's ear.*

FERDINAND   Antonio, the great master of her household,
            Had been far fitter.

CARDINAL   You are deceived in him,   235
            His nature is too honest for such business.
            He comes. I'll leave you.

Enter BOSOLA.

                                        Exit CARDINAL.

BOSOLA   I was lured to you.

FERDINAND   My brother here, the Cardinal, could never
            Abide you.

BOSOLA   Never since he was in my debt.

FERDINAND   May be some oblique character in your face   240
            Made him suspect you?

BOSOLA   Doth he study physiognomy?
            There's no more credit to be given to th'face
            Than to a sick man's urine, which some call
            The physician's whore, because she cozens him.
            He did suspect me wrongfully.

FERDINAND   For that   245
            You must give great men leave to take their times:
            Distrust doth cause us seldom be deceived;
            You see, the oft shaking of the cedar tree
            Fastens it more at root.

BOSOLA   Yet take heed:
            For to suspect a friend unworthily   250
            Instructs him the next way to suspect you,
            And prompts him to deceive you.

FERDINAND   There's gold.

BOSOLA   So:
            What follows? Never rained such showers as these
            Without thunderbolts i'th'tail of them.
            Whose throat must I cut?   255

1.1 *Ferdinand tells Bosola the gold is payment for spying on the Duchess, as he doesn't want his sister to remarry. Bosola refuses to be an informer, but Ferdinand then offers him a position in the Duchess's household*

256 **post** in haste; faster *(the adverb comes from delivering post fast by relays of horses)*

257 **that** the gold

259 **particulars** personal relations

haviour behaviour

261 **best affects** likes best

265 **familiars** (1) household servants; (2) officers of the Inquisition of the Roman Catholic Church who arrested and imprisoned those accused; (3) *it was believed that witches had* **familiars**, *often in the shape of an animal, who did magical services for them*; (4) intimate friends

266 **quaint** clever; cunning

266–267 **invisible...intelligencer** *Bosola likens a spy to a witch's familiar (the latter was sometimes thought to have been given to a witch by the devil).*

269–270 **devils...angels** *Old English gold coins were called angels or angel-nobles because they had on them an image of the archangel Michael and a dragon.*

271 **impudent** shameless

277 **bounty** munificence; generosity

279 **ingratitude** *'ingratitude is monstrous' (Shakespeare:* Coriolanus *2.3)*

Ferdinand (Simon Russell Beale) and the Cardinal (Robert Demeger) warn the Duchess (Juliet Stevenson) against marrying in secret (Greenwich/Wyndham's Theatres, 1995)

Ferdinand

261–264 What is Ferdinand's motive for not wanting the Duchess to remarry? No one has believed Ferdinand's reason in 4.2 about *treasure* (280–284). Today it seems taken for granted that his motive derives from incestuous jealousy, but some critics have wondered if Webster knew Ferdinand's motive. James L Calderwood, however, says: 'it is Ferdinand who is unsure of himself, not Webster...Ferdinand's brusqueness here suggests a lack of self-awareness, not so much an irritation at being questioned as a failure ever to have asked himself the same question.'

Bosola

269–272 'Bosola cannot be said to be merely greedy for gain...we need to understand what more he wants' (Frank Whigham). This critic then suggests that Bosola longs for personal service – like the service Cariola gives the Duchess – which Ferdinand denies him, even though 'Bosola offers up to Ferdinand all he has' (see 4.2.327–332).

FERDINAND   Your inclination to shed blood rides post
Before my occasion to use you. I give you that
To live i'th'court here and observe the Duchess,
To note all the particulars of her haviour:
What suitors do solicit her for marriage   260
And whom she best affects. She's a young widow,
I would not have her marry again.

BOSOLA   No, sir?

FERDINAND   Do not you ask the reason, but be satisfied
I say I would not.

BOSOLA   It seems you would create me
One of your familiars.

FERDINAND   Familiar? What's that?   265

BOSOLA   Why, a very quaint invisible devil in flesh:
An intelligencer.

FERDINAND   Such a kind of thriving thing
I would wish thee: and ere long thou mayst arrive
At a higher place by't.

BOSOLA   Take your devils,
Which hell calls angels: these cursed gifts would
    make   270
You a corrupter, me an impudent traitor,
And should I take these they'd take me to hell.

FERDINAND   Sir, I'll take nothing from you that I have given.
There is a place that I procured for you
This morning, the provisorship o'th'horse.   275
Have you heard on't?

BOSOLA   No.

FERDINAND   'Tis yours: is't not worth thanks?

BOSOLA   I would have you curse yourself now, that your
    bounty,
Which makes men truly noble, e'er should make
Me a villain: oh, that to avoid ingratitude
For the good deed you have done me, I must do   280

Bosola agrees to accept the position and to inform Ferdinand about the Duchess. The Cardinal and Ferdinand, who are about to go back to Rome, give their sister advice about marrying again

282 **Candies** sugars

283 **complemental** a polite accomplishment; a refinement which completes a gentleman

284 **garb** (1) clothes *(black in the case of melancholy)*; (2) manner

285 **envy** feel a grudge against; have malevolent feelings towards

288 **politic** shrewd; cunning

289 **Feed...dish** dine at a lord's table

293 **creature** *i.e. he owes his position to Ferdinand; another example of animal imagery that pervades the play*

295–296 **Let...shame** a good name/reputation can only be got by a good person doing good deeds; a powerful well-paid job doesn't give a person a good name since it was probably obtained by a shameful bribe *(Ferdinand could turn away at line 294 so that these lines are an aside to the audience)*

297 **Sometimes...preach** sometimes the devil can teach a good moral message *(proverb: 'the devil sometimes speaks the truth')*

301 **promotion** advancement in rank

303 **high blood** noble descent *(Ferdinand then picks up on **blood** as: the seat of passion; sexual appetite)*

luxurious lecherous

304 **O fie!** *This expression of disgust could be directed at Ferdinand or the Duchess (see page 260).*

304–305 **Their...sheep** *from the Bible: Genesis 30.31–43: Jacob, twin of Esau, was sent to his uncle Laban to work as a shepherd. After twenty years he made a deal with Laban to divide up the sheep; goats and cattle based on spots; Laban tried to trick him, but Jacob ingeniously increased his share of the flock. He is seen as the ancestor of all the Israelites.*

304 **livers** seat of love and passion

Bosola

295–297 Bosola 'ironically voices an attitude which will more and more become a sign of the hypocritical court itself' (R S White). *Sometimes...preach:* either Bosola is commenting on the moralising maxim he has just stated, or on what Ferdinand has just said – or both.

Duchess

302–304 These lines suggest that the Cardinal would allow her to remarry as long as it is with *honour*, but Ferdinand rejects any idea of remarriage.

303–311 The 'lusty widow' (see 344) was a cultural stereotype. A tract against 'lewd' women published in 1615 declared: 'it is more easy for a young man or maid to forbear carnal acts than it is for a widow'. Ferdinand comments again on the apparent sexual voraciousness of women at 340–1 *(women like that part...).*

303–305 In this period a brother had authority over his sister, but it was seen as wrong to forbid a young widow from remarrying. Widows were a threat to male authority: they were economically independent and sexually experienced. Remarriage, however, might be an economic problem to her former husband's family and any children they had had.

All the ill man can invent. Thus the devil
Candies all sins o'er: and what heaven terms vile,
That names he complemental.

FERDINAND   Be yourself:
Keep your old garb of melancholy, 'twill express
You envy those that stand above your reach,   285
Yet strive not to come near 'em. This will gain
Access to private lodgings, where yourself
May, like a politic dormouse –

BOSOLA   As I have seen some
Feed in a lord's dish, half asleep, not seeming
To listen to any talk, and yet these rogues   290
Have cut his throat in a dream. What's my place?
The provisorship o'th'horse? Say then my
       corruption
Grew out of horse dung. I am your creature.

FERDINAND   Away!

BOSOLA   Let good men, for good deeds, covet good fame,   295
Since place and riches oft are bribes of shame.
Sometimes the devil doth preach.

                                                    Exit BOSOLA.

Enter CARDINAL and DUCHESS.

CARDINAL   We are to part from you, and your own discretion
Must now be your director.

FERDINAND   You are a widow:
You know already what man is, and therefore   · 300
Let not youth, high promotion, eloquence –

CARDINAL   No, nor any thing without the addition, honour,
Sway your high blood.

FERDINAND   Marry? They are most luxurious
Will wed twice.

CARDINAL   O fie!

FERDINAND   Their livers are more spotted
Than Laban's sheep.

Ferdinand and the Cardinal warn their sister against any thought of marrying in secret

309 **motion** impulse; inclination; emotion

312 **rank** (1) grossly fertile, lustful; (2) corrupt, festering; (3) *wordplay:* social position

313 **honey-dew** *literally:* a sweet substance that forms on leaves; *so:* something that is ideally sweet

314 **poison your fame** *This recalls Antonio's lines above (11–15) and is one of the main themes of the play.*

   cunning (1) crafty; (2) having magical knowledge *(which connects with his next lines)*

315 **they...hearts** those women whose faces disguise what they really feel

316 **witches** *see note to 3.1.78*

   ere...years before they reach the age of twenty

317 **give...suck** *It was believed that a witch had a teat on her body so that her familiar – often in the shape of an animal – could suck her blood for nourishment.*

318 **Hypocrisy** *appearing to be virtuous or good while hiding your real character*

319 **Subtler...engine** finer than Vulcan's device *(in Roman mythology the god Vulcan trapped his wife Venus and the god Mars in a net as they made love; he is thus a patron of cuckolds)*

321 **flatter** happily delude

323 **Under...night** *This phrase was connected with bats and owls and secrecy, as in Thomas Dekker's anti-Catholic play Whore of Babylon (1607): 'Fly with the bat under the eaves of night'.*

324–326 **irregular...backward** *the crab seems to look one way and go another; see Hamlet's remark to Polonius (2.2): 'yourself, sir, shall grow old as I am...if like a crab you could go backward'*

328 **executed** *wordplay:* (1) legally carried out; (2) put to death

Duchess

308 In the 1623 quarto there is a colon after *marry,* which often means a full stop. But the colon might instead mean that the Duchess was interrupted by the Cardinal before she had a chance to qualify her statement. Webster may not have intended her to tell a blatant lie.

Ideas and interpretations

324–326 James L Calderwood says that the *irregular crab* image 'is essentially an argument from Degree: the reliance upon private choice, especially when that choice descends upon an inferior, constitutes an infringement of the rigidly established social hierarchy'.

327–332 Michael Neill points to these lines as one of many 'prolepses' that prepare us for the Duchess's death in Act 4 (a prolepsis is a figurative device that indicates what is going to happen). See also the Language note on page 30.

DUCHESS	Diamonds are of most value 305
	They say, that have passed through most jewellers'
	hands.

FERDINAND   Whores, by that rule, are precious.

DUCHESS   Will you hear me?
I'll never marry.

CARDINAL   So most widows say,
But commonly that motion lasts no longer
Than the turning of an hourglass: the funeral
  sermon,   310
And it, end both together.

FERDINAND   Now hear me:
You live in a rank pasture here, i'th'court.
There is a kind of honey-dew that's deadly:
'Twill poison your fame. Look to't. Be not cunning:
For they whose faces do belie their hearts   315
Are witches ere they arrive at twenty years,
Ay, and give the devil suck.

DUCHESS   This is terrible good counsel.

FERDINAND   Hypocrisy is woven of a fine small thread
Subtler than Vulcan's engine: yet, believe't,
Your darkest actions, nay, your privat'st thoughts,   320
Will come to light.

CARDINAL   You may flatter yourself
And take your own choice: privately be married
Under the eaves of night.

FERDINAND   Think't the best voyage
That e'er you made, like the irregular crab
Which, though't goes backward, thinks that it goes
  right   325
Because it goes its own way; but observe:
Such weddings may more properly be said
To be executed than celebrated.

CARDINAL   · The marriage night
Is the entrance into some prison.

The Cardinal leaves; Ferdinand threatens his sister with their father's dagger. After he has gone, however, the Duchess says she is determined to marry again

330 **heavy** sorrowful

331 **do forerun** are the precursor of

mischief misfortune

333 **studied** rehearsed

334 **roundly off** fluent; glib

335 **my...poniard** *Michael Neill comments that the 'sexual innuendo of Ferdinand's threats is underlined by the explicitly phallic menace' of the poniard (dagger). See also 3.2.70 and 149–153.*

336 **rusty** *i.e. by being used*

337 **chargeable revels** expensive celebrations *(the Duchess has provided lavish entertainments for her brothers' visit to her court just like those provided at James I's court)*

338–339 **visor...goodness** *Wordplay on* **visor** *(mask) and* **masque** *(a dramatic performance at court; see page 238) shows Ferdinand's unease about the*

sexual activities of people at masked entertainments (see also 4.2.103–105).

340–342 **women like...tongue** *The Duchess thinks at first he means a penis;* **lamprey** = eel-like fish.

343 **neat knave** elegant rogue

smooth agreeable

tale *wordplay:* (1) story; (2) penis

347 **foot-steps** steps *(up to the altar for the wedding)*

349 **apprehending** anticipating with fear

351 **assay** attempt

352 **old wives** *'Old wives' tales' are trivial or superstitious stories supposedly spread by old women; see also note below.*

353 **I winked** (1) I shut my eyes to something improper; (2) I gave a glance of sexual invitation

---

Duchess in performance

333–335 In the 2003 National Theatre production, Ferdinand (Will Keen) got a small dagger out from his jacket which the Duchess (Janet McTeer) shrugged off without much fear: as if she had seen him do this before. In the 1995 Cheek by Jowl production, the Duchess (Anastasia Hille) lit a cigarette, smacked her brother's face, and when he flourished the dagger at her she seized it from him and then threw it back (see cartoon on page 100).

Ferdinand

334–344 'The reference to his father suggests that Ferdinand is invoking some notion of family honour, but the remainder of the speech, together with the physical image of Ferdinand holding the dagger, dramatises the sexual aggression of his remarks' (Kathleen McLuskie); she adds that his 'dirty-minded joke' (at 340–342) 'suggests an obsessive hatred of sexuality which sees all courtship as deception'.

Duchess

345–353 This speech has 'the unmistakably male tone of the Renaissance hero' (Frank Whigham) (see also note to 363–365). Judith Haber, however, says that Whigham misses the significance of *old wives*, which is a 'crucial' phrase: 'the effect of juxtaposing the heroic lines that build to a crescendo in the description of "this dangerous venture" with the blunt statement that follows...seems inescapably comic' – 'old wives are despised because of class, gender, age, and lack of education...and their frivolous, fabulous tales are conventionally opposed to the knowledge of learned men' – the Duchess is instead mocking conventional heroic values.

FERDINAND   And those joys,
Those lustful pleasures, are like heavy sleeps   330
Which do forerun man's mischief.

CARDINAL   Fare you well.
Wisdom begins at the end: remember it.

Exit CARDINAL.

DUCHESS   I think this speech between you both was studied,
It came so roundly off.

FERDINAND   You are my sister.
This was my father's poniard: do you see?   335
I'd be loath to see't look rusty, 'cause 'twas his.
I would have you to give o'er these chargeable
            revels;
A visor and a masque are whispering rooms
That were ne'er built for goodness. Fare ye well –
And women like that part which, like the lamprey,   340
Hath ne'er a bone in't.

DUCHESS   Fie sir!

FERDINAND   Nay,
I mean the tongue: variety of courtship.
What cannot a neat knave with a smooth tale
Make a woman believe? Farewell, lusty widow.

Exit FERDINAND.

DUCHESS   Shall this move me? If all my royal kindred   345
Lay in my way unto this marriage
I'd make them my low foot-steps, and even now,
Even in this hate, as men in some great battles,
By apprehending danger have achieved
Almost impossible actions – I have heard soldiers
            say so –   350
So I, through frights and threat'nings will assay
This dangerous venture. Let old wives report
I winked and chose a husband.

Enter CARIOLA.

1.1

The Duchess tells her waiting woman (Cariola) to conceal herself and listen to what takes place between herself and Antonio, the master of her household

355 **fame** reputation *(see e.g. note to 1.1.463–465)*

357 **warily** carefully; watchfully

358–359 **Thy...hearty** your solemn affirmation is clever and sincere

361 **arras** tapestry *(which hung on the Jacobean stage in front of the discovery space/the middle entrance on to the stage from backstage)*

362 **speed** luck; fortune

363–365 **For I am...guide** *The Duchess again uses the language of the male hero (see note to 345–353). In Greek mythology, Theseus was given a ball of thread by Ariadne to help guide him through the paths of a labyrinth,* where the hybrid monster, the Minotaur, was hidden. The story is in Metamorphoses by the Roman poet Ovid (43 BC–AD 17).

364 **clew** ball of thread *(figuratively: something that guides one through a maze or difficulty – the original meaning of 'clue')*

369 **triumphs** public festivities; tournaments

370 **husbands** stewards; managers of a household *(as well as the normal meaning)*

373 **for your sake** (1) thanks to you; (2) for love of you

The Duchess (Anastasia Hille) gives Antonio (Matthew Macfadyen) her wedding ring: 1.1.407–417 (Cheek by Jowl, 1995–6)

Performance

361 There are several occasions in the play where people hide to watch what is going on (e.g. in 3.2 and 5.2). In the 2003 National Theatre production Cariola went behind the glass screen which also served as the screen for projections.

Duchess and Antonio

367 In the same production there was a long pause before the Duchess said *What did I say?* – she was wondering how to begin; meanwhile it was clear that Antonio enjoyed being with her. At *large expense* (369) he nodded in sympathy, both knowing how much it had cost to entertain her brothers; *beauteous excellence* (372) was said with obvious admiration, flirting, though knowing his place as her steward. After *I look young for your sake* (373) she quickly stopped herself – had she said to much? – and tried to explain it away (374).

Cariola,
To thy known secrecy I have given up
More than my life, my fame.

CARIOLA   Both shall be safe: 355
For I'll conceal this secret from the world
As warily as those that trade in poison
Keep poison from their children.

DUCHESS   Thy protestation
Is ingenious and hearty: I believe it.
Is Antonio come?

CARIOLA   He attends you.

DUCHESS   Good dear soul,   360
Leave me: but place thyself behind the arras,
Where thou mayst overhear us. Wish me good speed,
For I am going into a wilderness
Where I shall find nor path, nor friendly clew
To be my guide.

CARIOLA goes behind the arras. Enter ANTONIO.

I sent for you. Sit down: 365
Take pen and ink and write. Are you ready?

ANTONIO   Yes.

DUCHESS   What did I say?

ANTONIO   That I should write somewhat.

DUCHESS   Oh, I remember:
After these triumphs and this large expense
It's fit – like thrifty husbands – we enquire   370
What's laid up for tomorrow.

ANTONIO   So please your beauteous excellence.

DUCHESS   Beauteous?
Indeed I thank you: I look young for your sake.
You have ta'en my cares upon you.

ANTONIO   I'll fetch your grace
The particulars of your revenue and expense.   375

The Duchess tells Antonio she is making her will; Antonio raises the subject of her marrying again

376 **upright** *wordplay:* (1) honest; (2) standing up *(lines 374–375 suggest Antonio has stood up to fetch the* **particulars** *– and he does so in most productions)*

380 **will** *wordplay:* (1) testament *(the legal document)*; (2) carnal desire

387 **overseer** person who supervised the executors of a will

393 **winding sheet** burial sheet for a corpse *(with wordplay on 'wedding sheet'. There was a fashion for women to be buried in the sheets used on their wedding night. Here the Duchess brings the subject back to death.)*

couple (1) couple of sheets; (2) coupling in marriage; sexual union

394 **St Winifred** patron saint of North Wales *(her well was famous, so there may be wordplay on 'will' and 'well'; see note below)*

397 **purgatory** *Catholics believe in a place or state of punishment after death where people undergo spiritual purification before they go to heaven. This was rejected by Protestants.*

398 **locally** *with the idea of in a small place, i.e. all of heaven or hell just in that married couple*

or...or either...or

399 **affect** feel about

Performance

In the 2003 National Theatre production this scene was hugely enjoyed by the audience, partly because they were one step ahead of Antonio (Charles Edwards) – understanding all the Duchess's 'double entendres' – but also because of the obvious great liking between the characters. The 1995 Cheek by Jowl version, however, was bleak: there was no hint of love between the Duchess and Antonio (Matthew Macfadyen), and after Antonio's *Would often reason thus –* (401) there was a very long pause as he seemed to remember something he didn't wish to share with either the Duchess or the audience.

Language

380, 393 Much of the language in the Duchess's wooing is, ominously, to do with death. The mood is one of 'morbid anticipation...where wedding-sheets are identified with winding-sheets and courtship is conducted under the ominous pretence of making a will' (Michael Neill). (The image of the Duchess's will is repeated in 4.2.199 and 369.)

Ideas and interpretations

394 The Welsh saint Winifred lived in the seventh century. According to legend she loved chastity and when she refused the advances of a chieftain's son he cut off her head; he was then swallowed up by the earth. Her uncle, St Beuno, replaced her head on her shoulders and she became a nun. Holywell in Clwyd, Wales – the healing spring where her head fell – is the only Catholic pilgrimage site in Britain that has lasted uninterrupted since the early Middle Ages. Various kings prayed there before major battles, including Henry V (before Agincourt) and Henry VII (before Bosworth). It had a reputation for curing diseases and other ailments, and was hugely important after the Reformation as a centre for Catholics, despite attempts to stop the practice – some of the Gunpowder Plot conspirators were known to have made a pilgrimage there in 1605. The Duchess's mention of this saint, therefore, had many resonances for Webster's audience.

DUCHESS   Oh, you are an upright treasurer: but you mistook,
               For when I said I meant to make enquiry
               What's laid up for tomorrow, I did mean
               What's laid up yonder for me.

ANTONIO   Where?

DUCHESS   In heaven.
               I am making my will, as 'tis fit princes should   380
               In perfect memory, and I pray sir, tell me
               Were not one better make it smiling, thus,
               Than in deep groans and terrible ghastly looks,
               As if the gifts we parted with procured
               That violent distraction?

ANTONIO   Oh, much better.   385

DUCHESS   If I had a husband now, this care were quit:
               But I intend to make you overseer.
               What good deed shall we first remember? Say.

ANTONIO   Begin with that first good deed began i'th'world
               After man's creation, the sacrament of marriage.   390
               I'd have you first provide for a good husband,
               Give him all.

DUCHESS   All?

ANTONIO   Yes, your excellent self.

DUCHESS   In a winding sheet?

ANTONIO   In a couple.

DUCHESS   St Winifred, that were a strange will!

ANTONIO   'Twere strange if there were no will in you   395
               To marry again.

DUCHESS   What do you think of marriage?

ANTONIO   I take't as those that deny purgatory:
               It locally contains or heaven or hell;
               There's no third place in't.

DUCHESS   How do you affect it?

1.1

Antonio indicates that he would love to be a father. The Duchess gives him her wedding ring to help his 'eyesight'. Suddenly realising what she means, Antonio kneels

400   **My banishment** *see 1.1.2*

402–407 **Say...starling** *Webster took this speech, though changing some of the phrasing, from Sir Thomas Elyot's book,* The Image of Governance *(1541).*

403   **bare** *simple*

405   **wanton** *rogue*

    a-cock-horse *mounted; on a hobby-horse (this was a child's toy – a* **painted stick** *with a horse's head)*

407   **taught starling** *Starlings were popular as caged birds and taught to mimic human speech; Hotspur mentions this in Shakespeare's Henry IV Part 1 1.3 – which led to starlings (now seen as a pest) being introduced into North America in the 1890s, in order to have all the birds he mentions. Webster added this image: see note to 402–407 above.*

408   **use my ring to't** *gold was seen as a remedy*

409   **sovereign** *effective*

414   **stark blind** *completely blind (with wordplay: (1) blind = the opposite of seeing; (2) blind = reckless)*

416   **saucy** *insolent; presumptious*

416–417 **devil...circle** *Magicians – like Marlowe's Doctor Faustus – drew a circle when conjuring up devils or spirits.*

417   **this circle** *the ring*

418   **There...small** *you don't need much*

    conjuration *magical conjuring; magic spell (note also the imagery of witchcraft, which is so frequent in this play)*

419   **is it fit?** *(1) does it fit? (2) is this right/proper?*

s.d.   **He kneels** *In a scene full of funereal imagery, Antonio's kneeling is an ominous parallel to the Duchess kneeling at her husband's tomb (lines 458–459).*

420–422 **This goodly roof...higher** *There are two meanings here: (1) because he is kneeling and she is standing she cannot discuss the matter unless (**without**) she helps him to stand; (2) she is acknowledging that he is of lower birth and she must raise him in rank – by marrying him – because otherwise she cannot maintain her integrity/her honour (**stand upright**).*

421   **discourse** *discuss the matter; communicate*

Structure

Jacqueline Pearson remarks on how often this wooing scene is repeated and parodied: in 3.2 – when Ferdinand bursts into her bedroom and Antonio is 'banished'; in 4.2 – the madmen and the Duchess's death scene; and 5.2 – when Julia woos Bosola: 'These reflected images of the wooing scene become increasingly grotesque and disturbing as the play progresses, so that the Duchess' secret marriage is examined and re-examined through the play.'

Antonio

402–407 Antonio presents the argument by which he tried to convince himself – when in a depressed state in banishment – that marriage wasn't important, but this picture of a child at play convinces the Duchess that Antonio approves of marriage. It is interesting that in talking about what marriage means to him, Antonio focuses on being a father.

ANTONIO   My banishment, feeding my melancholy,   400
              Would often reason thus –

DUCHESS   Pray let's hear it.

ANTONIO   Say a man never marry, nor have children,
              What takes that from him? Only the bare name
              Of being a father, or the weak delight
              To see the little wanton ride a-cock-horse   405
              Upon a painted stick, or hear him chatter
              Like a taught starling.

DUCHESS   Fie, fie, what's all this?
              One of your eyes is bloodshot, use my ring to't,
              They say 'tis very sovereign: 'twas my wedding ring,
              And I did vow never to part with it   410
              But to my second husband.

ANTONIO   You have parted with it now.

DUCHESS   Yes, to help your eyesight.

ANTONIO   You have made me stark blind.

DUCHESS   How?   415

ANTONIO   There is a saucy and ambitious devil
              Is dancing in this circle.

DUCHESS   Remove him.

ANTONIO   How?

DUCHESS   There needs small conjuration when your finger
              May do it: thus – is it fit?

She puts the ring on his finger. He kneels.

ANTONIO   What said you?

DUCHESS   Sir,
              This goodly roof of yours is too low built,   420
              I cannot stand upright in't, nor discourse,
              Without I raise it higher. Raise yourself,
              Or if you please, my hand to help you: so.

Antonio insists he is not ambitious and feels unworthy of the honour. The Duchess in exasperation tells him not be afraid

422–428 **Ambition...cure** *It was a conventional idea to link ambition with madness; this also anticipates Act 4.*

425 **close-pent** closely shut up

426 **lightsome** bright; elegant

girt surrounded; besieged

427 **prattling visitants** idly chattering visitors *(i.e. people who throng to the court hoping for favours, jobs etc.)*

430 **but** since; for

433 **mine** (1) *wordplay on* **ground's broke**: gold mine etc.; (2) me

435 **You...yourself** you wouldn't be any good at selling yourself

436–438 **This...wares off** making yourself out not to be worth very much is different from the trick that tradesmen try in the city, who literally 'darken' their goods – use a faint light to hide the defects in their goods *(i.e. Antonio has no defects to hide)*

441 **progress...yourself** *Monarchs made a* **progress** *(journey through their kingdom) to show themselves off to their subjects, but Antonio doesn't need to make a display to be known as a worthy man.*

442–443 **Were...honest** I would be an honest man even if heaven and hell didn't exist

443 **honest** (1) truthful; (2) honourable

446 **forced to woo** *wordplay:* (1) forced into woe *(following* **misery** *on line 445);* (2) forced to woo/court *('woo' and 'woe' were pronounced similarly)*

447 **doubles** speaks evasively; deceives

448 **equivocates** says one thing and means another

455–459 **Make...tomb** *This has been called 'the emotional climax of this episode' which also prefigures the Duchess's kneeling before her death (4.2.233) and the echo scene (5.3) (Michael Neill).*

Antonio

424–430 Some critics see Antonio as one of the increasing number of men in Tudor and Stuart England who advanced through education and ability rather than birth. 'Whether Antonio's motives for marrying the Duchess are ambitious is arguable, but it is clear that his valuable skills are administrative rather than military; and that his managerial abilities match those that became increasingly important to upwardly mobile men in sixteenth-century England' (Mary Beth Rose). (See also Delio on Antonio's *ambition* at 2.4.80–81.)

Duchess

439–441 'The idea of royalty suggested by "progress" (a king's journey to survey his realm) and the neoplatonic union of action, passion and contemplation in the notion of a "complete" man places the Duchess's attraction to him on a far higher plane than the ticklish instigations of her wanton flesh suggested by Painter, one of Webster's sources, as the reason for her love' (Kathleen McLuskie). Here the Duchess idealises Antonio, just as he idealised her (see 1.1.195–217).

Performance

435–452 In the 2003 National Theatre production the Duchess was cross at *You were ill to sell yourself;* they kissed at *Now she pays it* (444); in the next line she was exasperated with him and her situation, but it was clear how attracted they were. In the 1995 Cheek by Jowl production their relationship seemed to be a business relationship with an undercurrent of lust. At *ne'er ta'en wages of her* (444) Antonio gave the wedding ring back by placing it on a chair; *Go, go* (452) was really telling him to go.

She raises him.

ANTONIO   Ambition, madam, is a great man's madness,
That is not kept in chains and close-pent rooms   425
But in fair lightsome lodgings, and is girt
With the wild noise of prattling visitants
Which makes it lunatic beyond all cure.
Conceive not I am so stupid but I aim
Whereto your favours tend: but he's a fool   430
That being a-cold would thrust his hands i'th'fire
To warm them.

DUCHESS   So now the ground's broke
You may discover what a wealthy mine
I make you lord of.

ANTONIO   O my unworthiness.

DUCHESS   You were ill to sell yourself.   435
This dark'ning of your worth is not like that
Which tradesmen use i'th'city: their false lights
Are to rid bad wares off; and I must tell you,
If you will know where breathes a complete man –
I speak it without flattery – turn your eyes   440
And progress through yourself.

ANTONIO   Were there nor heaven nor hell
I should be honest: I have long served virtue
And ne'er ta'en wages of her.

DUCHESS   Now she pays it.
The misery of us that are born great,   445
We are forced to woo because none dare woo us:
And as a tyrant doubles with his words,
And fearfully equivocates, so we
Are forced to express our violent passions
In riddles and in dreams, and leave the path   450
Of simple virtue which was never made
To seem the thing it is not. Go, go brag
You have left me heartless, mine is in your bosom,
I hope 'twill multiply love there. You do tremble.
Make not your heart so dead a piece of flesh   455
To fear more than to love me. Sir, be confident,
What is't distracts you? This is flesh and blood, sir,
'Tis not the figure cut in alabaster

1.1 *The Duchess implores Antonio to see her as a woman. He agrees to be her husband, and she lightly dismisses his fears about her brothers. Cariola comes out of hiding to witness their private marriage*

460   **vain** worthless

464–465 **I...name** *With the word* **sanctuary** *Antonio picks up her reference to her* **husband's tomb** *(line 459): he will protect her reputation, just as a holy place protects a person who seeks sanctuary in it.*

466   **'cause** because: in order that

468   ***Quietus est*** *Latin:* he is quit: (1) acquitted of a debt; (2) discharged from an office; (3) death *(the last is not meant by the Duchess and is another ominous phrase in a scene full of images of death; see also 3.2.185)*

470   **sweetmeats** sugared food; sweets

471   **As fearful** as if afraid

473   **discord** (1) lack of agreement; (2) lack of harmony *(the music image is picked up in line 485 and 2.5.61–62)*

    without this circumference outside this circle *(i.e. their embracing bodies or arms, and the ring on his finger; it could also refer to the room/palace or even the theatre they are in; see also note below)*

475–476 **Yet...tempest** *but see 2.5.16–21*

477   **parts** *perhaps wordplay:* (1) parts of speech; (2) roles *(e.g. in wooing, in reassuring)*; (3) particulars

478   **savoured flattery** *perhaps:* looked like a pleasing delusion

481   ***Per verba de presenti*** *Latin:* by words, as from the present *(a phrase used in the verbal contract of marriage since at least the thirteenth century. Though the authorities encouraged marriage as a public act in church, this informal declaration was valid, if unusual and irregular; but see note to 488.)*

482–483 **Gordian...untwine** *In 333 BC Alexander the Great arrived in Gordium (in modern Turkey) and heard the legend that the man who undid an ancient knot on a chariot there would rule Asia; he slashed through it with his sword. The Duchess refers to the meaning of knot = marriage tie; bond of union, and perhaps also to their entwined hands.*

483–485 **spheres...music** *It used to be thought that the moon, sun, stars and planets were fixed to concentric hollow globes that revolved around the earth, and made music as they moved.*

484   **still** *wordplay:* (1) motionless; (2) soft *(e.g. music)*; (3) always

    motion *wordplay:* (1) movement; tempo *(music)*; (2) emotion; desire

Ideas and interpretations

463–465 'If an overarching fable were to be sought for the whole play, it could be a masque of Good Fame. This was a favourite figure in masques...good fame is immortality' (Muriel Bradbrook). In accepting to be her husband, Antonio puts as his main aim to protect her reputation/her fame: *your good name.*

468 Michael Neill says that after Antonio offers himself (463–465) 'as a kind of living memorial to her fame' this gesture is 'subtly discomposed' by 'the quietus which his mistress signs upon his lips – a gesture that anticipates the "perfect peace" signed for the Duchess herself in the dirge with which Bosola announces her death at the terminal hour of midnight' (see 4.2.184 and 193).

Duchess

472–476 The Duchess dismisses Antonio's fears about her brothers; Muriel Bradbrook comments: 'The noblest courage feeds and fuels the blindest egoism; the Duchess of Malfi, dismissing any threat to her wishes, reveals to the spectators her dangerous over-security.'

Kneels at my husband's tomb. Awake, awake, man,
I do here put off all vain ceremony   460
And only do appear to you a young widow
That claims you for her husband; and like a widow,
I use but half a blush in't.

ANTONIO   Truth speak for me,
I will remain the constant sanctuary
Of your good name.

DUCHESS   I thank you, gentle love,   465
And 'cause you shall not come to me in debt,
Being now my steward, here upon your lips
I sign your *Quietus est.* (*She kisses him*)
This you should have begged now.
I have seen children oft eat sweetmeats thus   470
As fearful to devour them too soon.

ANTONIO   But for your brothers?

DUCHESS   Do not think of them.
All discord, without this circumference,
Is only to be pitied and not feared.
Yet, should they know it, time will easily   475
Scatter the tempest.

ANTONIO   These words should be mine,
And all the parts you have spoke, if some part of it
Would not have savoured flattery.

DUCHESS   Kneel.

Enter CARIOLA.

ANTONIO   Ha?

DUCHESS   Be not amazed, this woman's of my counsel.
I have heard lawyers say a contract in a chamber,   480
Per verba de presenti, is absolute marriage:
Bless, heaven, this sacred Gordian, which let
        violence
Never untwine.

ANTONIO   And may our sweet affections, like the spheres,
Be still in motion –

The Duchess declares that they are now man and wife and asks Antonio
to lead her to their marriage bed. Alone, Cariola expresses her fears

484   **Quick'ning** animating; stimulating

485   **soft** (1) quiet; unheard by humans; (2) melodious

485–487   **loving...divided** *Single palm trees cannot bear fruit: this idea was often used at the time in reference to marriage.*

489   **That Fortune** so that Fortune *(continuing from his lines at 483–484)*

       accident event

492   **We now...wife** *It is not clear by what wording they are actually married.*

492–493   **Church...echo this** *It will be echoed in 5.3 (this is known as a figurative prolepsis: see page 24), but one critic takes it more literally and suggests that here the Duchess 'appears to signal that the marriage will be solemnised by the church at some*

future date' (Dympna Callaghan), which never happens.

494   **conceit** idea; notion

499   **humorous** full of the humours *(it was thought the body consisted of four humours or fluids: blood, phlegm, choler and melancholy)*; capricious

500–501   ***Alexander...chaste*** *Two faithful friends looked so like each other that no one could tell them apart. Lodowick married a princess in Alexander's name and each night laid a sword between them in order not to wrong his friend. There was a ballad about the story and a play at the Rose playhouse in 1597 and 1599.*

502   **shroud** (1) hide; (2) prepare for burial *(a **shroud** is a winding sheet – see line 393; another funereal image)*

Duchess in performance

488   In the 2003 National Theatre production the Duchess (Janet McTeer) addressed this line to Cariola, as if really wanting to know if there was anything else she and Antonio ought to do in their private ceremony.

500–501   This is normally played as sexual teasing; but the Duchess in the 1995 Cheek by Jowl production (Anastasia Hille) made it more blatant by stripping down to just her pants and shoes.

Duchess

504–505   'Cariola's opposition between "greatness" and "woman" reveals a great deal about the values of the world in which the Duchess has to act' (Kathleen McLuskie), who says that the Duchess's greatness 'consists of an independent spirit and an awareness of her own sexuality'.

505–506   Cariola identifies madness with social transgression, but her speech 'is rather incongruous, for the behaviour to which it refers manifestly does *not* show "a fearful madness". Indeed...the Duchess has conducted her courtship of Antonio with an air of legalistic calm and practicality' (Karin Coddon).

DUCHESS	Quick'ning, and make The like soft music –
ANTONIO	That we may imitate the loving palms, 485 Best emblem of a peaceful marriage, That ne'er bore fruit divided.
DUCHESS	What can the Church force more?
ANTONIO	That Fortune may not know an accident Either of joy, or sorrow, to divide 490 Our fixed wishes.
DUCHESS	How can the Church build faster? We now are man and wife, and 'tis the Church That must but echo this. Maid, stand apart, I now am blind.
ANTONIO	What's your conceit in this?
DUCHESS	I would have you lead your Fortune by the hand 495 Unto your marriage bed. You speak in me this, for we now are one. We'll only lie, and talk together, and plot T'appease my humorous kindred; and if you please, Like the old tale in *Alexander and Lodowick,* 500 Lay a naked sword between us, keep us chaste. Oh, let me shroud my blushes in your bosom, Since 'tis the treasury of all my secrets.

Exeunt DUCHESS and ANTONIO.

CARIOLA	Whether the spirit of greatness or of woman Reign most in her, I know not, but it shows 505 A fearful madness. I owe her much of pity.

Exit.

2.1 *In the Duchess's presence chamber, nine months later, Bosola passes the time by mocking the old lord Castruchio and railing at an old lady*

s.d. **Enter…CASTRUCHIO** *His only purpose in this scene is as a foil for Bosola's satirical comments.*

1 **fain be** like to be

2 **courtier** lawyer; judge; person who attends a law court *(this unusual meaning is because of the legal satire from Bosola that follows; perhaps Castruchio is dressed as a lawyer, e.g. with a skullcap)*

3 **main** aim; purpose

5–6 **nightcap…largely** *His lawyer's skullcap exposes his large ass-like ears (i.e. he's stupid); also, cuckolds were often shown wearing nightcaps.*

7 **band** neck band; collar; ruff

8 **set** public; formal

11 **president** presiding judge

19 **roaring boys** noisy, riotous lads *(so-called since the end of the sixteenth century; perhaps equivalent to 'lager louts')*

19–20 **eat…valiant** *It was believed that meat made one valiant (e.g. see 3.3.14–15), so presumably this is sarcastic – i.e. roaring boys (who were perhaps mainly apprentices) probably couldn't afford much meat and were noisy but cowardly.*

25–26 **prime nightcaps** chief lawyers

29 **scurvy face physic** (1) medicine for your skin-diseased face; (2) contemptible medicine for your face

31–32 **were deep…progress** *The image is to do with the king's annual summer travels* (**progress**) *outside the capital along rutted and muddy roads.*

Plot

We learn only from Bosola's soliloquy (73–81) that about nine months have passed. At the indoor Blackfriars theatre there would have been a pause before Act 2 started (see page 231).

Performance

The beginning of 2.1 was cut in the National Theatre's 2003 production, which started with: *What thing is in this outward form* (54) which Bosola (Lorcan Cranitch) said to the audience while getting ready for the day's work: first shaving, and then putting on his shirt at 67 (hiding his body *in rich tissue*). The 1995 Cheek by Jowl production was even more radical – further emphasising that for them Bosola (George Anton) was not a central character – since this scene started with *I observe our Duchess* (73).

Old Lady

The figure of the old court lady who paints her face also appears in Webster's funeral poem on Prince Henry (see page 233): she paints herself 'to add a grace, / To the deformity of her wrinkled face'. Webster here aligns himself with puritan preachers who railed against the falsehood of face painting. This character's only purpose seems to be as an excuse for Bosola's diatribe against women, which leads into his meditation (53–69), but the Old Lady also appears at 2.2.5, and could be one of the midwives Antonio has arranged to attend the Duchess (see 2.1.181–184). Mary Beth Rose suggests: 'like the character Julia…the old lady seems to be in the play as a comment on and warning about the Duchess's marriage. Her odd appearances…can be linked with the complex of witch imagery that pervades the play.'

Act 2

Scene 1

Enter BOSOLA and CASTRUCHIO.

BOSOLA   You say you would fain be taken for an eminent
courtier?

CASTRUCHIO   'Tis the very main of my ambition.

BOSOLA   Let me see: you have a reasonable good face
for't already, and your nightcap expresses your ears   5
sufficient largely. I would have you learn to twirl
the strings of your band with a good grace; and in
a set speech, at th'end of every sentence, to hum
three or four times, or blow your nose till it smart
again, to recover your memory. When you come   10
to be a president in criminal causes, if you smile
upon a prisoner, hang him, but if you frown upon
him, and threaten him, let him be sure to 'scape
the gallows.

CASTRUCHIO   I would be a very merry president.   15

BOSOLA   Do not sup a-nights, 'twill beget you an admirable
wit.

CASTRUCHIO   Rather it would make me have a good stomach to
quarrel, for they say your roaring boys eat meat
seldom, and that makes them so valiant. But how   20
shall I know whether the people take me for an
eminent fellow?

BOSOLA   I will teach a trick to know it: give out you lie
a-dying, and if you hear the common people curse
you, be sure you are taken for one of the prime   25
nightcaps.

Enter OLD LADY.

You come from painting now?

OLD LADY   From what?

BOSOLA   Why, from your scurvy face physic. To behold
thee not painted inclines somewhat near a miracle.   30
These in thy face, here, were deep ruts and foul

32 **sloughs** (1) wet muddy holes in the road; (2) skin *(e.g. of a snake)*; (3) layers of dead tissue covering a wound or sore *(this wordplay would only be noticed when reading the play since meaning (1) is pronounced to rhyme with 'cows', and (2) and (3) as 'sloffs')*

33 **flayed** stripped; peeled *(Webster probably read about the French lady in Montaigne's* Essays*)*

35 **nutmeg grater** *Nutmeg seeds were an exotic spice brought to Britain by ship and overland from Indonesia and grated to make spices for food and in medicines.*

36 **abortive** aborted; born before its time

38 **careening** *nautical image:* turning a ship over on one side for cleaning, repairing or caulking *(caulking is using oakum and melted pitch to stop a ship leaking)*

   morphewed covered with leprous eruptions

39 **disembogue** *nautical image:* come out of a river into the open sea *(the image is that after applying make-up a woman then steps out into the world to seek new adventures)*

40 **rough-cast...plastic** *Bosola refers back to the old lady's term* **painting** *(line 37) by comparing* **rough-cast** *(a coat of lime and gravel roughly applied to walls) to* **plastic** *(fine, artistic modelling of figures); the 1995 Cambridge edition suggests:* 'And that's a rough phrase; coarse plaster compared to your fine moulding in clay.'

41 **closet** private dressing-room; cabinet

43–44 **fat...ordures** *perhaps from a satire by the Italian writer Ariosto (1474–1535). It is also reminiscent of the contents of the witches' cauldron in* Macbeth *4.3* (**ordures** = excrement).

45–47 **dead...plague** *A suggested remedy for a plague sore was to hold the bared rump of a bird to it in order to draw the poison from the sore.*

47 **kiss...fasting** *i.e. because their breath smelt so bad*

47–48 **two of you** the old lady and Castruchio

48–49 **sin...physician** *Their sexual activity and other indulgences in their youth (causing venereal disease etc.) have now in their old age brought their doctor so much work it's like an inheritance* (**patrimony**) *for him.*

50 **footcloth** expensive cloth laid over a horse to protect the rider from dirt

63 **wolf** *disease that ate away the flesh, or a cancerous growth; it prefigures the wolf 'disease' that Ferdinand will get (see 5.2.5–12)*

   swinish measle *measles is also a disease in pigs*

67 **tissue** rich cloth

71 **wells at Lucca** *spa at Bagni di Lucca, in northern Italy, noted for its warm sulphur waters since the twelfth century*

   recover get better from

Bosola's meditation

53 'The term *meditation* signals the introspective and implicitly religious nature of the passage which follows: a dark vision of the brevity and nastiness of human existence cast in the tradition whose origin is Innocent III's famous tract, *De Contemptu Mundi*' (Innocent was Pope from 1198 to 1216) (1995 Cambridge edition of *The Duchess*).

53–69 Michael Neill: 'Webster's imagery...links Bosola and the Aragonian brothers to the corruptions of the grave. For Bosola in his vein of melancholy satire, the body is...a vessel of mortal corruption, given the false semblance of life by the bravery of its decoration' (see also Bosola's lines about rottenness at 4.2.318–319).

sloughs the last progress. There was a lady in
France that, having had the smallpox, flayed the
skin off her face to make it more level; and
whereas before she looked like a nutmeg grater,   35
after she resembled an abortive hedgehog.

OLD LADY   Do you call this painting?

BOSOLA   No, no, but careening of an old morphewed
             lady, to make her disembogue again. There's
             rough-cast phrase to your plastic.   40

OLD LADY   It seems you are well acquainted with my closet?

BOSOLA   One would suspect it for a shop of witchcraft, to
             find in it the fat of serpents, spawn of snakes, Jews'
             spittle, and their young children's ordures, and all
             these for the face: I would sooner eat a dead pigeon, 45
             taken from the soles of the feet of one sick of the
             plague, than kiss one of you fasting. Here are two
             of you whose sin of your youth is the very
             patrimony of the physician, makes him renew his
             footcloth with the spring, and change his high-   50
             priced courtesan with the fall of the leaf. I do
             wonder you do not loathe yourselves.
             Observe my meditation now.
             What thing is in this outward form of man
             To be beloved? We account it ominous   55
             If nature do produce a colt, or lamb,
             A fawn, or goat, in any limb resembling
             A man; and fly from't as a prodigy.
             Man stands amazed to see his deformity
             In any other creature but himself;   60
             But in our own flesh, though we bear diseases
             Which have their true names only ta'en from beasts –
             As the most ulcerous wolf, and swinish measle –
             Though we are eaten up of lice, and worms,
             And though continually we bear about us   65
             A rotten and dead body, we delight
             To hide it in rich tissue; all our fear –
             Nay all our terror – is lest our physician
             Should put us in the ground, to be made sweet.
             (To CASTRUCHIO) Your wife's gone to Rome: you two   70
             couple, and get you to the wells at Lucca, to recover
             your aches.

2.1 *Bosola is going to try a trick with apricots to discover if the Duchess is pregnant. Antonio enters with Delio, having told him of his marriage, and Bosola spars with Antonio about ambition*

74 **a-days** by day; in the daytime

75 **fins** *also meant eyelids, so perhaps:* skin, *or* rims; edges

teeming pregnant; fertile

76 **wanes...waxes** *like the moon*

78 **loose-bodied** loosely fitting (*with innuendo:* dissolute; immoral)

There's...in't (1) there's something going on; (2) there's something inside her dress (*usually gets a laugh from the audience*)

80 **pretty** clever

apricots *The original spelling in the play is 'apricocks'. Various herbs were used to speed up delivery of a baby, but the herbalist Nicholas Culpeper warned that apricots could instead produce an abortion. King Henry VIII's gardener was the first to grow them in England in 1542 (he got them from Italy). They can ripen in England in May.*

81 **spring** *At the end of 2.3 we are told the baby is born in December.*

88–92 **the opinion...wisdom** *perhaps:* a wise person's opinion is like a foul skin disease (**tetter**) all over a man's body. If an unsophisticated, simple person can guide us to be good, then he guides us to happiness, because the most wickedly cunning (**subtlest**) stupidity actually comes from the cleverest (**subtlest**) wisdom *(Webster adapted this from Montaigne's Essays)*

92 **Let...honest** *i.e.* rather than 'a great wise fellow' (with the emphasis on **simply**)

93 **inside** meaning; inward nature

96 **preferment** high office; advanced status

97 **out of fashion** old-fashioned (*because he has now got preferment*)

leave it give it up; stop it

99–100 **Give...whatsoever** (*Bosola replies sarcastically with wordplay on* **leave**) give me permission to be honest with any words or praise you choose

103 **disposition** inclination; mood

Bosola

73–76 Kathleen McLuskie contrasts the way Bosola describes the Duchess's body: *sick a-days...pukes...stomach seethes...* with the Duchess's actual appearance (122): 'Her body has changed from its first youthful beauty but it has done so for the sake of the procreation which undermines the pessimism of Bosola's vision of human frailty.'

Performance

81 onwards: In the 2003 National Theatre production Antonio and Delio were setting up a photoshoot of the Duchess; Delio was the photographer. (See page 48.)

82–85 In the 1995 Cheek by Jowl production Antonio physically threatened Delio, though it was followed by a hug. (The lines were also moved to after the Duchess is hurried off to her chamber at 177.)

Antonio and Bosola

100–101 'This small-talk – opinionated, ironic, and complimental – presents two ambitious men sparring for advantage. Bosola out-plays Antonio by pretending at one point to reveal all and then turning defence into attack' (John Russell Brown).

Exeunt CASTRUCHIO and OLD LADY.

I have other work on foot. I observe our Duchess
Is sick a-days, she pukes, her stomach seethes,
The fins of her eyelids look most teeming blue,   75
She wanes i'th'cheek, and waxes fat i'th'flank;
And contrary to our Italian fashion
Wears a loose-bodied gown. There's somewhat in't.
I have a trick may chance discover it,
A pretty one: I have bought some apricots,   80
The first our spring yields.

Enter ANTONIO and DELIO.

DELIO   And so long since married?
You amaze me.

ANTONIO   Let me seal your lips for ever,
For did I think that anything but th'air
Could carry these words from you, I should wish
You had no breath at all.   85
(*To BOSOLA*) Now sir, in your contemplation?
You are studying to become a great wise fellow?

BOSOLA   Oh sir, the opinion of wisdom is a foul tetter
that runs all over a man's body: if simplicity direct
us to have no evil, it directs us to a happy being.   90
For the subtlest folly proceeds from the subtlest
wisdom. Let me be simply honest.

ANTONIO   I do understand your inside.

BOSOLA   Do you so?

ANTONIO   Because you would not seem to appear to   95
th'world puffed up with your preferment, you
continue this out of fashion melancholy; leave it,
leave it.

BOSOLA   Give me leave to be honest in any phrase, in any
compliment whatsoever. Shall I confess myself to   100
you? I look no higher than I can reach: they are the
gods that must ride on winged horses, a lawyer's
mule of a slow pace will both suit my disposition
and business, for, mark me, when a man's mind

2.1 *Bosola tells Antonio that great people are no different from anyone else. The Duchess enters, wearing a loose dress to conceal her advanced stage of pregnancy*

107 **You...heaven** *Antonio is disagreeing with what Bosola has just said about himself, i.e.* I believe you *are* ambitious for higher honours

107–108 **the devil...light** *see note below*

109–121 **Oh...cannon** *i.e. it doesn't matter what his or anyone's past is, what matters is what a person does now. People are essentially equal.*

109 **lord...ascendant** *astrological term: the sky is divided into twelve houses: the 'house of the* **ascendant***' is the part rising above the horizon; the* **lord** *is the planet whose linked sign of the zodiac is entering that house (there is of course unintentional irony here)*

110–111 **cousin...removed** *sarcastic:* first cousin once removed

112 **King Pippin** King of the Franks (751–68), father of Charlemagne and founder of the Carolingian dynasty of French kings *(the relevance may be that he was a steward, or 'Mayor of the Palace', to the previous king)*

116 **meaner** of lower social class

117 **there's...them** the same God created them

118 **like** same

119 **tithe-pig** a pig taken as a tithe *(a tenth part of the annual produce of agriculture had to be given to the Church)*

120 **makes...spoil** makes princes lay waste

129 **tedious** annoying; slow

130 **lemon peels** *used to sweeten bad breath*

132 **mother** *wordplay:* (1) hysteria; (2) pregnancy

134–135 **I...King** *an issue much debated at the time; the Duchess may also want to see Antonio with his hat on as her equal*

137 **In the presence?** in the presence chamber? *(see note to 1.1.85)*

Antonio and Bosola

107–121 These two speeches sum up the major theme of the play: where does greatness lie? In Painter, Webster's source for the story (see page 237), it is the Duchess who gives a version of Bosola's speech as she thinks about wooing Antonio: 'But from whence issue the monarchs, princes and greater lords, but from the natural and common mass of earth, whereof other men do come? What maketh these differences between those that love each other, if not the sottish opinion which we conceive of greatness and preeminence?' (See also note to 4.2.27–28.)

Language

114–121 Webster adapted this from Montaigne's *Essays*, but added the detail of the *tithe-pig*. Commenting on this addition, Rupert Brooke admiringly wrote: 'Bosola has the vision of an artist.'

Ideas and interpretations

107–108 The devil is described as ruling 'in the air' in St Paul's letter to the Ephesians (2.2) in the English 'Bishops' Bible' published in 1568. St Paul tells the people of Ephesus that before they were converted to Christianity they were sinful people, ruled by the devil. Thus Antonio is saying that Bosola's sinful past is keeping him down.

	rides faster than his horse can gallop, they quickly both tire. 105
ANTONIO	You would look up to heaven, but I think the devil that rules i'th'air stands in your light.
BOSOLA	Oh, sir, you are lord of the ascendant, chief man with the Duchess, a duke was your cousin-german, 110 removed. Say you were lineally descended from King Pippin, or he himself, what of this? Search the heads of the greatest rivers in the world, you shall find them but bubbles of water. Some would think the souls of princes were brought forth by some 115 more weighty cause than those of meaner persons; they are deceived, there's the same hand to them, the like passions sway them; the same reason that makes a vicar go to law for a tithe-pig, and undo his neighbours, makes them spoil a whole province, 120 and batter down goodly cities with the cannon.

Enter DUCHESS with attendants.

DUCHESS	Your arm, Antonio. Do I not grow fat? I am ⌐ exceeding short-winded. Bosola, I would have you, sir, provide for me a litter, such a one as the Duchess of Florence rode in. 125
BOSOLA	The Duchess used one when she was great with child.
DUCHESS	I think she did. (*To an attendant*) Come hither, mend my ruff, here, when? Thou art such a tedious lady, and thy breath smells of lemon peels, would 130 thou hadst done; shall I swoon under thy fingers? I am so troubled with the mother.
BOSOLA	(*Aside*) I fear too much.
DUCHESS	(*To ANTONIO*)I have heard you say that the French courtiers wear their hats on 'fore the King. 135
ANTONIO	I have seen it.
DUCHESS	In the presence?
ANTONIO	Yes.

144   **colder...France** *probably England is meant*

145   **bare** (1) bare-headed; (2) *innuendo: naked (Antonio is teasing the Duchess – but did Webster also have someone in mind in James's court?)*

149   **to-year** this year

153   **pare** take the skin off

162   **dainties** *sexual innuendo:* (1) delicacies *(food)*; (2) delightful things *(sexual)*

163   **restorative** a food which restores health

A photoshoot staging of 2.1: Delio (Jonathan Slinger) takes photographs of the Duchess (Janet McTeer), as Antonio (far left) and other attendants watch (National Theatre, 2003)

Ideas and interpretations

According to Dympna Callaghan, one of the main arguments of the time to show that women were inferior and dependent on others, and should not have power, was that they became pregnant: 'That Webster shows us the Duchess on stage and pregnant is a factor of the utmost significance, since woman's sexuality constituted in the Renaissance the single and most intransigent obstacles to any argument which countered the belief in innate female inferiority.'

DUCHESS   Why should not we bring up that fashion?
                 'Tis ceremony more than duty that consists   140
                 In the removing of a piece of felt.
                 Be you the example to the rest o'th'court,
                 Put on your hat first.

ANTONIO   You must pardon me:
                 I have seen, in colder countries than in France,
                 Nobles stand bare to th'prince; and the distinction 145
                 Methought showed reverently.

BOSOLA   I have a present for your grace.

DUCHESS   For me sir?

BOSOLA   Apricots, madam.

DUCHESS   O sir, where are they?
                 I have heard of none to-year.

BOSOLA   (Aside)   Good, her colour rises.

DUCHESS   Indeed I thank you, they are wondrous fair ones.   150
                 What an unskilful fellow is our gardener,
                 We shall have none this month.

BOSOLA   Will not your grace pare them?

DUCHESS   No – they taste of musk, methinks, indeed they do.

BOSOLA   I know not: yet I wish your grace had pared 'em.   155

DUCHESS   Why?

BOSOLA   I forgot to tell you, the knave gardener,
                 Only to raise his profit by them the sooner,
                 Did ripen them in horse dung.

DUCHESS   Oh you jest.
                 (To ANTONIO) You shall judge: pray taste one.

ANTONIO   Indeed madam,   160
                 I do not love the fruit.

DUCHESS   Sir, you are loath
                 To rob us of our dainties: 'tis a delicate fruit,
                 They say they are restorative?

2.1 *The apricots make the Duchess feel unwell and she is rushed off. Antonio is afraid she has gone into labour because they were planning for her to give birth somewhere else more secretly*

164 **grafting** *Some plants, such as apricot trees, are propagated by grafting rather than seed – i.e. joining a 'scion' (one or more buds of one plant) on to a 'stock' (another, rooted, plant, e.g. a tree); one reason for grafting is to increase the productivity of a fruit tree (see also note below).*

166 **pippin...crab** *types of apple and apple tree;* **pippin** *also echoes* **King Pippin** *(line 112)*

167 **damson...blackthorn** *types of plum and plum tree/shrub*

168 **bawd** deceiving; disguising *(a bawd was a person in charge of prostitutes)*

farthingales frameworks of whalebone hoops under a woman's petticoat

170 **apparently** visibly

171 **springal...caper** youth dancing fantastically

178 **undone** ruined; destroyed

181 **for her remove** to take her away *(from Malfi)*

183 **politic** (1) skilfully contrived; (2) crafty

conveyance means of transport; means of entry

184 **plotted** (1) planned; (2) schemed *(with a less innocent sense)*

185 **forced** unsought

Ideas and Interpretations

164–167 Bosola has deliberately raised the topic of *grafting* with the Duchess since it was a familiar metaphor applied to the sexual relationship of nobles with those of lower social status. There was hierarchy in the natural world as well: one contemporary author wrote that damson trees were superior to blackthorn trees, and pippin trees above crab apple trees. In Shakespeare's *Winter's Tale*, written two years before *The Duchess*, there is a debate about grafting between Perdita, who is thought to be a shepherd's daughter, and King Polixenes, whose son wants to marry her (4.4.79–103 in the Longman edition). Polixenes and the Duchess believe grafting improves nature.

BOSOLA	'Tis a pretty art, this grafting.
DUCHESS	'Tis so: a bett'ring of nature. 165
BOSOLA	To make a pippin grow upon a crab,
	A damson on a blackthorn. (*Aside*) – How greedily
	she eats them!
	A whirlwind strike off these bawd farthingales!
	For, but for that, and the loose-bodied gown,
	I should have discovered apparently 170
	The young springal cutting a caper in her belly.
DUCHESS	I thank you, Bosola, they were right good ones,
	If they do not make me sick.
ANTONIO	How now madam?
DUCHESS	This green fruit and my stomach are not friends.
	How they swell me!
BOSOLA	(*Aside*) Nay, you are too much swelled already. 175
DUCHESS	Oh, I am in an extreme cold sweat.
BOSOLA	I am very sorry.
DUCHESS	Lights to my chamber! Oh, good Antonio,
	I fear I am undone.
DELIO	Lights there, lights!

Exeunt all but ANTONIO and DELIO.

ANTONIO	Oh my most trusty Delio, we are lost.
	I fear she's fall'n in labour, and there's left 180
	No time for her remove.
DELIO	Have you prepared
	Those ladies to attend her, and procured
	That politic safe conveyance for the midwife
	Your Duchess plotted?
ANTONIO	I have.
DELIO	Make use then of this forced occasion. 185
	Give out that Bosola hath poisoned her

2.2 *Delio advises Antonio to pretend that Bosola's apricots have poisoned the Duchess. Bosola is now certain the Duchess is pregnant and can't resist being abusive about women to the old lady*

187   **colour** excuse; reason

188   **close** confined; hidden *(i.e. keeping to her rooms in the palace)*

      physicians doctors

1   **tetchiness** irritableness

2   **vulturous** *The Oxford English Dictionary gives 1623 for the first use of this adjective, and for* **tetchiness** *– which is the date of the first printing of this play.*

s.d.   **Enter** OLD LADY *She may be one of the midwife's helpers.*

7   **glass-house** glass furnace *(one was built near the Blackfriars theatre c. 1600 and closed in 1614; glassblowing was quite new and strange to the English, and glass was only just beginning to be available to more than the very wealthy; see also 4.2.77–79)*

10   **fashion** shape

15   **your** women's

16   **altogether** at the same time

17   **entertainment** sexual pleasure

Delio in performance

185–191 In the 2003 National Theatre production, Delio was here desperately coming up with ideas to help his friend.

Antonio

192 Many critics feel that Antonio is weak and the Duchess takes the lead in everything: 'Antonio repeatedly demonstrates his helpless inability either to confront the dreaded brothers or to outwit their villainy' (Mary Beth Rose); she adds that this line could 'stand as a summary statement of his position'. The editors of the 1995 Cambridge edition agree: 'Antonio's panicky response to the emergency, highlighted by Delio's calm resourcefulness, is the first evidence of weakness in the Duchess's beloved.' But Delio need not be 'calm' (see note above), and Philip Franks, the director of the 1995 Greenwich/Wyndham's Theatres production, felt Antonio's reaction was quite normal in the situation (see note to 2.2.72–76). Antonio's line was, however, cut in the 2003 National Theatre production.

Performance

The beginning of 2.2 – Bosola's exchange with the Old Lady – is often cut in productions.

With these apricots: that will give some colour
For her keeping close.

ANTONIO   Fie, fie, the physicians
Will then flock to her.

DELIO   For that you may pretend
She'll use some prepared antidote of her own,   190
Lest the physicians should repoison her.

ANTONIO   I am lost in amazement. I know not what to
think on't.

Exeunt.

Scene 2

Enter BOSOLA.

BOSOLA   So, so: there's no question but her tetchiness,
and most vulturous eating of the apricots, are
apparent signs of breeding.

Enter OLD LADY.

Now?

OLD LADY   I am in haste, sir.   5

BOSOLA   There was a young waiting-woman had a
monstrous desire to see the glass-house –

OLD LADY   Nay, pray let me go –

BOSOLA   And it was only to know what strange instrument
it was should swell up a glass to the fashion of a   10
woman's belly.

OLD LADY   I will hear no more of the glass-house, you are still
abusing women.

BOSOLA   Who I? No, only by the way, now and then,
mention your frailties. The orange tree bears ripe   15
and green fruit and blossoms altogether, and some
of you give entertainment for pure love; but more,

2.2 *Bosola continues to rail against promiscuous women. Antonio orders the palace gates to be shut and all the officers to be summoned*

18   **more...reward** *e.g. money*

18–19   **lusty...tastes well** *contrasting young and mature women*

19–22   **If we...receive them** *In Greek myth, Danae was the daughter of the King of Argos who put her in prison because an oracle said her son would kill him. Jupiter (Zeus) desired Danae; he transformed himself into a shower of gold and poured through the roof of her prison into her lap. She bore a son, Perseus, who later killed the King by accident. Renaissance writers and artists often depicted Danae as an expensive prostitute. (See also 1.1.253–254.)*

25–26   **to make...centre** *proverbial: e.g. 'many ways meet in one town', with sexual innuendo*

26–27   **foster-daughters** *girls she has nursed at the breast (noble ladies usually employed a wet nurse to breastfeed their children)*

28   **girdle** *belt*

32   **posterns** *doors and gates other than the main entrance*

presently *immediately*

34   **Forobosco** *He is listed with the other characters in the 1623 quarto, but never appears: Webster presumably revised this scene.*

39   **Switzer** *Swiss guard (mercenary soldiers often used at Italian and French courts, and still used to guard the Pope at the Vatican)*

for more precious reward. The lusty spring smells
well, but drooping autumn tastes well. If we have
the same golden showers that rained in the time   20
of Jupiter the Thunderer, you have the same
Danaes still, to hold up their laps to receive them.
Didst thou never study the mathematics?

OLD LADY   What's that, sir?

BOSOLA   Why, to know the trick how to make a many lines   25
meet in one centre. Go, go; give your foster-
daughters good council: tell them that the devil
takes delight to hang at a woman's girdle like a
false rusty watch, that she cannot discern how the
time passes.   30

Exit OLD LADY.

Enter ANTONIO, DELIO, RODERIGO, GRISOLAN.

ANTONIO   Shut up the court gates.

RODERIGO   Why sir, what's the danger?

ANTONIO   Shut up the posterns presently, and call
All the officers o'th'court.

GRISOLAN   I shall, instantly.

Exit.

ANTONIO   Who keeps the key o'th'park gate?

RODERIGO   Forobosco.

ANTONIO   Let him bring't presently.   35

Exeunt ANTONIO and RODERIGO.

Enter SERVANTS.

1 SERVANT   Oh gentlemen o'th'court, the foulest treason!

BOSOLA   (*Aside*) If that these apricots should be poisoned,
now, without my knowledge!

1 SERVANT   There was taken even now a Switzer in the
Duchess' bedchamber.   40

2.2 *The servants/officers make bawdy jokes. Antonio enters and tells them that jewels and plate have been stolen and that they are all to be locked into their rooms until the next morning*

42   **pistol** *was pronounced like 'pizzle' = penis, which explains Bosola's laughter*

      codpiece pouch that covers the genitals on a man's breeches *(no longer in fashion in 1614; some were so large they could hold pistols)*

47   **if he...chambers** *i.e. only women would have searched his codpiece*

48   **moulds** wooden disks *(which were then covered with cloth)*

50   **cannibal...fire-lock** *wordplay to do with venereal disease:* **cannibal** = syphilis;

      fire-lock = diseased penis *(and type of pistol)*

51   **French** *Syphilis was called the 'French disease'.*

54   **plate** silver and gold tableware

      but just

55   **ducats** gold and silver coins used in many European countries

56   **cabinet** cupboard *or* private room

64   **approved** proved; confirmed

2 SERVANT	A Switzer?
1 SERVANT	With a pistol in his great codpiece!
BOSOLA	Ha, ha, ha.
1 SERVANT	The codpiece was the case for't.
2 SERVANT	There was a cunning traitor: who would have 45 searched his codpiece?
1 SERVANT	True, if he had kept out of the ladies' chambers; and all the moulds of his buttons were leaden bullets.
2 SERVANT	Oh wicked cannibal: a fire-lock in's codpiece? 50
1 SERVANT	'Twas a French plot, upon my life!
2 SERVANT	To see what the devil can do!

Enter ANTONIO, RODERIGO, GRISOLAN.

ANTONIO	All the officers here?
SERVANTS	We are.
ANTONIO	Gentlemen, We have lost much plate, you know; and but this evening Jewels to the value of four thousand ducats 55 Are missing in the Duchess' cabinet. Are the gates shut?
1 SERVANT	Yes.
ANTONIO	'Tis the Duchess' pleasure Each officer be locked into his chamber Till the sun-rising, and to send the keys Of all their chests, and of their outward doors, 60 Into her bedchamber: she is very sick.
RODERIGO	At her pleasure.
ANTONIO	She entreats you take't not ill. The innocent Shall be the more approved by it.

Antonio is afraid and tells Delio that the Duchess is too. Delio reassures him of his loyal friendship, and leaves for Rome. Cariola tells Antonio that his wife has had a boy

65 **Gentleman...woodyard** *mocking echo of line 36; working in the* **woodyard** *of Whitehall Palace near the Thames was a menial occupation (see also 2.5.43)*

68 **Black-guard** *a joke: the lowest menial in a nobleman's court (dirty from scrubbing pots and pans and, in common with most lowlife at this time, a synonym for untrustworthiness)*

73 **post** *travel with speed*

74 **service** *perhaps: friendship (see note to 73–74 below)*

76 **Somewhat** *something*

77 **shadow...fear** *i.e. it doesn't exist, it's just caused by your fear*

78 **mind** *consider; notice*

evils *disasters; misfortunes*

79 **throwing down salt** *Spilling salt has been an unlucky omen since the time of the Romans.*

crossing of a hare *It was unlucky for a hare to cross your path because witches were said to change into hares.*

80 **Bleeding at nose** *see 2.3.42–44*

80–81 **stumbling...cricket** *omens of death*

82 **daunt...us** *overcome our resolution; dash our spirits*

84 **for my faith** *as for you trusting me*

89 **set...nativity** *cast a horoscope for his birth (see page 236)*

Antonio

72–76 Jacqueline Pearson says: '"Fear" and a desire for "safety" at any cost become key characteristics of his in the second half of the play' (e.g. 2.3.11–12; 3.1.18). But Antonio is in danger, and of the thirteen uses of the word 'danger/dangerous' in the play, the majority are either said by him or used of his relationship with the Duchess. Philip Franks, the director of the 1995 Greenwich/Wyndham's production, also defends Antonio in this scene: 'Yes, he's gone to pieces, but it seems terribly naturalistic: his wife's having a baby at the worst possible time.'

Delio

73–74 Delio does go to Rome (see 2.4) but doesn't perform any service for Antonio. Either Webster revised the play and forgot to change these lines, or Antonio is merely acknowledging that Delio is leaving for Rome (where the brothers are) that night, and *My life lies in your service* means that his life depends on Delio keeping quiet about the birth (although Delio leaves before the news that Antonio has a son!). Webster may have deliberately written these lines so dramatically in order to keep the tension at a high level.

Performance

86–89 In the 1995 Cheek by Jowl production Cariola actually came on with the baby and sat down. Antonio didn't go near them; he hovered uncertainly and then went off to arrange the horoscope. In the much less bleak 2003 National Theatre production, Cariola appeared without the baby (as is normal), and Antonio greeted her news with delight.

BOSOLA	Gentleman o'th'woodyard, where's your Switzer now?	65

1 SERVANT	By this hand, 'twas credibly reported by one o'th' Black-guard.	

Exeunt all but DELIO and ANTONIO.

DELIO	How fares it with the Duchess?	

ANTONIO	She's exposed	
	Unto the worst of torture, pain, and fear.	70

DELIO	Speak to her all happy comfort.	

ANTONIO	How I do play the fool with mine own danger!	
	You are this night, dear friend, to post to Rome,	
	My life lies in your service.	

DELIO	Do not doubt me.	

ANTONIO	Oh, 'tis far from me: and yet fear presents me	75
	Somewhat that looks like danger.	

DELIO	Believe it,	
	'Tis but the shadow of your fear, no more:	
	How superstitiously we mind our evils!	
	The throwing down salt, or crossing of a hare,	
	Bleeding at nose, the stumbling of a horse	80
	Or singing of a cricket, are of power	
	To daunt whole man in us. Sir, fare you well:	
	I wish you all the joys of a blessed father	
	And, for my faith, lay this unto your breast:	
	Old friends, like old swords, still are trusted best.	85

Exit.

Enter CARIOLA.

CARIOLA	Sir, you are the happy father of a son.	
	Your wife commends him to you.	

ANTONIO	Blessed comfort:	
	For heaven' sake tend her well. I'll presently	
	Go set a figure for's nativity.	

Exeunt.

2.3 *Just after one o'clock in the morning Bosola and Antonio run into each other in a dark courtyard of the palace*

s.d. *dark lantern* a lantern with a shutter than can conceal its light

1 **list** listen

4 **In the confining** in imprisoning

5 **several wards** *possibly sarcastic:* various prison departments

    part of it a share in the knowledge of the stratagem

6 **My...freeze else** *i.e. I will not advance in my role as a spy*

9 **owl** *see note to 3.2.89*

10 **...who's there...** *Antonio may be carrying only a candle.*

12 **forced...fear** *Antonio's expression of (real) fear is so unusual to Bosola that he comments on it as* **forced** = unnatural.

14 **mole** *This burrowing animal was also used of those who worked in the dark.*

    undermine me work secretly against me

20 **figure** horoscope *(see page 236)*

    jewels *another lie, following his earlier one at 2.2.55–56 (and again at line 34)*

Ideas and interpretations

1–9 The first *shriek* (1) that Bosola heard before he entered was presumably the Duchess, but now that she has given birth he may be hearing an owl (6). It is interesting that he might be confusing the Duchess's cry and the call of an owl since Ferdinand later calls the Duchess a *screech owl* (see note to 3.2.89).

Language

10–42 The shared lines (e.g. three speeches make up line 15), short speeches and diction are clearly inspired by the night scene (2.2) between Macbeth and Lady Macbeth after he has just killed Duncan. Webster probably saw Shakespeare's *Macbeth* at the Globe in 1606.

Performance

This night scene is normally played with the stage lights dimmed or even with no other light than from the torches (or lanterns) the two men are holding. Candlelight was probably reduced at the Blackfriars theatre to enhance the atmosphere, but it couldn't be as effective on the stage of the Globe in the afternoon.

Scene 3

Enter BOSOLA with a dark lantern.

BOSOLA   Sure I did hear a woman shriek: list, ha?
And the sound came, if I received it right,
From the Duchess' lodgings. There's some stratagem
In the confining all our courtiers
To their several wards. I must have part of it,   5
My intelligence will freeze else. List again:
It may be 'twas the melancholy bird,
Best friend of silence, and of solitariness,
The owl, that screamed so – Ha? Antonio?

Enter ANTONIO with a horoscope.

ANTONIO   I heard some noise: who's there? What art thou?
       Speak.   10

BOSOLA   Antonio? Put not your face nor body
To such a forced expression of fear;
I am Bosola, your friend.

ANTONIO   Bosola?
     (*Aside*) This mole does undermine me – heard you
       not
     A noise even now?

BOSOLA   From whence?

ANTONIO   From the Duchess' lodging.   15

BOSOLA   Not I. Did you?

ANTONIO   I did, or else I dreamed.

BOSOLA   Let's walk towards it.

ANTONIO   No. It may be 'twas
     But the rising of the wind.

BOSOLA   Very likely.
     Methinks 'tis very cold, and yet you sweat.
     You look wildly.

ANTONIO   I have been setting a figure   20
     For the Duchess' jewels.

2.3

Antonio implies that Bosola gave the Duchess poisoned apricots and accuses him of stealing the jewels. They quarrel and Antonio drops the horoscope by mistake

22 **radical** *astrological term:* fit to be judged *(i.e. Is the timing suitable?)*

23 **design** purpose

25 **night-walker** person who walks about by night with criminal intentions *(the term was common in the seventeenth century)*

32 **Spanish fig** *wordplay:* (1) an expression of contempt *(Bosola may accompany it with a rude hand gesture in which his thumb is inserted between his two first fingers and pointed at Antonio);* (2) a notorious poison

   imputation accusation

35 **conceit** opinion

38 **ruin** falling down

40 **scarce...sting** *This is a dig at Bosola who has only been in his post for nine months.*

40–41 **sting...You libel** *Editors have suggested that Bosola must be missing a line here, because the 1623 quarto repeats 'Antonio' for lines 39 and 41.*

41 **libel** make a malicious accusation; defame

41–42 **Copy...to't** write it out and I will sign it as a true statement *(this either refers to the missing line or to* **false steward** *at line 36)*

45 **wrought** embroidered *(i.e. his initials on the handkerchief)*

Performance

In the 2003 National Theatre production Antonio and Bosola were friendly at first – behaving as courtiers who had got on quite well for the preceding nine months, but their attitude to each other suddenly changed. At *You are a false steward* (36) Bosola hit out at Antonio, who dropped one of the papers he was carrying – the horoscope (see page 259).

BOSOLA   Ah: and how falls your question?
Do you find it radical?
                     What's that to you?

ANTONIO   'Tis rather to be questioned what design,
When all men were commanded to their lodgings,
Makes you a night-walker.

BOSOLA   In sooth I'll tell you: 25
Now all the court's asleep, I thought the devil
Had least to do here. I came to say my prayers,
And if it do offend you I do so,
You are a fine courtier.

ANTONIO   (*Aside*)   This fellow will undo me. –
You gave the Duchess apricots today,   30
Pray heaven they were not poisoned.

BOSOLA   Poisoned?
A Spanish fig for the imputation.

ANTONIO   Traitors are ever confident till they
Are discovered. There were jewels stolen too.
In my conceit none are to be suspected   35
More than yourself.

BOSOLA   You are a false steward.

ANTONIO   Saucy slave, I'll pull thee up by the roots!

BOSOLA   May be the ruin will crush you to pieces.

ANTONIO   You are an impudent snake indeed, sir!
Are you scarce warm and do you show your sting?   40

[BOSOLA   …]

ANTONIO   You libel well, sir.

BOSOLA   No, sir. Copy it out
And I will set my hand to't.

ANTONIO   (*Aside*)   My nose bleeds.
     (*Takes out handkerchief and drops paper*)
One that were superstitious would count
This ominous, when it merely comes by chance:
Two letters that are wrought here for my name   45

2.3 Antonio warns Bosola that he will be imprisoned in the morning and leaves. Bosola finds the paper Antonio dropped and discovers it is a horoscope for the Duchess's son born that night. Bosola will inform the brothers of this by letter

47 **accident** chance

I'll take order I'll make arrangements

48 **safe** kept in custody

colour render plausible; explain

51 **quit yourself** proved your innocence

52–53 **'The great...shame'** This *'sententia'* shows that Antonio is ashamed of his lies.

55 **false friend** the lantern

56 **nativity** *'The horoscope, with its dire prognostication of a violent death, is astrological gibberish' (John Russell Brown).*

58 ***Anno Dom*** *usual written abbreviation of Anno Domini = AD (Latin: in the year of the Lord)*

59 ***decimo...Decembris*** *Latin:* on the 19th December *(see note to 2.1.81)*

60 ***meridian*** circle of longitude

61–62 ***Lord...ascendant*** see 2.1.109

62 ***combust*** burnt up

63 ***Mars*** god of war *(and the planet)*

human sign *e.g. Sagittarius*

64 ***tail of the Dragon*** part of the moon's path

65 ***Caetera non scrutantur*** *Latin:* the rest is not investigated

66 **precise** who strictly follows rules; particular *(ironically it also had the meaning:* complete; perfect – *see 1.1.439)*

67 **bawd** go-between; pimp

68 **parcel of intelligency** piece of news

70 **committed** imprisoned

72–73 **If one...discover** *It takes Bosola at least two more years to find out what the audience already know (see page 256).*

75–76 **her...livers** *i.e. her brothers will be extremely bitter and angry (see notes to 1.1.23 and 304)*

76 **thrifty** successful; fortunate

77–78 **'Though...wise'** *Bosola is mistaken about the Duchess, and Webster will deliberately connect* **lust** *and* **witty** *with Julia: see 2.4.5.*

77 **masque** mask

Bosola

66–67 Despite having been a spy in the household for about nine months, Bosola has no idea that Antonio is the Duchess's lover. This is perhaps because it would be unbelievable that an aristocratic lady would choose such a *base, low fellow* (his description of Antonio at 3.5.113), rather than that Bosola is useless at spying (it also suggests that Bosola's admiration for Antonio in 3.2 – e.g. 245–255 – is feigned). See also pages 254, 256 and 259.

Language

52–53 'Sententiae' (the plural of the Latin word) was the term used for wise sayings like this, which were used by many writers. They occur several times in the play, often in inverted commas. (See other examples at 3.5.137 and 140.) John Russell Brown suggests that these 'sententiae' 'are like signposts, provided by the play's characters as they step out of character and out of dramatic time'. See also Kathleen McLuskie's comments on page 250.

Are drowned in blood:
Mere accident. (*Aloud*) For you, sir, I'll take order:
I'th'morn you shall be safe. (*Aside*) 'Tis that must
    colour
Her lying in: (*Aloud*) sir, this door you pass not.
I do not hold it fit that you come near   50
The Duchess' lodgings till you have quit yourself.
(*Aside*) 'The great are like the base, nay, they are the
    same,
When they seek shameful ways to avoid shame.'

Exit.

BOSOLA   Antonio here about did drop a paper:
Some of your help, false friend: oh, here it is.   55
What's here? A child's nativity calculated?
(*Reads*) *The Duchess was delivered of a son, 'tween the*
hours twelve and one, in the night, Anno Dom: 1504,
(that's this year) *decimo nono Decembris,* (that's
this night) *taken according to the meridian of Malfi*   60
(that's our Duchess: happy discovery). *The Lord of the*
first house, being combust in the ascendant, signifies
short life; and Mars being in a human sign, joined to
the tail of the Dragon, in the eighth house, doth
threaten a violent death. Caetera non scrutantur.   65
Why now 'tis most apparent. This precise fellow
Is the Duchess' bawd. I have it to my wish.
This is a parcel of intelligency
Our courtiers were cased up for. It needs must
    follow
That I must be committed on pretence   70
Of poisoning her, which I'll endure, and laugh at.
If one could find the father now: but that
Time will discover. Old Castruchio
I'th'morning posts to Rome; by him I'll send
A letter that shall make her brothers' galls   75
O'erflow their livers. This was a thrifty way.
'Though lust do masque in ne'er so strange disguise
She's oft found witty, but is never wise.'

Exit.

In the Cardinal's palace at Rome, Julia tells the Cardinal that she will be his mistress

4   **anchorite** an extreme ascetic Christian (both men and women) who lived withdrawn from the world in a small cell

5   **devotion** religious reverence *(also wordplay on non-religious sense)*

    witty *see note to 2.3.77–78*

11 **approved** found; experienced

13 **Did...them?** have you ever found me inconstant?

    Sooth truly; truth to say

14–15 **A man...fixed** *The idea is that glass is not malleable – it will just break if you* try to change its form – so a man will never *(***Ere*** = ever) find a constant (***fixed***) woman.*

16 **glass** telescope

17 **Galileo** *In 1610 Galileo Galilei, the Italian astronomer, published his famous account of the moon as seen through his new, powerful telescope.*

18 **moon** *an image of inconstancy (used e.g. in* Romeo and Juliet *2.2)*

21 **justification** defence *(for being inconstant)*

The Cardinal and Julia (Edward Petherbridge and Sheila Hancock) (National Theatre, 1985)

Julia

Webster did not find Julia in his source; he invented her. Bradbrook describes her as 'a foil to the Duchess...who takes a man if she feels the impulse'. As the Duchess will agree to, later (see 3.2.304–316), Julia pretends she is on a religious pilgrimage (3–5). Julia is escaping her husband to meet a lover; the Duchess escaping her brother to meet her husband.

Cardinal

5–6 The Cardinal's amused reaction to Julia feigning a religious pilgrimage contrasts with his reaction to the Duchess feigning one (3.3.61–62). The Cardinal, as a Roman Catholic priest, ought to be celibate and unmarried. Protestant English audiences particularly enjoyed Catholic priests depicted as immoral monsters, and Cardinals and Popes as villains, especially after the failed Gunpowder Plot of 1605.

Scene 4

Enter CARDINAL and JULIA.

CARDINAL   Sit: thou art my best of wishes.Prithee tell me
What trick didst thou invent to come to Rome
Without thy husband?

JULIA   Why, my lord, I told him
I came to visit an old anchorite
Here, for devotion.

CARDINAL   Thou art a witty false one –   5
I mean, to him.

JULIA   You have prevailed with me
Beyond my strongest thoughts; I would not now
Find you inconstant.

CARDINAL   Do not put thyself
To such a voluntary torture, which proceeds
Out of your own guilt.

JULIA   How, my lord?   10

CARDINAL   You fear my constancy because you have approved
Those giddy and wild turnings in yourself.

JULIA   Did you e'er find them?

CARDINAL   Sooth, generally, for women,
A man might strive to make glass malleable
Ere he should make them fixed.

JULIA   So, my lord.   15

CARDINAL   We had need go borrow that fantastic glass
Invented by Galileo the Florentine
To view another spacious world i'th'moon,
And look to find a constant woman there.

JULIA   This is very well, my lord.

CARDINAL   Why do you weep?   20
Are tears your justification? The selfsame tears
Will fall into your husband's bosom, lady,

2.4 *Julia is upset at the Cardinal's words but he assures her of his passion. A servant tells them that a man has come from Malfi to see her and that her husband has arrived in Rome*

25–26 **jealously...cuckold** *The only way to make sense of this is as an ironic comment: it is not wise for husbands to love jealously, but he can since he can't be cuckolded (because he is not a husband).*

28–30 **I...fly at it** *imagery from falconry: see note to 27–36 below*

31–32 **watched...elephant** *see note to 31–32 below*

33 **high feeding** rich, luxurious food

38 **liver** *i.e. as the seat of love*

39 **in physic** receiving medical treatment

41 **lightning...to't** lightning moves slow in comparison to my passion *(but lightning also usually symbolised impermanence)*

45 **post** fast *(see note to 1.1.256)*

Cardinal and Julia

27–36 'It is clear that the Cardinal's description of the affair expresses only satisfaction at his sexual prowess. He compares Julia to a falcon, a creature whose flight is completely controlled by the falconer who is, of course, the Cardinal himself...The repeated "still you are to thank me" with which the Cardinal punctuates this speech indicates a pose of complete self-satisfaction; he regards Julia as completely his creature with no independent contribution to make to the affair' (Kathleen McLuskie).

31–32 King James established a menagerie of wild animals in St James's Park, near Whitehall Palace, including an elephant sent to him by King Philip of Spain. It is said to have been fed on burgundy wine during the winter! The image suggests that Julia has been kept simply as an exotic object by her husband.

Performance

There is normally some kind of sexual activity between the Cardinal and Julia in this scene. In the 2003 National Theatre production Julia sat on his desk with her legs open. In the 1980 Manchester Royal Exchange production they mimed sexual intercourse. In the 1995 Cheek by Jowl production the Cardinal (Paul Brennen) hurt her breast in a way that suggested their relationship was sado-masochistic. At a performance in 1618 the Cardinal was shown 'with a harlot on his knee' – when Julia was played by a boy, of course.

With a loud protestation that you love him
Above the world. Come, I'll love you wisely,
That's jealously, since I am very certain   25
You cannot me make cuckold.

JULIA   I'll go home
          To my husband.

CARDINAL   You may thank me, lady:
          I have taken you off your melancholy perch,
          Bore you upon my fist, and showed you game,
          And let you fly at it. I pray thee kiss me.   30
          When thou wast with thy husband thou wast
               watched
          Like a tame elephant – still you are to thank me –
          Thou hadst only kisses from him, and high feeding,
          But what delight was that? 'Twas just like one
          That hath a little fingering on the lute,   35
          Yet cannot tune it – still you are to thank me.

JULIA   You told me of a piteous wound i'th'heart
          And a sick liver, when you wooed me first,
          And spake like one in physic.

          Knocking.

CARDINAL   Who's that?
          Rest firm: for my affection to thee,   40
          Lightning moves slow to't.

          Enter SERVANT.

SERVANT   Madam, a gentleman
          That's come post from Malfi, desires to see you.

CARDINAL   Let him enter, I'll withdraw.

                                             Exit.

SERVANT   He says
          Your husband, old Castruchio, is come to Rome,
          Most pitifully tired with riding post.   45

                                             Exit.

2.4 *To the audience's, and Julia's, surprise, Delio enters and tells Julia he has brought her some money*

48 **lie** stay; sleep

49 **Roman prelates** Roman Catholic bishops, archbishops etc.

51 **commendations** greetings

54 **good back** *Delio is mocking Castruchio as impotent as well as weak and a bad horseman*

56 **breech** breeches *(breeches were like long tight shorts, so this means his thighs and bottom were sore)*

56–57 **Your...pity** what you laugh at you should instead pity me for, since I have to deal with him

64 **cassia** herb similar to cinnamon *(i.e. one of great fragrance)*

civet musky perfume taken from the scent glands of a civet cat

65 **physical** used in medicine; good for one's health

fond foolish

Delio

'I think Delio is very interesting because he's so slippery. He's somebody surfing on the top of this world, and you can make moral judgements about him if you like, but he survives, and he survives without getting his hands *too* dirty, but what you see with him is somebody playing the game of the time: "It might do me a great deal of good if I had a mistress – if she was powerful, it just might."' (Philip Franks, director of the 1995 Greenwich/Wyndham's Theatres production).

Enter DELIO.

JULIA	Signior Delio? (*Aside*) 'Tis one of my old suitors.
DELIO	I was bold to come and see you.
JULIA	Sir, you are welcome.
DELIO	Do you lie here?
JULIA	Sure, your own experience Will satisfy you no, our Roman prelates Do not keep lodging for làdies.
DELIO	Very well: 50 I have brought you no commendations from your husband, For I know none by him.
JULIA	I hear he's come to Rome?
DELIO	I never knew man and beast, of a horse and a knight, So weary of each other; if he had had a good back He would have undertook to have borne his horse, 55 His breech was so pitifully sore.
JULIA	Your laughter Is my pity.
DELIO	Lady, I know not whether You want money, but I have brought you some.
JULIA	From my husband?
DELIO	No, from mine own allowance.
JULIA	I must hear the condition ere I be bound to take it. 60
DELIO	Look on't, 'tis gold, hath it not a fine colour?
JULIA	I have a bird more beautiful.
DELIO	Try the sound on't.
JULIA	A lute-string far exceeds it, It hath no smell, like cassia or civet, Nor is it physical, though some fond doctors 65

2.5 *It is reported that Bosola's letter about the Duchess's child has made Ferdinand mad; Julia rejects Delio; Ferdinand and the Cardinal enter with the letter as Delio exits*

66 **seeth't in cullisses** cook it *(gold coins)* in strong broths

67 **bred by –** *'Julia intended to complete the sentence with some such phrase as "unnatural means", alluding to the traditional comparison of usury and an unnatural breeding of gold' (1995 Cambridge edition).*

Your husband Castruchio *(Webster has ironically finished line 67 with mention of her husband, who is incapable of breeding)*

Duke of Calabria Ferdinand

82–83 **'They...done'** 'those who think hard before they undertake an action will go safely through whirlpools and avoid great troubles'

1 **mandrake** mandragora *(see note to 4.2.234 and below)*

2 **What's the prodigy?** what does the omen say?

Delio and Julia

74 *my mistress:* This has always surprised audiences (see note to 2.2.73–74). Some critics have suggested that Webster intended to use Julia to spy on the brothers, but this is never stated. It is more likely that Webster wanted to make Delio a more complex character and to develop the atmosphere of intrigue, with characters being not all that they seem to be.

77 Kathleen McLuskie says that Delio, to his astonishment, has been rejected: 'Both Julia and the Duchess assert their independence in the only way open to them, by sexual choice.'

Antonio and Delio

79–83 Delio is Antonio's *noble friend* (3.1.1) – the only man Antonio can confide in (e.g. 2.1.81–92, 179–192). Here he says Antonio's marriage was due to *ambition*, and in the couplet he suggests Antonio should have thought hard before marrying. But Delio's proposition to Julia shows his unromantic attitude to women: Julia can be bought – as a fashionable accessory? This suggests it has not crossed his mind that Antonio might love the Duchess and is not in the relationship for either money or ambition.

Language

82–83 The strict ten syllables and simple rhyme – *shun...done* – seem to give an old-fashioned moral message, but to a sophisticated Jacobean audience this style would undermine the supposed weight of Delio's thoughts, and make them question what he had said.

1 Written about since biblical and classical times, the mandrake plant is connected with madness, sex, fertility, witchcraft, foretelling the future and sleep. The root of the plant is forked and thus resembles a man; it was said to shriek when pulled out of the ground – and produce madness in the person who heard it. It was well known as a love potion. As a narcotic it links with Ferdinand's unusual need for sleep – see 2.5.76 and comments by the actor Will Keen on page 262.

Persuade us seeth't in cullisses; I'll tell you,
This is a creature bred by –

Enter SERVANT.

SERVANT   Your husband's come,
Hath delivered a letter to the Duke of Calabria that,
To my thinking, hath put him out of his wits.

                                          Exit.

JULIA   Sir, you hear: 70
Pray let me know your business, and your suit,
As briefly as can be.

DELIO   With good speed. I would wish you,
At such time as you are non-resident
With your husband, my mistress.

JULIA   Sir, I'll go ask my husband if I shall,   75
And straight return your answer.

                                          Exit.

DELIO   Very fine.
Is this her wit, or honesty, that speaks thus?
I heard one say the Duke was highly moved
With a letter sent from Malfi. I do fear
Antonio is betrayed. How fearfully   80
Shows his ambition now: unfortunate Fortune!
'They pass through whirlpools, and deep woes do shun,
Who the event weigh, ere the action's done.'

                                          Exit.

Scene 5

Enter CARDINAL and FERDINAND, with a letter.

FERDINAND   I have this night digged up a mandrake.

CARDINAL   Say you?

FERDINAND   And I am grown mad with't.

CARDINAL   What's the prodigy?

Ferdinand is filled with fury at the news; the Cardinal is in control but appalled that their royal blood has been tainted

3 **loose i'th'hilts** promiscuous; unchaste *(this sexual reference is to the blade of a sword which was 'inserted' into the hilt – the handle of the sword)*

4 **strumpet** prostitute; promiscuous woman *(see also 3.1.26)*

5 **publish't** make it publicly known

6 **bounty** gifts

7 **Aloud...covetous** *This seems to refer to the* **rogues**, *not the* **servants**; *the former are* **covetous** *'because they hope to be paid for future silence, or further information' (John Russell Brown).*

8 **confusion** ruin

9 **cunning bawds** clever pimps *(***cunning** *also has the idea of magical knowledge and witchcraft)*

10–11 **more...service** *perhaps:* more safe means of providing her with a sexual partner than a garrison of soldiers have

11 **service** (1) army supplies; (2) sexual satisfaction

12 **this** the letter from Bosola

Rhubarb *This bitter, medicinal root was used as a purgative.*

13 **choler** anger *(see note to 1.1.499)*

Here's *may refer to the horoscope Bosola has sent them, or to his brain*

16–21 **Why...honours** *The Cardinal uses* **tempest** *as a metaphor, but Ferdinand wishes he were one. The motifs of storm and tempest run through the play (e.g. 1.1.476; 3.1.22).*

19 **meads** meadows

20 **general** whole

22 **Aragon and Castile** *The Duchess and her brothers are of the royal family that ruled Spain, the kingdom of Naples (Italy south of the papal states, including Sicily) and Sardinia. The two Spanish kingdoms of Aragon and Castile had united to include most of modern Spain in 1479.*

23 **attainted** tainted: infected with corruption, poison etc.

physic medicine

24 **balsamum** balm *(a fragrant ointment used for wounds or embalming the dead)*

25 **cupping-glass** surgical vessel to draw off blood

Cardinal and Ferdinand

20–26 The brothers are incensed that the Duchess has destroyed the honour of their family and polluted their noble blood (see also, for example, 33–36). According to some critics, and to Jacobean ideas of social hierarchy, she is at fault. But the critic Karin Coddon points out that Webster gives these views to the brothers who represent 'dissemblance, corruption, even madness'.

21–23 Muriel Bradbrook suggests that the Cardinal's belief in pride and honour was a particularly Spanish belief of Webster's time, and that Webster added 'contemporary colour' to the story of the Duchess: 'The Spanish rulers of the Kingdom of Naples could be interpreted in the light of contemporary Spanish honour and Spanish pride.'

Language

21–26 *blood:* The Cardinal means 'lineage'; Ferdinand means 'sexual desire, passion'. Note also that the former says *our*, meaning the family; Ferdinand says *hers*. He also uses medical imagery that distances himself from his sister.

FERDINAND   Read there: a sister damned, she's loose i'th'hilts,
Grown a notorious strumpet!

CARDINAL   Speak lower.

FERDINAND   Lower?
Rogues do not whisper't now, but seek to publish't, 5
As servants do the bounty of their lords,
Aloud; and with a covetous searching eye
To mark who note them. Oh confusion seize her!
She hath had most cunning bawds to serve her turn,
And more secure conveyances for lust   10
Than towns of garrison for service.

CARDINAL   Is't possible?
Can this be certain?

FERDINAND   Rhubarb, oh, for rhubarb
To purge this choler! Here's the cursèd day
To prompt my memory, and here it shall stick
Till of her bleeding heart I make a sponge   15
To wipe it out.

CARDINAL   Why do you make yourself
So wild a tempest?

FERDINAND   Would I could be one,
That I might toss her palace 'bout her ears,
Root up her goodly forests, blast her meads,
And lay her general territory as waste   20
As she hath done her honours.

CARDINAL   Shall our blood,
The royal blood of Aragon and Castile,
Be thus attainted?

FERDINAND   Apply desperate physic!
We must not now use balsamum, but fire,
The smarting cupping-glass, for that's the mean 25
To purge infected blood, such blood as hers.
There is a kind of pity in mine eye,
I'll give it to my handkercher – and now 'tis here,
I'll bequeath this to her bastard.

CARDINAL   What to do?

2.5 *Ferdinand seems to be going mad as he imagines his sister's lover, and the Cardinal criticises him*

32 **Unequal** unjust

32–33 **place...side** *It was said that because the hearts of humans are on the left side of our bodies we tend to be deceitful, and that women's hearts are even more to the left.*

34 **bark** boat

37–38 **Ignorance...wield it** *This comes from the character description of a truly noble man by Joseph Hall, published in 1608.*

38–39 **laughing...hyena** *The spotted hyena has a high 'giggle' when chased; these predators were also seen as sexually ambiguous, because not only do the females dominate the males, but the females appear to have a penis (see also the comment on Antonio at 3.2.218).*

42 **Happily** haply: perhaps

43 **woodyard** *see note to 2.2.65*

quoit the sledge *a sport:* throw the hammer *(a* **sledge** *is a heavy hammer used by blacksmiths, usually wielded with both hands)*

44 **toss the bar** throw the bar *(= piece of wood/tree trunk, i.e. 'toss the caber', a*

traditional Highland game like throwing the hammer, and therefore Ferdinand/Webster is dangerously suggesting that the Duchess's supposed lover is Scottish – as James's lover was at this time: see page 234)

squire young man; lover

45 **coals** *Coal is of course burnt wood and may continue an allusion from* **woodyard** *and* **bar** *with some satirical, topical meaning, or may simply imply a menial servant.*

privy lodgings *wordplay:* (1) private rooms; (2) sexual private parts/penetrations

46 **Go to, mistress** come, come, madam

47 **wild-fire** destructive fire or passion *(see also 3.2.116)*

51 **whirlwinds** *Ferdinand is again connected with storm imagery: see note to 2.5.16–21.*

intemperate excessive; violent

55 **palsy** powerless tremors

Ferdinand

47–48 Ferdinand had indirectly suggested his sister was a *whore* when advising her not to remarry (1.1.307); now he directly calls her a *whore*, twice. 'One way to contain women who acted in ways contrary to accepted patterns of female behaviour was to label them "whores" or "witches"' (Theodora Jankowski). Ferdinand also links his sister with witchcraft (see note to 3.1.78). The 1995 Cambridge editors add: 'The identification of Ferdinand with fire, which began at [1.1.127–130], is carried a stage further here, with the *wild-fire* burning within. The references to *milk* and *blood* again show Ferdinand's obsession with his sister's body.'

FERDINAND	Why, to make soft lint for his mother's wounds,	30
	When I have hewed her to pieces.	

CARDINAL   Cursed creature!
Unequal nature, to place women's hearts
So far upon the left side.

FERDINAND   Foolish men,
That e'er will trust their honour in a bark
Made of so slight weak bullrush as is woman,   35
Apt every minute to sink it!

CARDINAL   Thus
Ignorance, when it hath purchased honour,
It cannot wield it.

FERDINAND   Methinks I see her laughing –
Excellent hyena! Talk to me somewhat quickly,
Or my imagination will carry me   40
To see her in the shameful act of sin.

CARDINAL   With whom?

FERDINAND   Happily with some strong-thighed bargeman;
Or one o'th'woodyard that can quoit the sledge
Or toss the bar; or else some lovely squire
That carries coals up to her privy lodgings.   45

CARDINAL   You fly beyond your reason.

FERDINAND   Go to, mistress,
'Tis not your whore's milk that shall quench my
    wild-fire,
But your whore's blood!

CARDINAL   How idly shows this rage, which carries you
As men conveyed by witches through the air   50
On violent whirlwinds! This intemperate noise
Fitly resembles deaf men's shrill discourse,
Who talk aloud, thinking all other men
To have their imperfection.

FERDINAND   Have not you
My palsy?

CARDINAL   Yes. I can be angry   55

2.5 *The Cardinal is alarmed at his brother's reaction; Ferdinand finally calms down and decides not to do anything until he knows who his sister's lover is*

56 **rupture** bursting; breaking

56–57 **there...beastly** *This recalls Bosola's lines (2.1.54–60), and prefigures Ferdinand's lycanthropy (5.2.5–19).*

58 **Chide** scold; rebuke

59–61 **You...themselves** There are several men who have shown their strong need for peace only by being troublesome to (or distressing) themselves and others. *(Note the rhymes:* **expressed**; **rest**; **unrest** *– these suggest a proverbial expression conveying some generalised moral statement.)*

61–62 **Come...tune** *This musical metaphor picks up on the 'discord' the Duchess felt might happen (see note to 1.1.473).*

62–63 **study...am not** *Appearance and reality is one of the major themes of the play.*

67 **coal pit** pit where charcoal is made

ventage air-hole

69–70 **dip...match** *a death inflicted on a servant by an Italian prince, described by Painter, Webster's source*

71 **cullis** meat-based broth

76 **I'll go sleep** *see page 262*

77 **leaps** copulates with *(a verb normally used of animals)*

78 **scorpions** knotted cords, lead balls, or steel spikes on a whip *(an instrument of torture which inflicted extreme pain)*

79 **general** total

Cardinal and Ferdinand

66 *Are you stark mad?:* The Cardinal is calm compared to Ferdinand; he doesn't understand Ferdinand's reaction (see also 46: *You fly beyond your reason*). 'Only if we accept the unmistakable suggestion of incestuous jealousy in this scene does Ferdinand's behaviour become more understandable for us than for the Cardinal' (James L Calderwood). (See also page 249.)

Language

66–70 'The linking, in this ferocious piece of imagining, of sex, fire, and religion, marks the culmination...of several lines of metaphoric suggestion, where fire and storm, the traditional metaphors for choler, also suggest the fires and storms of desire...and, at the deepest level, the identification of Ferdinand with hell, witchcraft, and the Devil; wind and fire being traditional attributes of hell' (1995 Cambridge edition).

Without this rupture; there is not in nature
A thing that makes man so deformed, so beastly,
As doth intemperate anger. Chide yourself.
You have diverse men who never yet expressed
Their strong desire of rest, but by unrest –   60
By vexing of themselves. Come, put yourself
In tune.

FERDINAND   So, I will only study to seem
The thing I am not. I could kill her now
In you, or in myself, for I do think
It is some sin in us heaven doth revenge   65
By her.

CARDINAL   Are you stark mad?

FERDINAND   I would have their bodies
Burnt in a coal pit with the ventage stopped,
That their cursed smoke might not ascend to
        heaven;
Or dip the sheets they lie in, in pitch or sulphur,
Wrap them in't and then light them like a match;   70
Or else to boil their bastard to a cullis
And give't his lecherous father to renew
The sin of his back.

CARDINAL   I'll leave you.

FERDINAND   Nay, I have done.
I am confident, had I been damned in hell
And should have heard of this, it would have
        put me   75
Into a cold sweat. In, in, I'll go sleep.
Till I know who leaps my sister, I'll not stir:
That known, I'll find scorpions to string my whips,
And fix her in a general eclipse.

Exeunt.

3.1 *Malfi, at least two or three years later. Delio has returned to the Duchess's palace after a long absence, accompanying Duke Ferdinand*

8 **wink** close my eyes

12–15 **You...wife** *matters which took a long time in the early seventeenth century, which would raise laughs of recognition in the audience*

14 **reversion** right of succession to an office after the holder has retired or died

16 **insensibly** (1) imperceptibly; (2) without meaning

21–22 **sleep...winter** *Ferdinand has taken over from Bosola as the dormouse: see 1.1.286–291; for the tempest metaphor see note to 2.5.16–21.*

25 **directly** plainly

Delio

1–3 'One important thing about this scene is that we find out that Delio is working for Ferdinand – it's very interesting. Webster describes very deftly a world where you absolutely *had* to work in court if you wanted to get on at all. Delio maintains a certain amount of integrity, but he also has very grey areas' (Philip Franks, director).

Structure

6–11 Webster is mocking the classical unities, one of which was that a drama should take place within twenty-four hours. This rule was largely ignored by English dramatists, though Shakespeare set *The Tempest* (written about two years before *The Duchess*) within one day.

Act 3

Scene 1

Enter ANTONIO and DELIO.

ANTONIO   Our noble friend, my most beloved Delio,
Oh you have been a stranger long at court;
Came you along with the Lord Ferdinand?

DELIO   I did sir; and how fares your noble Duchess?

ANTONIO   Right fortunately well. She's an excellent   5
Feeder of pedigrees: since you last saw her,
She hath had two children more, a son and
    daughter.

DELIO   Methinks 'twas yesterday – let me but wink
And not behold your face, which to mine eye
Is somewhat leaner, verily I should dream   10
It were within this half hour.

ANTONIO   You have not been in law, friend Delio,
Nor in prison, nor a suitor at the court,
Nor begged the reversion of some great man's place,
Nor troubled with an old wife, which doth make   15
Your time so insensibly hasten.

DELIO   Pray sir tell me,
Hath not this news arrived yet to the ear
Of the Lord Cardinal?

ANTONIO   I fear it hath.
The Lord Ferdinand that's newly come to court
Doth bear himself right dangerously.

DELIO   Pray why?   20

ANTONIO   He is so quiet that he seems to sleep
The tempest out as dormice do in winter.
Those houses that are haunted are most still
Till the devil be up.

DELIO   What say the common people?

ANTONIO   The common rabble do directly say   25
She is a strumpet.

81

3.1

Antonio tells Delio that he is under suspicion about his growing wealth but that no one has guessed that he and the Duchess are married. Ferdinand enters and tells his sister he has thought of a husband for her

25–35 **common rabble...people** *an ironic parallel to Antonio's speech in 1.1.4–22*

27 **politic** prudent

censure judge

28 **purchase** wealth; gains; acquisitions

29 **left-hand** questionable; irregular; corrupt

31–35 **Great...people** *Webster took this from the poet John Donne's attack on Jesuit priests:* Ignatius his Conclave *(1611). Interestingly, in 1613 Donne was promised court employment by Robert Carr (see page 234) – a promise that was not met, and so Donne became a clergyman and began his celebrated career as a preacher as well as poet.*

31 **grudge** grumble that

34 **Lest...odious** in case, by complaining, the princes make the officers hateful

35 **obligation** contract; moral or legal tie

39 **bespeak** speak for; arrange for

41 **Malateste** *This count does appear – in 3.3 and Act 5 – but not as a suitor to the Duchess.*

43 **thorough** through

49 **Pasquil's...bullets** *Pasquillo or Pasquino was the name given to an ancient statue in Rome, dug up in 1501, which was used as a site for anonymous satiric verses – here called* **paper bullets** *because of the harm they could do.*

calumny malicious slander

52 **I pour...bosom** I assure you

53 **extenuate** lessen

Ferdinand

39–41 Has Ferdinand changed his mind about not wanting his sister to remarry? (See his lines at e.g. 1.1.262–264; 303–304.) His behaviour in 3.2 (e.g. 111–114) suggests that he is testing her here: he knows she has a lover and has had a child, so he wants to see her reaction. It is probably a lie, especially as when we actually see the *great Count Malateste* (41) in 3.3 he is thoroughly disparaged by Delio and other courtiers as an effete poseur. (See also the actor Will Keen's comments on pages 261–262.)

Duchess

43–44 Is the Duchess lying, or does she mean a different kind of honour from that believed in by her brothers? 'Honour' is part of the play's theme of 'who is greatest'. On the one hand there is *painted* and *seeming* honour, and supposed honour in war (see note to 1.1.67–68), on the other hand there is real honour, upheld by the Duchess and Antonio, and praised by Bosola (see note to 3.2.275–276). As to the Duchess's use of the future tense, she might well defend it as *a noble lie* (see 3.2.178–179).

DELIO   And your graver heads,
Which would be politic, what censure they?

ANTONIO   They do observe I grow to infinite purchase
The left-hand way, and all suppose the Duchess
Would amend it if she could. For, say they,   30
Great princes, though they grudge their officers
Should have such large and unconfinèd means
To get wealth under them, will not complain
Lest thereby they should make them odious
Unto the people; for other obligation –   35
Of love, or marriage, between her and me –
They never dream of.

Enter FERDINAND, DUCHESS and BOSOLA.

DELIO   The Lord Ferdinand
Is going to bed.

FERDINAND   I'll instantly to bed,
For I am weary. I am to bespeak
A husband for you.

DUCHESS   For me, sir? Pray who is't?   40

FERDINAND   The great Count Malateste.

DUCHESS   Fie upon him!
A Count? He's a mere stick of sugar candy,
You may look quite thorough him. When I choose
A husband, I will marry for your honour.

FERDINAND   You shall do well in't. – How is't, worthy Antonio? 45

DUCHESS   But, sir, I am to have private conference with you
About a scandalous report is spread
Touching mine honour.

FERDINAND   Let me be ever deaf to't:
One of Pasquil's paper bullets, court calumny,
A pestilent air which princes' palaces   50
Are seldom purged of. Yet, say that it were true:
I pour it in your bosom, my fixed love
Would strongly excuse, extenuate, nay deny
Faults, were they apparent in you. Go, be safe
In your own innocency.

3.1

The Duchess is relieved that her brother doesn't seem to mind about the rumours. After her exit Bosola tells Ferdinand he still doesn't know who the father of her children is but he has a skeleton key to her bedroom

57 **coulters** iron blades of ploughs *(in Old English law women could be forced to walk barefoot on red-hot coulters to prove they were chaste)*

60–62 **read...them** *see page 236*

70 **gulleries** tricks; deceptions

71 **mountebanks** itinerant quacks who sold useless medicines and potions by beguiling their audience with stories, juggling etc. *(from Italian:* monta in banco *– 'mount on a bench', because they stood on platforms in fairs and marketplaces)*

73 **will** (1) sexual desire; (2) intention

75 **lenitive** soothing *('Ferdinand means that these potions were sweet to take, but poisonous in that they rendered the takers crazy', John Russell Brown)*

of force powerful enough

77 **by equivocation** by being ambiguous in the words used

78 **rank** lustful; corrupt

80 **false key** skeleton key

Ferdinand

78 Ferdinand directly links his sister with witchcraft by actually denying witchcraft has anything to do with it: it's her *rank blood* – her lustful, lecherous nature rather than any magic potion. But perhaps he is trying to be rational here; his final speech to his sister in the bedchamber suggests the linking of his sister with witchcraft is powerfully present in his mind (3.2.139–140).

DUCHESS   Oh bless'd comfort, 55
This deadly air is purged.

Exeunt all but FERDINAND and BOSOLA.

FERDINAND   Her guilt treads on
Hot burning coulters. Now Bosola,
How thrives our intelligence?

BOSOLA   Sir, uncertainly:
'Tis rumoured she hath had three bastards, but
By whom, we may go read i'th'stars.

FERDINAND   Why some 60
Hold opinion all things are written there.

BOSOLA Yes, if we could find spectacles to read them.
I do suspect there hath been some sorcery
Used on the Duchess.

FERDINAND   Sorcery? To what purpose?

BOSOLA To make her dote on some desertless fellow 65
She shames to acknowledge.

FERDINAND   Can your faith give way
To think there's power in potions or in charms
To make us love, whether we will or no?

BOSOLA Most certainly.

FERDINAND Away! These are mere gulleries, horrid things 70
Invented by some cheating mountebanks
To abuse us. Do you think that herbs or charms
Can force the will? Some trials have been made
In this foolish practice, but the ingredients
Were lenitive poisons, such as are of force 75
To make the patient mad; and straight the witch
Swears, by equivocation, they are in love.
The witchcraft lies in her rank blood. This night
I will force confession from her. You told me
You had got, within these two days, a false key 80
Into her bedchamber?

BOSOLA   I have.

3.2 *Night-time at Malfi: Ferdinand prepares to visit the Duchess secretly; in the Duchess's bedchamber she prepares for bed*

84 **compass** *nautical image:* make a circuit of *(as around the world)*; navigate

drifts *wordplay:* (1) slow currents; (2) purposes

85 **put a girdle...world** *'a proverbial phrase, after Drake's circumnavigation of the world [1577–80], commonly used of daring actions and great ambitions'* *(John Russell Brown)*

86 **sounded** *nautical image:* discovered the depth of; investigated

88 **Your own chronicle** *i.e. blow your own trumpet* (**chronicle** = record of events in order of time)

90 **pension** wages; regular payment

91 **entertained** employed

92–93 **'That...defects'** 'the downfall of a great man is completely stopped by the friend who forces him to accept all his faults' *(Ferdinand's 'sententia' seems more out of touch with reality than others)*

1 **casket** box *(for her jewellery)*

glass mirror

5 **with cap and knee** *Removing one's cap and bending the knee showed respect.*

Bosola

84–91 Bosola deflates Ferdinand's self-aggrandisement with *I do not / Think so.* His next speech (88–90) could be dangerous in the light of the icy way Ferdinand can treat courtiers (see note to 1.1.126–130), even though Bosola is accepted as the *court-gall* (1.1.23) and speaks freely to Ferdinand elsewhere (e.g. 1.1.269–283). Bosola takes a risk also when he praises Antonio to the Duchess in the next scene (3.2.225–270).

Performance

In the 2003 National Theatre production, a bed was brought on, which showed it was their bedroom. At the beginning of the scene the Duchess played with her two elder children, dressed in their nightclothes. It was clear that the Duchess and Antonio had a very warm, happy relationship, which was shared by Cariola. In contrast this scene in the 1995 Cheek by Jowl production was quarrelsome; for example Antonio shouted crossly at the Duchess *my rule is only in the night* (8) – he was obviously unhappy about his subordinate relationship. (See also page 253 for the Greenwich/Wyndham's Theatres production.)

| FERDINAND | As I would wish. |

BOSOLA   What do you intend to do?

FERDINAND   Can you guess?

BOSOLA   No.

FERDINAND   Do not ask then.
He that can compass me, and know my drifts,
May say he hath put a girdle 'bout the world   85
And sounded all her quicksands.

BOSOLA   I do not
Think so.

FERDINAND   What do you think then, pray?

BOSOLA   That you are
Your own chronicle too much, and grossly
Flatter yourself.

FERDINAND   Give me thy hand, I thank thee.
I never gave pension but to flatterers   90
Till I entertained thee: farewell.
'That friend a great man's ruin strongly checks,
Who rails into his belief all his defects.'

Exeunt.

Scene 2

Enter DUCHESS, ANTONIO and CARIOLA.

DUCHESS   Bring me the casket hither, and the glass.
You get no lodging here tonight my lord.

ANTONIO   Indeed I must persuade one.

DUCHESS   Very good.
I hope in time 'twill grow into a custom
That noblemen shall come with cap and knee   5
To purchase a night's lodging of their wives.

ANTONIO   I must lie here.

7   **Lord of misrule** a young man elected at court, in some university colleges, Middle Temple *(see pages 231–232)* etc., to preside over the Christmas revels, e.g. mock ceremonies, banquets, masques (**misrule** = bad government)

9   **use** *sexual innuendo*

12 **disquiet** disturb

16–19 **Wherefore...ended** *Antonio has to rise early from his bed because of the 'need for secrecy, typical of adultery rather than of marriage'; in this scene 'lightheartedness is simultaneously present and painfully absent' (Frank Whigham).*

16 **still** always

18 **Count the clock** count the gongs of a striking clock *(usually on a church tower; the wealthy had table clocks, and both only had an hour hand – the minute hand was invented in the 1670s)*

20 **Venus** goddess of love

23–31 **Oh fie...stars** *These examples appear in Ovid's* Metamorphoses *(widely read in its original Latin in schools), but Webster took it mainly from George Whetstone's book of prose tales,* An Heptameron of Civil Discourses *(1582).*

24–25 **Daphne...bay-tree** *Daphne ran away from the god Apollo, who was in love with her; after her transformation he claimed the bay (the laurel) as his tree.*

24 **peevish** (1) senseless; (2) headstrong

25–26 **Syrinx...reed** *The god Pan pursued the nymph Syrinx; he made his panpipes from the reed.*

26–27 **Anaxarete...marble** *Humbly born Iphis fell in love with the princess Anaxarete; she scorned him so he hanged himself.*

28 **friends** lovers

30 **mulberry** *The tree's fruit turned red from the blood of Pyramus, who slew himself when he thought Thisbe was dead.*

Antonio and Duchess

7–8 Lord of misrule:

• Several recent critics see the public and private roles of the Duchess as important in the Renaissance context of the play. Susan Wells believes they are contradictory: 'She has established a family, but within that family she does not maintain her proper subordinate role. She has enforced a split between private life and public life, establishing Antonio as ruler of the night and lord of misrule, while she rules the public world of day.'

• Muriel Bradbrook, writing in 1980 from a pre-feminist viewpoint, says that Antonio jests about being a *Lord of misrule* but that he is indeed a social inferior who should not have married above his degree: 'He simply does not belong with the great ones; his role in the marriage is passive, indeed feminine; the Duchess, acting as the masculine half in the partnership, proposes the contract, directs their action, plans their flight, faces her brothers. At the end, Antonio hopes only to ask pardon of his new kinsmen. As a member of the Household, he should have respected its degrees.'

• A later, feminist reading of this scene by Theodora Jankowski has a different, positive, reading to Bradbrook's: 'The Duchess is...radically different from the traditional picture of the Renaissance wife in this scene': she is a woman who can command her husband as regards his sexual desires (4–6), and refuse him (2), but also 'thoroughly enjoys her sexuality' (10) and her children. Antonio is 'similarly radical for he is represented as not challenging his wife regarding his "rights" to her body or bed'.

DUCHESS	Must? You are a Lord of misrule.
ANTONIO	Indeed, my rule is only in the night.
DUCHESS	To what use will you put me?
ANTONIO	We'll sleep together.
DUCHESS	Alas, what pleasure can two lovers find in sleep? 10
CARIOLA	My lord, I lie with her often and I know She'll much disquiet you –
ANTONIO	See, you are complained of –
CARIOLA	For she's the sprawling'st bedfellow.
ANTONIO	I shall like her the better for that.
CARIOLA	Sir, shall I ask you a question?
ANTONIO	I pray thee Cariola. 15
CARIOLA	Wherefore still when you lie with my lady Do you rise so early?
ANTONIO	Labouring men Count the clock oft'nest, Cariola, Are glad when their task's ended.
DUCHESS	I'll stop your mouth (*Kisses him*).
ANTONIO	Nay, that's but one, Venus had two soft doves 20 To draw her chariot: I must have another (*She kisses him*). When wilt thou marry, Cariola?
CARIOLA	Never, my lord.
ANTONIO	Oh fie upon this single life! Forgo it: We read how Daphne, for her peevish flight, Became a fruitless bay-tree; Syrinx turn'd 25 To the pale empty reed; Anaxarete Was frozen into marble, whereas those Which married, or proved kind unto their friends, Were by a gracious influence transshaped Into the olive, pomegranate, mulberry, 30 Became flowers, precious stones or eminent stars.

3.2 *Antonio teases his wife and Cariola, then for a joke he and Cariola leave the Duchess on her own in the bedroom*

32 **vain** fruitless; ineffectual

33 **proposed me** put before me

34 **several** different

35 **Paris' case** *Paris, son of King Priam of Troy, was asked to judge who was the fairest of Minerva, Juno and Venus, who offered him* **wisdom**, **riches** *and the most beautiful woman, respectively. Paris chose Venus who helped him elope with Helen of Troy.*

36 **blind in't** lacking proper judgement

39 **motion** show

40 **Were...apprehension** that would cloud the brain

41 **severest counsellor** most unsparing barrister

44 **hard-favoured** ugly

48–51 **Did...undo him** *The area where Webster lived was home to several painters, including the royal portrait painter Robert Peake, whose painting of Prince Henry c. 1610 hangs in the National Portrait Gallery in London. Webster is writing from experience.*

55 **chafed** been angry

58 **wax** go

59 **arras** orris-root *(plant of the Iris genus, whose root was powdered to perfume or whiten hair)*

Antonio (Joe Dixon), the Duchess (Juliet Stevenson) and Cariola (Jane Galloway) (Greenwich/Wyndham's Theatres, 1995)

Ideas and interpretations

51–52 I prithee / When were we so merry?: 'Webster's characters have the trick of commenting on themselves when they are jesting...It is a trick that makes the transience or the unreality of their merriment stand out against the normal and real gloom' (Rupert Brooke). But there were also proverbs about merriment coming just before disaster, and Shakespeare refers to it: when Romeo has just killed Paris in the monument (5.3), he says: 'How oft when men are at the point of death / Have they been merry!'

CARIOLA	This is a vain poetry; but I pray you tell me,
	If there were proposed me wisdom, riches, and
	beauty,
	In three several young men, which should I choose?

ANTONIO	'Tis a hard question. This was Paris' case	35
	And he was blind in't, and there was great cause:
	For how was't possible he could judge right,
	Having three amorous goddesses in view,
	And they stark naked? 'Twas a motion
	Were able to benight the apprehension	40
	Of the severest counsellor of Europe.
	Now I look on both your faces so well formed
	It puts me in mind of a question I would ask.

| CARIOLA | What is't? |

ANTONIO	I do wonder why hard-favoured ladies
	For the most part keep worse-favoured waiting-
	women	45
	To attend them, and cannot endure fair ones.

DUCHESS	Oh, that's soon answered.
	Did you ever in your life know an ill painter
	Desire to have his dwelling next door to the shop
	Of an excellent picture-maker? 'Twould disgrace	50
	His face-making, and undo him. – I prithee
	When were we so merry? My hair tangles.

ANTONIO	(*Aside to* CARIOLA) Pray thee, Cariola, let's steal
	forth the room
	And let her talk to herself. I have divers times
	Served her the like, when she hath chafed extremely.	55
	I love to see her angry. Softly Cariola.

Exeunt ANTONIO and CARIOLA.

DUCHESS	Doth not the colour of my hair 'gin to change?
	When I wax grey I shall have all the court
	Powder their hair with arras, to be like me:
	You have cause to love me, I enter'd you into my
	heart	60

Enter FERDINAND, behind.

3.2   *Suddenly Ferdinand enters. He gives her a dagger and tells her to use it on herself. The Duchess tells him she is married*

61   **vouchsafe** graciously agree

62   **take you napping** catch you off your guard

65   **Love...sweetest** *Many see Antonio as passive, faceless and overshadowed by the Duchess – so this is an intriguingly different view.*

67   **gossips** godparents *(but with feminine resonances, see pages 247–248)*

68   **'Tis welcome** *This may refer to the poniard (dagger) (see also note to 1.1.335).*

s.d.   **FERDINAND...poniard** *a stage direction in the 1623 quarto*

71   **hid...hideous** *note the wordplay*

71–72   **What...eclipse thee?** *the answer is Ferdinand himself – see 2.5.79*

74   **essential** real

Performance

In the 2003 production at the National Theatre (see photograph above), Ferdinand (Will Keen) threatened the Duchess (Janet McTeer) with a pistol, which he then put in his mouth, as if he was going to shoot himself. In the 1995 Cheek by Jowl production, the Duchess (Anastasia Hille) was angry with Ferdinand at *Pray sir hear me* (72), slapped him, and when he fell on the floor she leapt on top of him and threatened him with the dagger (see cartoon on page 100).

Structure

s.d. after 67 An example of internal repetition: 'Ferdinand's gift of the poniard with its threatening phallic suggestions grimly recalls the Duchess' playful banter about the old tale in which a naked sword is placed between the two partners to keep them chaste [1.1.500–501]' (Jacqueline Pearson). (See the note on repetition of the wooing scene on page 32.)

Language

73–75 *Or is it true...essential thing?* Webster took this from Sidney's *Arcadia*: 'Or is it true that thou wert never but a vain name, and no essential thing?' in a long passage about Virtue. Rupert Brooke says: 'Webster makes it a shade more visual, and twenty times as impressive.' Lines 60–61, 69–70, 77–81, 84–85 in Ferdinand's interview with the Duchess are also adapted from *The Arcadia*: 'This detracts no whit from its tumultuous force' (Brooke).

Before you would vouchsafe to call for the keys.
We shall one day have my brothers take you
    napping:
Methinks his presence, being now in court,
Should make you keep your own bed; but you'll
    say
Love mixed with fear is sweetest. I'll assure you   65
You shall get no more children till my brothers
Consent to be your gossips. – Have you lost your
    tongue?

She sees FERDINAND.

'Tis welcome:
For know, whether I am doomed to live, or die,
I can do both like a prince.

FERDINAND gives her a poniard.

FERDINAND   Die then, quickly!   70
Virtue, where art thou hid? What hideous thing
Is it that doth eclipse thee?

DUCHESS   Pray sir hear me.

FERDINAND   Or is it true thou art but a bare name,
And no essential thing?

DUCHESS   Sir –

FERDINAND   Do not speak.

DUCHESS   No sir: 75
I will plant my soul in mine ears to hear you.

FERDINAND   Oh most imperfect light of human reason,
That mak'st so unhappy to foresee
What we can least prevent, pursue thy wishes
And glory in them: there's in shame no comfort   80
But to be past all bounds and sense of shame.

DUCHESS   I pray sir, hear me: I am married.

FERDINAND   So.

3.2 *Ferdinand calls out to the hidden Antonio that he does not want to know who he is now*

83 **Happily** haply: perhaps

84–85 **Alas...flown** from Sidney's Arcadia, with some slight changes of phrase

84 **shears** scissors *(there is perhaps also the idea here of the shears used by the Fates in classical mythology to cut the thread of a person's life)*

untimely before the natural time; badly timed

87 **basilisk** *(from Greek 'basileus' = king)* a mythical reptile: the king of serpents *(also known as a cockatrice, said to be hatched by a serpent from a cock's egg; its look lethal. According to the Roman writer Pliny the Elder it was so called because it had a crown-like spot on its head. Bosola applies it to the Cardinal at 5.2.147.)*

88 **By his confederacy** *i.e. in alliance with the basilisk* (**confederacy** = conspiracy; alliance)

howling of a wolf *Ironically Ferdinand will later believe he is a wolf (see note to 4.2.308–310).*

89 **to thee** compared to you

screech owl *The barn owl lets out a shrill cry and was thought of as a bird of evil omen; it was also applied figuratively to a person who had brought bad news or would bring misfortune (see also 2.3.7–9).*

93 **work** bring about

104–105 **let...converse** let only dogs and monkeys keep company

107 **paraquito** parakeet

109 **bewray** expose; betray

112–114 **And...heart** *This image is ominously echoed by Antonio at 3.5.88; see also 4.2.318–319.*

112 **massy** solid; weighty

sheet of lead *i.e. the tomb, coffin*

114 **Mine...for't** my heart bleeds for it *(a figurative expression simply meaning: I am very sorry, but in the next line Ferdinand seizes on the word she omitted)*

Structure

91 This scene is said to be a repetition or parody of the wooing scene in 1.1 because it 'repeats the stage-patterning of the earlier as an interview is watched from concealment' (Jacqueline Pearson): Cariola and Antonio are listening to this exchange, just as Cariola eavesdropped on the Duchess's wooing of Antonio.

Duchess in performance

'The sexual politics of twentieth-century theatre make it inevitable that a starring actress will also be a beautiful woman and in this production [Manchester Royal Exchange, 1981] Helen Mirren's dress and style emphasised her sexuality above all. The sexual sub-text of Ferdinand's feeling for her was allowed full rein, positioning the audience as voyeurs in a sexual drama...this is the most common positioning of an audience in realist spectacle and the one which affords the greatest pleasure, but it is a pleasure which needs to be examined' (Kathleen McLuskie). (McLuskie is a feminist and is concerned that the play's complexities – such as the oppression of women – are obscured when a production is a costume drama that focuses on a beautiful woman being tortured.)

Duchess

109–111 Frank Whigham says that her argument here is rational but false: she *is* doing something new.

DUCHESS	Happily, not to your liking; but for that,
	Alas, your shears do come untimely now
	To clip the bird's wings that's already flown. 85
	Will you see my husband?

FERDINAND   Yes, if I could change
Eyes with a basilisk.

DUCHESS   Sure, you came hither
By his confederacy.

FERDINAND   The howling of a wolf
Is music to thee, screech owl; prithee peace.
Whate'er thou art that hast enjoyed my sister –   90
For I am sure thou hear'st me – for thine own sake
Let me not know thee. I came hither prepared
To work thy discovery, yet am now persuaded
It would beget such violent effects
As would damn us both. I would not for ten
    millions   95
I had beheld thee, therefore use all means
I never may have knowledge of thy name.
Enjoy thy lust still, and a wretched life,
On that condition; and for thee, vile woman,
If thou do wish thy lecher may grow old   100
In thy embracements, I would have thee build
Such a room for him as our anchorites
To holier use inhabit. Let not the sun
Shine on him till he's dead, let dogs and monkeys
Only converse with him, and such dumb things   105
To whom nature denies use to sound his name.
Do not keep a paraquito lest she learn it.
If thou do love him cut out thine own tongue
Lest it bewray him.

DUCHESS   Why might not I marry?
I have not gone about in this to create   110
Any new world or custom.

FERDINAND   Thou art undone;
And thou hast ta'en that massy sheet of lead
That hid thy husband's bones, and folded it
About my heart.

DUCHESS   Mine bleeds for't.

3.2 *Ferdinand tells his sister a story about how reputation is lost, then leaves her saying he will never see her again*

115 **bullet** cannonball *(exploding cannonballs appeared in the sixteenth century)*

116 **wild-fire** highly inflammable substance used in warfare *(see also note to 2.5.47–48)*

118 **wilful** perverse; passionate *(see also 3.1.73)*

122 **Upon** once upon

128 **dowries** money or property brought by a bride to her husband

136 **I...you more** *see note to 140*

139–140 **virgins...witches** *see notes to 2.5.47–48 and 3.1.78*

140 **I...thee more** *'thee' is the familiar pronoun (accusative of 'thou') and also used to address inferiors – so can be an insult; 'you' is the plural pronoun which gradually replaced it in addressing superiors and equals (see also page 261)*

141 **apparition** (1) unexpected appearance; (2) ghost *(see line 146)*

Ferdinand's parable

119–135 One of the main themes of the play is the opposition of true fame to worldly greatness (e.g. see note to 4.2.231–233):
• Muriel Bradbrook agrees with Ferdinand: the Duchess, 'by failing to publish her marriage, destroys her own good fame'.
• Michael Neill sees irony: 'Ironically enough Ferdinand, in his parable of Reputation, Love, and Death, ends by implicitly identifying himself with Reputation.'
• Kathleen McLuskie describes his speech as 'moralising platitudes' which 'have no reality in the world of the play' (see also page 250).
• Rupert Brooke also disliked this speech: 'In the tremendous scene in the bedchamber...the mad frenzy of his reproaches is excellently rendered. She replies with short sentences, bursting from her heart. Each of his taunts carries flame. The whole is living, terse, and affecting. In the middle of this Ferdinand breaks into a long old-fashioned allegory about Love, Reputation, and Death, a tale that (but for a fine line or two) might have appeared in any Elizabethan collection of rhymed parables. The point of it is that Reputation is very easy to lose, and the Duchess has lost hers.'
• See the actor Will Keen's defence of the speech on page 261.

Language

138 *cased up like a holy relic:* This is one of the many images that contrasts what is fair on the outside with a rotting inside – such as in tombs, palaces or clothes (see also 3.2.197). In this line the palace in which the Duchess lives is like a precious box to hold parts of a corpse; and it is an image like the *dead man's skull* she refers to when she and Antonio finally part (3.5.85–87).

FERDINAND   Thine? Thy heart?
What should I name't, unless a hollow bullet   115
Filled with unquenchable wild-fire?

DUCHESS   You are in this
Too strict, and were you not my princely brother
I would say too wilful. My reputation
Is safe.

FERDINAND   Dost thou know what reputation is?
I'll tell thee – to small purpose, since th'instruction   120
Comes now too late.
Upon a time Reputation, Love and Death
Would travel o'er the world; and it was concluded
That they should part, and take three several ways:
Death told them they should find him in great
           battles   125
Or cities plagued with plagues; Love gives them
           counsel
To enquire for him 'mongst unambitious shepherds,
Where dowries were not talked of, and sometimes
'Mongst quiet kindred that had nothing left
By their dead parents. 'Stay', quoth Reputation,   130
'Do not forsake me: for it is my nature
If once I part from any man I meet
I am never found again.' And so, for you:
You have shook hands with Reputation
And made him invisible. So fare you well.   135
I will never see you more.

DUCHESS   Why should only I
Of all the other princes of the world
Be cased up like a holy relic? I have youth,
And a little beauty.

FERDINAND   So you have some virgins
That are witches. I will never see thee more.   140

                                                        Exit.

Enter CARIOLA and ANTONIO with a pistol.

DUCHESS   You saw this apparition?

3.2 *Antonio accuses Cariola of betraying them and wishes Ferdinand would return, but he has to hide again when Bosola enters to tell the Duchess that Ferdinand has rushed off to Rome*

144 **cleft** split

145 **gallery** hall *(in the palace; see note to 1.1.218)*

147 **on my guard** *originally a fencing term*: in a defensive position

148 **warrantable** permitted; guaranteed as genuine

153 **rank gall** (1) *literally*: swollen gall-bladder; (2) *perhaps*: loathsome body *(see also 3.1.78)*

154 **earthquakes** *There was a memorable, and large, earthquake in* England in 1580, which killed two people in London and damaged St Paul's Cathedral. Webster may have had a childhood memory of it.

155 **mine** *military image*: underground passage dug under a besieged castle's walls in which gunpowder was placed

157 **unjust** dishonest

158 **masks and curtains** *both objects one hides behind*

160 **whirlwind** *see note to 2.5.51*

Antonio in performance

146–148 There is disappointment by some critics in Antonio's behaviour here: 'He listens in hiding while Ferdinand threatens his wife, but takes no action to protect her' (Andrea Henderson), and indeed he suggests to his wife that *she* should kill her brother (152); he doesn't offer to himself. But in his defence, this could be because he is not known to be her husband and no longer knows what role he should play. This last interpretation came across in the 1995 Cheek by Jowl production – Antonio was a subordinate, the Duchess obviously much stronger than he was. A stronger Antonio could perhaps play his re-entry as if he has gone to find a pistol and just come too late to use it on Ferdinand. In the 2003 National Theatre production it was as if Antonio was being discreet by not interfering.

ANTONIO	Yes, we are
	Betrayed. How came he hither? I should turn
	This to thee, for that. (*Points the pistol at* CARIOLA)

CARIOLA	Pray sir do: and when
	That you have cleft my heart you shall read there
	Mine innocence.

| DUCHESS | That gallery gave him entrance.   145 |

ANTONIO	I would this terrible thing would come again
	That, standing on my guard, I might relate
	My warrantable love. Ha, what means this?

| DUCHESS | He left this with me – (*She shows the poniard*) |

| ANTONIO | And it seems did wish |
| | You would use it on yourself? |

| DUCHESS | His action   150 |
| | Seemed to intend so much. |

ANTONIO	This hath a handle to't
	As well as a point, turn it towards him
	And so fasten the keen edge in his rank gall. (*Knocking*)
	How now? Who knocks? More earthquakes?

DUCHESS	I stand
	As if a mine beneath my feet were ready 155
	To be blown up.

| CARIOLA | 'Tis Bosola. |

DUCHESS	Away!
	Oh misery, methinks unjust actions
	Should wear these masks and curtains, and not we:
	You must instantly part hence: I have fashioned it
	already.

Exit ANTONIO.

Enter BOSOLA.

| BOSOLA | The Duke your brother is ta'en up in a whirlwind: 160 |
| | Hath took horse and's rid post to Rome. |

| DUCHESS | So late? |

99

3.2 Ferdinand has told Bosola that his sister is 'undone'. The Duchess pretends to Bosola that Antonio has damaged her and her brother's finances. Secretly she tells Antonio to go to Ancona, where she will follow him

163 **undone** ruined

166–168 **My...forfeit** *The Duchess borrowed money from Jews in Naples, using Ferdinand as security; since Antonio failed to pay either the interest or the sum borrowed, Ferdinand is now liable.*

170–171 **My...against** *The Jews have made a declaration that Ferdinand's bills of exchange are not acceptable.*

172 **Ancona** *seaport on the opposite, Adriatic, coast of Italy, about 200 miles north of Amalfi; it was a free city during the time of the historical Duchess (see page 237)*

175 **enginous** crafty; deceitful *(or perhaps* **enginous wheels** = wheels of an engine. *There was a proverb 'The world runs on wheels', suggesting impermanence and speed.)*

176 **periods** full sentences

177 **Tasso** *the Italian playwright and poet Torquato Tasso (1544–95)*

178 *Magnanima...lie* *the phrase comes from Tasso's epic poem on the First Crusade, Jerusalem Delivered; see also note to 3.1.43–44*

181 **I...you** *the first in a series of innuendoes between Antonio and the Duchess*

184 **audit** official examination of accounts

185 *Quietus* clearing of accounts; receipt *(this innuendo recalls the kiss in the wooing scene; see note to 1.1.468)*

Cartoon of the Duchess and Ferdinand in the 1995–6 Cheek by Jowl production (from The Times *newspaper*)

BOSOLA	He told me as he mounted into th'saddle You were undone.
DUCHESS	Indeed I am very near it.
BOSOLA	What's the matter?
DUCHESS	Antonio, the master of our household, Hath dealt so falsely with me in's accounts. 165 My brother stood engaged with me for money Ta'en up of certain Neapolitan Jews, And Antonio lets the bonds be forfeit.
BOSOLA	Strange! (*Aside*) This is cunning.
DUCHESS	And hereupon My brother's bills at Naples are protested 170 Against. Call up our officers.
BOSOLA	I shall.

Exit.

Enter ANTONIO.

DUCHESS	The place that you must fly to is Ancona: Hire a house there. I'll send after you My treasure and my jewels. Our weak safety Runs upon enginous wheels, short syllables 175 Must stand for periods. I must now accuse you Of such a feigned crime as Tasso calls *Magnanima mensogna*, a noble lie, 'Cause it must shield our honours. Hark, they are coming.

Enter BOSOLA and OFFICERS.

ANTONIO	Will your grace hear me? 180
DUCHESS	I have got well by you: you have yielded me A million of loss; I am like to inherit The people's curses for your stewardship. You had the trick in audit time to be sick Till I had signed your *Quietus*; and that cured you 185 Without help of a doctor. Gentlemen,

3.2 *The Duchess dismisses Antonio from her service, using words that Antonio will understand very differently as confirming her love*

187–188   **I would...favour** *innuendo*

188   **let him** *either* let him be an example *or* let him go

189   **h'as done...of** *innuendo*

191   **publish** *innuendo:* announce it officially *(i.e. dismissal/marriage)*

        Use...elsewhere *innuendo (see lines 172–174)*

192   **brook** put up with; bear

195   **malevolent star** star that exercises an evil influence

196   **humour** mental disposition; state of mind

197   **rotten** *a stronger word in Webster's day, here invoking an image of rotting corpses in a graveyard*

198–201   **'Tis...sat down** *recalls his fire image at 1.1.430-432*

200   **As loath** as if unwilling

203–204   **I am...be so** *innuendo*

204   **pass** permission to go

205–206   **what 'tis...soul** *innuendo*

207–209   **Here's...sea again** Antonio's punishment is quite a warning against unlawfully taking money! Just as, when there's bad weather, all the moisture that evaporates from the sea rains back into the sea again *(a commonplace Renaissance image)*

212–213   **pig's head...Jew** *i.e. Antonio is like a Jew: Jews are not allowed to eat pork and therefore the officer says they don't like to see a cooked pig's head on the table. Also, Jews were often involved in lending money and were stereotyped as untrustworthy.*

Language

197 The *rotten ground of service* is one of the many images in the play that contrasts what is fair on the outside with a rotting inside – in tombs, palaces or clothes.

I would have this man be an example to you all,
So shall you hold my favour. I pray let him,
For h'as done that, alas, you would not think of,
And, because I intend to be rid of him,   190
I mean not to publish. – Use your fortune elsewhere.

ANTONIO   I am strongly armed to brook my overthrow,
As commonly men bear with a hard year.
I will not blame the cause on't but do think
The necessity of my malevolent star   195
Procures this, not her humour. Oh the inconstant
And rotten ground of service you may see:
'Tis ev'n like him that in a winter night
Takes a long slumber o'er a dying fire
As loath to part from't, yet parts thence as cold   200
As when he first sat down.

DUCHESS   We do confiscate,
Towards the satisfying of your accounts,
All that you have.

ANTONIO   I am all yours: and 'tis very fit
All mine should be so.

DUCHESS   So, sir; you have your pass.

ANTONIO   You may see, gentlemen, what 'tis to serve   205
A prince with body and soul.

                                                    Exit.

BOSOLA   Here's an example for extortion! What moisture
is drawn out of the sea, when foul weather comes,
pours down and runs into the sea again.

DUCHESS   I would know what are your opinions of this   210
Antonio.

2 OFFICER   He could not abide to see a pig's head gaping; I
thought your grace would find him a Jew.

3 OFFICER   I would you had been his officer, for your own sake.

4 OFFICER   You would have had more money.   215

The officers continue to revile Antonio. Bosola, in contrast, speaks highly of him

216 **black wool** *actually said to be used with fox's 'grease' to try to cure deafness*

218 **hermaphrodite** a human or animal that has both male and female organs *(see note below)*

220 **scurvy** contemptibly; shabbily

222 **chippings** bread crumbs *(i.e. may the crumbs fly after him)*

butt'ry *the buttery was the storeroom for bread, butter, ale etc.*

223 **gold chain** *this showed his office as steward – like Malvolio in* Twelfth Night *2.3*

225–226 **in's...wished** when he was doing well, merely just to have attended him as a servant would have wished

228 **after's mule** after his packhorse

bear in a ring *A new bearbaiting ring (that doubled as a theatre) opened on Bankside near the Globe in 1614.*

230 **intelligencers** informers; spies

232 **livery** distinctive clothing or badge worn by a noble's servants

234 **sort** group

236–237 **flatterers...lies** flatterers hide the vices of princes, and princes hide the lies of flatterers *(taken from a 1612 translation of the French writer Pierre Matthieu's* Henry IV*)*

239 **coffers** chests; strongboxes *(especially for money or valuables)*

240 **Pluto...riches** *Plutus was the god of wealth, but he was sometimes called Pluto, who was the god of the underworld.*

244 **scuttles** *alternative explanations:* (1) short hurried runs; (2) large baskets; (3) stage trapdoors

245 **unvalued** (1) not valued as he should have been; (2) invaluable

246 **wanton** petulant; reckless

Ideas and interpretations

218 *hermaphrodite:* Antonio is called this probably because he doesn't appear to be a 'real' man: (a) he serves a woman, as a secretary/administrator, at a time when a female ruler was regarded as unnatural, and (b) Antonio has presumably taken no interest in the women at court, since he is secretly married to the Duchess. See note to 2.5.38–39, where the Duchess is also seen as sexually ambiguous.

Bosola

230 The worst job that Bosola can think of for a boy *(first born)* is to be an informer – like himself.

232 *do these lice drop off now?* He is obviously being hypocritical: see 1.1.53–55. And the only *flatt'ring rogue* (234) is Bosola, in the rest of this scene. Critics are, however, unsure how far Bosola is genuine in what he says about Antonio in lines 240–270. Actors will work out how much is genuine, how much is playing a game, and this will vary: see the comments of Lorcan Cranitch who played Bosola in the 2003 National Theatre production (pages 258–259).

1 OFFICER	He stopped his ears with black wool, and to those came to him for money, said he was thick of hearing.

2 OFFICER   Some said he was an hermaphrodite, for he
             could not abide a woman.

4 OFFICER   How scurvy proud he would look when the   220
             treasury was full! Well, let him go.

1 OFFICER   Yes, and the chippings of the butt'ry fly after
             him, to scour his gold chain!

DUCHESS   Leave us.

Exeunt OFFICERS.

             (*To* BOSOLA) What do you think of these?

BOSOLA   That these are rogues that, in's prosperity,   225
             But to have waited on his fortune, could have
                 wished
             His dirty stirrup riveted through their noses
             And followed after's mule like a bear in a ring;
             Would have prostituted their daughters to his lust,
             Made their first born intelligencers, thought none
                 happy   230
             But such as were born under his blessed planet
             And wore his livery; and do these lice drop off
                 now?
             Well, never look to have the like again.
             He hath left a sort of flatt'ring rogues behind him:
             Their doom must follow. Princes pay flatterers   235
             In their own money: flatterers dissemble their vices,
             And they dissemble their lies: that's justice.
             Alas, poor gentleman.

DUCHESS   Poor? He hath amply filled his coffers.

BOSOLA   Sure he was too honest. Pluto the god of riches, 240
             When he's sent by Jupiter to any man,
             He goes limping, to signify that wealth
             That comes on god's name, comes slowly; but
                 when he's sent
             On the devil's errand he rides post and comes in
                 by scuttles.
             Let me show you what a most unvalued jewel   245
             You have in a wanton humour thrown away

3.2 *Bosola continues to praise Antonio, and the Duchess reveals the news that Bosola has for some years been searching for*

247 **To bless...him** to make prosperous the man who will next employ him

248–250 **a soldier...much** *i.e. as a soldier he was confident of his worth, but downplayed it*

251 **virtue and form** *perhaps:* moral excellence and outward behaviour

252 **His discourse...itself** *i.e. he preferred to use his intelligence to criticise himself rather than show off (from Sidney's* Arcadia *– who uses 'wit' = faculty of reasoning, a synonym of 'discourse' here)*

256–257 **Will you...virtues?** *This contrast is central to the play: who a person is descended from v. what they do themselves.*

256 **mercenary** working only for money

herald one who records pedigrees of people *(i.e. a family tree of their ancestors – to show their rank in society)*

258 **want** miss

259–262 **an honest...shadow** *i.e. for a prince, an honest man who runs the affairs of*

a state is like a spring that nourishes a tree (the prince); the prince rewards this man by protecting him

260 **cedar** *see note to 1.1.248*

263 **Bermoothes** Bermuda *(this group of islands in the Atlantic became famous in Britain when the flagship of the largest colonising expedition ever undertaken was wrecked there in 1609; it has been a British colony ever since, and it inspired Shakespeare's* The Tempest*)*

264 **rotten** *'implies both corruption and disease (probably venereal)' (1995 Cambridge edition)*

267–270 **malice...virtue** *mainly from Sidney's* Arcadia

275 **shadows** ephemeral delusions

276 **painted honours** false, artificial titles of rank *(also alluding to painted coats-of-arms, which anyone with money would buy along with the titles that King James and his noblemen were selling – see page 233)*

Bosola

256–270 Michael Neill (see page 245) says that Bosola begins this speech with what at first appears 'a piece of stock moralization', but that 'the sentiment answers closely to a rankling sense of neglect in the world of courtly reward which is not at all feigned'.

273–276 'His reply registers genuine wonder, an emotion compounded of astonishment at this profound shock to his habitual construction of the world' (Michael Neill).

275–276 The play debates the meaning of 'honour', as well as 'who is greatest'. There is false *painted* honour(s), which Bosola finally rejects at 4.2.335 (see also the same idea at 5.2.302–304), and which he contrasts in this scene with the true honour that Antonio has (288–295) and which the Duchess believes in.

To bless the man shall find him. He was an
   excellent
Courtier, and most faithful, a soldier that thought
   it
As beastly to know his own value too little
As devilish to acknowledge it too much;   250
Both his virtue and form deserved a far better fortune;
His discourse rather delighted to judge itself than
   show itself,
His breast was filled with all perfection
And yet it seemed a private whisp'ring room,
It made so little noise of't.

DUCHESS   But he was basely descended. 255

BOSOLA   Will you make yourself a mercenary herald,
Rather to examine men's pedigrees than virtues?
You shall want him,
For know: an honest statesman to a prince
Is like a cedar planted by a spring;   260
The spring bathes the tree's root, the grateful tree
Rewards it with his shadow. You have not done so:
I would sooner swim to the Bermoothes on
Two politicians' rotten bladders, tied
Together with an intelligencer's heart-string,   265
Than depend on so changeable a prince's favour!
Fare thee well, Antonio: since the malice of the
   world
Would needs down with thee, it cannot be said yet
That any ill happened unto thee,
Considering thy fall was accompanied with virtue. 270

DUCHESS   Oh, you render me excellent music.

BOSOLA   Say you?

DUCHESS   This good one that you speak of is my husband.

BOSOLA   Do I not dream? Can this ambitious age
Have so much goodness in't as to prefer
A man merely for worth, without these shadows 275
Of wealth and painted honours? Possible?

DUCHESS   I have had three children by him.

3.2 *Bosola praises the Duchess, who tells him to join Antonio in Ancona. Bosola advises the Duchess to pretend she is on a pilgrimage to a famous shrine near Ancona*

278 **nuptial** marriage

279 **seminary** *literally:* seed plot; nursery garden *(with wordplay on* **bed** *= flower bed)*

280 **unbeneficed** without a church living *(i.e. with no church office to provide an income)*

286 **Moors** Muslims *(e.g. from North Africa; Shakespeare's Othello is a Moor converted to Christianity)*

288 **neglected poets** *Bosola feels strongly his neglect by Ferdinand and the Cardinal (see note to 1.1.76–77), so it is interesting that here he talks of* **neglected poets** *(which meant playwrights as well) – did Webster feel he himself had been neglected?*

289 **trophy** *'Anything serving as a token or evidence of victory, valour, skill, power, etc.; a monument, memorial' (Oxford English Dictionary)*

290 **curious engine** beautifully made instrument

291–292 **make...cabinets** make your grave more worthy of respect than all the lodgings *(an ominous phrase that prefigures the tragedy)*

293 **For** as for

295 **want coats** run out of coats of arms *(another satiric comment on the sale of titles by James I – see page 233)*

305 **Loretto** *the small town of Loreto, about 15 miles south of Ancona (see note to 3.2.172), a famous pilgrimage site since the fifteenth century (see note to 3.4.1–2)*

leagues *1 league = about 3 miles*

307 **country** territory; land

308 **progress** *see note to 1.1.441*

309 **train** retinue; attendants

Bosola

277–295 Michael Neill says of this speech that 'there is a degree of comic exaggeration...as though the old sardonic Bosola were reasserting his ironic control' but that his irony is 'self-mockery directed at an emotion as dangerous as it is unfamiliar'. This interpretation, he says, is shown by 288–295, which echoes what Webster says in his dedication (see page 233): that greatness lies in virtue, not in blood, and that it is the writer who brings lasting fame to people. Frank Whigham comments on Bosola's speech: 'Many readers accept Bosola's speech as sincere; others presume it to be a ploy designed to unlock the Duchess's tongue. I think it is both: his own sincere response managed in pursuit of his employer's [Ferdinand's] goal.'

280–283 Delio's recollection of Bosola as a university student in the next scene (3.3.40–47) may suggest that Bosola is talking about himself.

Duchess

304–315 In Webster's source by Painter (see page 237), it is the Duchess's gentlewoman who advises her to go to Loretto on pilgrimage. The Duchess approves of the plan, but Painter comments: 'It was not sufficient for this foolish woman to take a husband, more to glut her libidinous appetite than for other occasion, except she added to her sin another execrable impiety, making holy places and duties of devotion to be as it were the ministers of her folly.' This is also her brothers' reaction, see 3.3.61–63.

BOSOLA   Fortunate lady,
For you have made your private nuptial bed
The humble and fair seminary of peace.
No question but many an unbeneficed scholar   280
Shall pray for you, for this deed, and rejoice
That some preferment in the world can yet
Arise from merit. The virgins of your land
That have no dowries, shall hope your example
Will raise them to rich husbands; should you want   285
Soldiers 'twould make the very Turks and Moors
Turn Christians and serve you, for this act.
Last, the neglected poets of your time,
In honour of this trophy of a man
Raised by that curious engine, your white hand,   290
Shall thank you, in your grave, for't, and make that
More reverend than all the cabinets
Of living princes. For Antonio,
His fame shall likewise flow from many a pen
When heralds shall want coats to sell to men.   295

DUCHESS   As I taste comfort in this friendly speech,
So would I find concealment.

BOSOLA   Oh the secret of my prince,
Which I will wear on th'inside of my heart.

DUCHESS   You shall take charge of all my coin, and jewels,   300
And follow him, for he retires himself
To Ancona.

BOSOLA   So.

DUCHESS   Whither, within few days,
I mean to follow thee.

BOSOLA   Let me think:
I would wish your grace to feign a pilgrimage
To Our Lady of Loretto, scarce seven leagues   305
From fair Ancona: so may you depart
Your country with more honour, and your flight
Will seem a princely progress, retaining
Your usual train about you.

DUCHESS   Sir, your direction
Shall lead me by the hand.

3.3

In a soliloquy, Bosola says he will tell Ferdinand that Antonio is the Duchess's husband. Scene 3 is set in Rome: the Emperor has asked the Cardinal to resume, for a time, his profession as a soldier

311–312 **baths At Lucca** *see note to 2.1.71*

312 **Spa** town in modern Belgium famous for its mineral springs since the fourteenth century *(it gave its name to similar resorts)*

319 **politician** schemer; intriguer *(it had this meaning into the eighteenth century, though the modern meaning was also in use)*

quilted cushioned; padded

319–321 **devil's...heard** *Other authors also used imagery involving anvils and the devil as a blacksmith. Webster grew up to the sound of metal being shaped on anvils: see page 228.*

323 **quality** occupation; profession *(especially used of an actor)*

324–325 **every...commendation** every occupation in the world helps to bring about (**Prefers**) only (**but**) profit or praise

326 **raised** promoted

327 **weeds** wild plants *(the point is that they are troublesome and not valued for their beauty or use, so painting them so well is a useless activity)*

to the life faithful to the original; realistic

s.d. **Enter...PESCARA** the Marquis of Pescara *(1489–1525; see note on page 174)*

1 **turn soldier** *In the 'Italian Wars', 1494–1559, France and Spain fought for control of the small independent states of Italy.*

Emperor *Since the events in the play historically took place between 1504–13, this should be Maximilian I, Holy Roman Emperor 1493–1519 (who made Innsbruck in Austria the imperial residence), but Webster is referring to his grandson, Charles V, Emperor 1519–56, and King of Spain from 1516, who was also ruler of the Kingdom of Naples.*

5 **Lannoy** *Charles de Lannoy (c. 1487–1527, led the Spanish forces to victory over Francis I in 1525)*

6 **French king prisoner** *Francis I, King of France 1515–47, was captured by Imperial troops in 1525.*

Bosola

322–327 Bosola is filled with self-loathing *(What rests...lord?)* shown by the line that follows: *Oh, this base...intelligencer!* But he argues with himself that he's not behaving worse than others do *(Why, every...commendation)* and ends on a cynical note – he will be advanced for this information, which is similar to an artist being praised for something inferior simply because it is realistic. The rhyming couplet not only rounds off the scene, but ends it on a jauntily cynical shrug.

Performance

Scene 3 is often cut in productions, but it does give additional insight into the Cardinal, Delio and Bosola, as well as more of the unsavoury flavour of court life. The 2003 National Theatre production kept lines 61–77.

Cardinal

1–5 Muriel Bradbrook remarks on the Cardinal's 'effortless use of Ferdinand as his pawn. He even usurps Ferdinand's part as a soldier, for there is nothing priestly about him except his vestments – themselves of course a sign of diabolic intrusion to the more Puritanically minded members of the English Church.'

| CARIOLA | In my opinion | 310 |

CARIOLA   In my opinion   310
She were better progress to the baths
At Lucca, or go visit the Spa
In Germany, for, if you will believe me,
I do not like this jesting with religion,
This feigned pilgrimage.

DUCHESS   Thou art a superstitious fool. 315
Prepare us instantly for our departure.
Past sorrows, let us moderately lament them,
For those to come, seek wisely to prevent them.

Exeunt DUCHESS and CARIOLA.

BOSOLA   A politician is the devil's quilted anvil,
He fashions all sins on him and the blows   320
Are never heard – he may work in a lady's chamber,
As here for proof. What rests, but I reveal
All to my lord? Oh, this base quality
Of intelligencer! Why, every quality i'th'world
Prefers but gain or commendation: 325
Now for this act I am certain to be raised,
And men that paint weeds to the life are praised.

Exit.

Scene 3

Enter CARDINAL, FERDINAND, MALATESTE, PESCARA, SILVIO, DELIO.

CARDINAL   Must we turn soldier then?

MALATESTE   The Emperor
Hearing your worth that way, ere you attained
This reverend garment, joins you in commission
With the right fortunate soldier, the Marquis of
    Pescara,
And the famous Lannoy.

CARDINAL   He that had the honour   5
Of taking the French King prisoner?

MALATESTE   The same.

3.3 *In Rome, Delio and Silvio make satirical comments on a would-be soldier, Count Malateste*

7 **plot** ground plan; map

10 **muster-book** book in which the muster-rolls *(registers of officers and men)* were copied out

11 **voluntary** serving as a volunteer soldier

12–13 **gunpowder...toothache** *i.e. he's not a real soldier: he uses gunpowder to ease toothache and not for military purposes. Traditional 'black' gunpowder was used as a remedy into the twentieth century; it was also used by soldiers to treat gonorrhoea, which may also be alluded to here.*

14 **leaguer** military camp *(often engaged in a siege)*

16 **scent** (1) of military excitement; (2) of garlic

17 **late service** recent military campaign

18 **chronicle** list of day-to-day events

19–20 **express...in model** depict battles in scale drawing

20 **by the book** according to theory in a book and not learned by practical experience *(Iago accuses Cassio of this in* Othello *1.1)*

21 **almanac** annual calendar with astronomical data, astrological forecasts etc.

shun the critical avoid the ill-omened days

24 **taffeta** (1) type of silk *(the scarf)*; (2) *figuratively:* bombast

26 **from taking** from being taken

28 **pate** head

29 **pot-gun** (1) toy gun; (2) braggart; boaster

he the Dutchman

30 **bore** hole

musket hand-gun used by infantry soldiers

31 **touch-hole** hole in a firearm, through which one ignites the charge *(wordplay on* **bore***)*

32 **guarded sumpter-cloth** ornamented cloth covering a pack-horse

33 **remove of the court** change of residence of the court to a different palace/house

---

Language

The early twentieth-century poet Rupert Brooke commented: 'The one influence upon Webster that is always noticeable is that of satire. His nature tended to the outlook of satire; and his plays give evidence that he read Elizabethan, and in some form Latin satire with avidity. *Hamlet,* the *Malcontent* [see page 239], and all the heroes of that type of play, "railed" continually. But with Webster every character and nearly every speech has something of the satirical outlook...There are several little irrelevant scenes of satire, like the malevolent discussion of Count Malatesti. It is incessant. The topics are the ordinary ones, the painting of women, the ingratitude of princes, the swaggering of blusterers, the cowardice of pseudo-soldiers. It gives part of the peculiar atmosphere of these plays.' (Satire has been defined as a kind of protest; it is writing designed to ridicule and correct follies or vices. In Webster's time, the playwright Ben Jonson was well known for his satirical comedies.)

(*Shows plan*) Here's a plot drawn for a new
    fortification
At Naples.

FERDINAND   This great Count Malateste I perceive
Hath got employment?

DELIO   No employment, my lord,
A marginal note in the muster-book that he is   10
A voluntary lord.

FERDINAND   He's no soldier?

DELIO   He has worn gunpowder in's hollow tooth,
For the toothache.

SILVIO   He comes to the leaguer with a full intent
To eat fresh beef and garlic, means to stay   15
Till the scent be gone, and straight return to court.

DELIO   He hath read all the late service,
As the city chronicle relates it,
And keeps two painters going, only to express
Battles in model.

SILVIO   Then he'll fight by the book.   20

DELIO   By the almanac, I think,
To choose good days and shun the critical. –
That's his mistress' scarf.

SILVIO   Yes, he protests
He would do much for that taffeta.

DELIO   I think he would run away from a battle   25
To save it from taking prisoner.

SILVIO   He is horribly afraid
Gunpowder will spoil the perfume on't.

DELIO   I saw a Dutchman break his pate once
For calling him pot-gun: he made his head
Have a bore in't like a musket.   30

SILVIO   I would he had made a touch-hole to't.

DELIO   He is indeed a guarded sumpter-cloth
Only for the remove of the court.

36–38 like Foxes...tails *At a time of conflict between Israel and the Philistines, Samson caught 300 foxes, tied them in pairs, attached firebrands to their tails and sent them into the Philistines' wheatfields, destroying all their corn, vineyards and olives (see the Bible: Judges 15.3–5).*

37 when...divided *when they disagree among themselves*

39 wrack *disaster; ruin*

40 Padua *a famous university city in northern Italy*

fantastical scholar *one who studies eccentric, fanciful, pointless ideas (Delio is disparaging Bosola as a scholar)*

41–44 how many knots...toothache *Greek mythological heroes and warriors. Hercules' symbol was the oaken club; Achilles and Hector were famous opponents in the Trojan War, as told in Homer's Iliad. (Webster took some of this from another writer.)*

44 blear-eyed *bleary eyed (dull or blurred from lack of sleep)*

45 Caesar *Julius Caesar (died in 44 BC; see 5.5.55–57)*

46 shoeing-horn *shoe-horn (curved instrument of horn to help put shoes on)*

47 speculative man *thinking man*

49 salamander *mythical lizard able to live in fire which it quenched by the coldness of its body (linking Ferdinand with fire again; see note to 2.5.47–48)*

50 mock *mimic (i.e. Ferdinand is looking furious and dangerous)*

51–52 That...oppression *i.e. the news the Cardinal is hearing is causing him much mental distress, as shown by his grimaces*

52 Michael Angelo *the famous Italian artist Michelangelo (1475–1564, for whom the beauty of the human body symbolised divine beauty)*

57 pangs *spasms of pain*

Ideas and interpretations

34–60 The way Webster shows the brothers being told the identity of the Duchess's husband 'gives a curiously dislocated effect, emphasising not simply the brothers' anger and disapproval but the fact that neutral observers realise the error of what is taking place but do nothing to oppose the evil' (Kathleen McLuskie).

48–56 Rupert Brooke commented that Webster sometimes 'achieves a dramatic effect, which would be a little less in a theatre than in the book, by comment. When Bosola brings the terrible discovery of the secret to Ferdinand and the Cardinal, he communicates it to them, unheard by us, up-stage. We only know, in reading, how they take it, by the comments of Pescara, Silvio, and Delio, who are watching, down-stage. It goes straight to the nerves. "The Lord Ferdinand laughs." It is unforgettable.'

Bosola

40–47 This scene is often cut, so few audiences are given this glimpse of Bosola as a university man; some productions instead show him as a rough soldier, but that hardly squares with his speeches (e.g. 1.1.50–64). University men were (and are) recruited as spies: the playwright Christopher Marlowe (fatally stabbed in 1593) was recruited while a student at Cambridge University. Also, according to Martin Wiggins, the 'alienated intellectual' was an 'early Stuart social problem' because there were not enough jobs for graduates. Is there a clue here as to why Bosola became a hired killer? (See also 3.2.280–283.)

Enter BOSOLA, who speaks apart to FERDINAND and the CARDINAL.

PESCARA	Bosola arrived? What should be the business?
	Some falling out amongst the cardinals. 35
	These factions amongst great men, they are like
	Foxes: when their heads are divided
	They carry fire in their tails, and all the country
	About them goes to wrack for it.

SILVIO   What's that Bosola?

DELIO   I knew him in Padua, a fantastical scholar, like   40
          such who study to know how many knots was in
          Hercules' club, of what colour Achilles' beard was,
          or whether Hector were not troubled with the
          toothache. He hath studied himself half blear-eyed
          to know the true symmetry of Caesar's nose by a   45
          shoeing-horn, and this he did to gain the name of
          a speculative man.

PESCARA   Mark Prince Ferdinand,
           A very salamander lives in's eye
           To mock the eager violence of fire.   50

SILVIO   That Cardinal hath made more bad faces with his
           oppression than ever Michael Angelo made good
           ones; he lifts up's nose like a foul porpoise before
           a storm.

PESCARA   The Lord Ferdinand laughs.

DELIO   Like a deadly cannon   55
           That lightens ere it smokes.

PESCARA   These are your true pangs of death,
           The pangs of life that struggle with great
                statesmen.

DELIO   In such a deformed silence witches whisper their
           charms.   60

CARDINAL   Doth she make religion her riding-hood
           To keep her from the sun, and tempest?

FERDINAND   That –
           That damns her. Methinks her fault and beauty,

3.4 *As the Cardinal sets out for Loretto, Ferdinand orders Bosola to meet him with an armed force. Antonio and the Duchess are shown at the shrine*

64–65 **leprosy...fouler** *one of the many images of disease in the play (though leprosy had died out in Britain); Webster took it from his fellow playwright George Chapman*

70 **Duke of Malfi** *This is the only mention of this boy, which came from Webster's source. Possibly he forgot to revise this section.*

72 **honesty** *sarcastic:* (1) chastity; (2) truthfulness

73 **counters** disks used to count money

75 **audit** *see 3.2.184*

1–2 **I have...many** *According to legend, the house of the Virgin Mary was carried by angels to Loreto (the usual modern spelling) from Nazareth in 1294. The present sumptuous church, built over it, was begun in 1468.*

s.d. ***Here the ceremony...churchmen*** *This is Webster's stage direction describing the dumbshow. The pilgrims describe what else takes place in this scene (e.g. lines 35–36).*

Ferdinand

73–75 Ferdinand's reaction to the news that Antonio is his sister's husband 'is one of snobbish contempt' (Kathleen McLuskie).

Ideas and interpretations

The dumbshow in 3.4 is often cut in the theatre, and divides critics as to its merits:
- Christy Desmet: It is 'a superfluous piece of dramatic exposition'.
- Andrea Henderson: It shows 'theatricality is fundamental to aristocratic life' (she labels the brothers as 'aristocratic' and the Duchess as 'bourgeois'/'middle-class', because of the different values they hold, and adds that the play criticises this type of aristocratic, hollow display).
- Kathleen McLuskie: The effect of the dumbshow 'is that the Cardinal's military and political power are presented as sheer unopposed dramatic fact, emphasised in the visual contrast between the powerful Cardinal in military dress with his train of "divers Churchmen", and the vulnerable family group...the Duchess has now become and remains a victim'.

Blended together, show like leprosy,
The whiter, the fouler. I make it a question   65
Whether her beggarly brats were ever christened.

CARDINAL   I will instantly solicit the state of Ancona
To have them banished.

FERDINAND   You are for Loretto?
I shall not be at your ceremony: fare you well.
(*To* BOSOLA) Write to the Duke of Malfi, my young
          nephew   70
She had by her first husband, and acquaint him
With's mother's honesty.

BOSOLA   I will.

FERDINAND   Antonio!
A slave that only smelled of ink and counters,
And ne'er in's life looked like a gentleman
But in the audit time! Go, go presently,   75
Draw me out an hundred and fifty of our horse,
And meet me at the fort bridge.

Exeunt.

Scene 4

Enter TWO PILGRIMS to the shrine of Our Lady of Loretto.

1 PILGRIM   I have not seen a goodlier shrine than this,
Yet I have visited many.

2 PILGRIM   The Cardinal of Aragon
Is this day to resign his cardinal's hat,
His sister Duchess likewise is arrived
To pay her vow of pilgrimage. I expect   5
A noble ceremony.

1 PILGRIM   No question. – They come.

*Here the ceremony of the Cardinal's instalment in the habit of a soldier:
performed in delivering up his cross, hat, robes and ring at the shrine; and
investing him with sword, helmet, shield and spurs. Then ANTONIO,
the DUCHESS and their children, having presented themselves at the shrine,*

7–22 **Arms and honours...showers** *Webster had inserted that 'The author disclaims...' but the theme of fame and how it is to be achieved is central to the play: here the Cardinal intends that success in war will give him glory that will outlive him.*

7 **deck** adorn

11 **I alone...praises** I will sing only in praise of you

16 **arts** learning

19 **courses** encounters

20 **forces** military power

23 **turn** change

state status; rank

25 **mean** of low social rank; of low degree

28–29 **Ancona...state** *The town was a semi-independent republic under papal protection until 1532, when it was occupied by papal troops.*

30 **forehearing** hearing beforehand

32 **dowager** widow with a title or property from her deceased husband

---

Performance

• 1618: The Venetian envoy, Orazio Busino, wrote that the King's Men 'showed a cardinal in all his grandeur, in the formal robes appropriate to his station, splendid and rich, with his train in attendance, having an altar erected on the stage, where he pretended to make a prayer, organizing a procession...Moreover he goes to war, first laying down his cardinal's habit on the altar, with the help of his chaplains, with great ceremoniousness; finally he has his sword bound on and dons the soldier's sash with so much panache you could not imagine it better done. And all this acted in condemnation of the grandeur of the Church, which they despise and which in this kingdom they hate to the death.'
• 1995: The Cheek by Jowl production cut the pilgrims but did include part of the dumbshow: the Duchess and Antonio knelt to receive Communion, while priests swung censers and chanted in Latin, but the Cardinal silently refused it to them.

are by a form of banishment in dumbshow, expressed towards them by the
CARDINAL and the state of ANCONA, banished. During all which ceremony
this ditty is sung to very solemn music, by divers churchmen; and then

Exeunt.

Arms and honours deck thy story
To thy fame's eternal glory,
Adverse fortune ever fly thee,   The author
No disastrous fate come nigh thee.   disclaims this   10
                                          ditty to be his.
I alone will sing thy praises,
Whom to honour, virtue raises;
And thy study, that divine is,
Bent to martial discipline is.
Lay aside all those robes lie by thee,   15
Crown thy arts with arms: they'll beautify thee.

Oh worthy of worthiest name, adorned in this manner,
Lead bravely thy forces on, under war's warlike banner:
Oh mayest thou prove fortunate in all martial courses,
Guide thou still, by skill, in arts and forces: 20
Victory attend thee nigh, whilst fame sings loud thy powers,
Triumphant conquest crown thy head, and blessings pour down
    showers.

1 PILGRIM   Here's a strange turn of state: who would
                  have thought
              So great a lady would have matched herself
              Unto so mean a person? Yet the Cardinal   25
              Bears himself much too cruel.

2 PILGRIM   They are banished.

1 PILGRIM   But I would ask what power hath this state
              Of Ancona to determine of a free prince?

2 PILGRIM   They are a free state sir, and her brother showed
              How that the Pope, forehearing of her looseness,   30
              Hath seized into the protection of the Church
              The dukedom which she held as dowager.

1 PILGRIM   But by what justice?

3.5 *The pilgrims report that they saw the Cardinal tear the Duchess's wedding ring off her finger. She and Antonio are banished, and many of their servants have left them*

39–41 **If that...bottom** *taken from Montaigne's* Essays, *who applies it to losing his temper*

42 **general** universal; generally true

1 **Banished** *This is the first word of Webster's previous play,* The White Devil.

2 **Lightens** gives light to; kindles

5 **take your fortune** share whatever happens to you

buntings birds similar to larks

7–9 **physicians...patients** in such a way, doctors, once they have been paid, are accustomed to abandon *(with wordplay on 'pronounce incurable')* their patients

9 **Right...world** that is exactly the way of the world

10–11 **From decayed...sinks** *This rhyming, moralising platitude may be intended ironically.*

2 PILGRIM	Sure I think by none, Only her brother's instigation.	

1 PILGRIM	What was it with such violence he took Off from her finger?	35

2 PILGRIM	'Twas her wedding ring, Which he vowed shortly he would sacrifice To his revenge.	

1 PILGRIM	Alas, Antonio, If that a man be thrust into a well, No matter who sets hand to't, his own weight Will bring him sooner to th'bottom. Come, let's hence. Fortune makes this conclusion general, 'All things do help th'unhappy man to fall.'	40

Exeunt.

Scene 5

Enter ANTONIO, DUCHESS, CHILDREN, CARIOLA, SERVANTS.

DUCHESS	Banished Ancona?	

ANTONIO	Yes, you see what power Lightens in great men's breath.	

DUCHESS	Is all our train Shrunk to this poor remainder?	

ANTONIO	These poor men, Which have got little in your service, vow To take your fortune; but your wiser buntings, Now they are fledged, are gone.	5

DUCHESS	They have done wisely. This puts me in mind of death: physicians thus, With their hands full of money, use to give o'er Their patients.	

ANTONIO	Right the fashion of the world: From decayed fortunes every flatterer shrinks, Men cease to build where the foundation sinks.	10

12–17 **dream...tears** *taken from Pierre Matthieu's* Henry IV

12 **tonight** last night

18 **benefit** gifts

20 **carol** sing joyfully

21 **happily** fortunately

23 **blanch** whitewash; palliate

mischief evil-doing

25 **tempest** *see note to 2.5.16–21*

28 **politic equivocation** crafty ambiguity

33 **engaged** pledged

Duchess

17–20 The Duchess's envy of the birds is a melancholy echo of her defiant reaction to Ferdinand when he discovers that she has remarried (3.2.84–85), and also links up with Bosola's speech about *silly birds* who let themselves be caught (98–101). Muriel Bradbrook believes that this speech shows the start of her tragic awakening to her mistake in marrying secretly, for love, it is 'a pathetic variation on her brother's warning that happiness dwells only with unambitious shepherds' (see 3.2.126–130).

Performance

This is the first time that Bosola appears after he had convinced her he was on her side (3.2), but there are no obvious lines for the Duchess or Antonio to show their reaction to his duplicity. If Bosola is not yet in disguise (see page 259) then their reaction may be shown by looks and the way the Duchess says *Thou dost blanch mischief...false hearts...* (23–26). In the 1995 Cheek by Jowl production Antonio added 'Bosola!' in shock after *You are happily o'erta'en* (21) and forced him to the ground, holding a gun at his head.

DUCHESS   I had a very strange dream tonight.

ANTONIO   What was't?

DUCHESS   Methought I wore my coronet of state,
             And on a sudden all the diamonds
             Were changed to pearls.

ANTONIO   My interpretation   15
             Is, you'll weep shortly, for to me the pearls
             Do signify your tears.

DUCHESS   The birds that live i'th'field
             On the wild benefit of nature, live
             Happier than we; for they may choose their mates
             And carol their sweet pleasures to the spring.   20

         Enter BOSOLA with a letter which he presents to the DUCHESS.

BOSOLA   You are happily o'erta'en.

DUCHESS   From my brother?

BOSOLA   Yes, from the Lord Ferdinand your brother,
             All love, and safety.

DUCHESS   Thou dost blanch mischief,
             Wouldst make it white. See, see, like to calm
                 weather
             At sea before a tempest, false hearts speak fair   25
             To those they intend most mischief.
             (*Reads*) *Send Antonio to me, I want his head in a*
                 business –
             A politic equivocation:
             He doth not want your counsel but your head:
             That is, he cannot sleep till you be dead.   30
             And here's another pitfall that's strewed o'er
             With roses: mark it, 'tis a cunning one:
             (*Reads*) *I stand engaged for your husband for several*
             debts at Naples; let not that trouble him, I had rather
             have his heart than his money.   35
             And I believe so too.

BOSOLA   What do you believe?

123

3.5 *The Duchess and Antonio believe Ferdinand's letter is a trap. Bosola departs, and the Duchess advises Antonio to flee to Milan with their eldest son*

39 **devil** *linking Ferdinand with the devil: see note to 2.5.66–70*

40 **circumvent** *try to trap; get the better of*

41 **free league** *generous alliance*

42 **amity** *friendship*

45 **be our after-ruin** *destroy us afterwards*

47 **And...this?** *either* and what follows? *or* and what of the letter?

48 **Bloodhounds** *murderers (a fairly common name for paid killers in the early seventeenth century)*

49 **hatched** *contrived; devise*

53 **adamant** *loadstone; magnet*

56 **Milan** *250 miles north-west of Ancona*

57–58 **venture...bottom** *nautical image and proverbial expression*

58 **bottom** *hold of a ship*

61 **curious artist** *skilful craftsman*

in sunder *asunder: in pieces*

62 **out of frame** *out of order*

'I am your adventure, am I not?' (3.5.95): in the 2003 National Theatre production, Bosola (far right) and the armed guard have ambushed the Duchess. A few moments before, Antonio swapped his coat and hat with the man on the left, and fled with his eldest son. Cariola comforts the daughter; the Duchess challenges Bosola – who does not yet realise that Antonio has escaped

Antonio

In Webster's source by Painter (see page 237) the Duchess also advises Antonio to flee with their eldest son, but Painter gives the reason that the Duchess believes her brothers intend harm only to Antonio and not to herself: 'if you do tarry, you will be the cause of the ruin and overthrow of us all'. Antonio in the source is reluctant to leave because of his love for the Duchess – he doesn't care about his own death, but he flees in order to save her. In Webster's play, the decision to flee comes straight after Bosola's accusation that Antonio is afraid because of his lowly birth (51–53).

DUCHESS	That he so much distrusts my husband's love He will by no means believe his heart is with him Until he see it. The devil is not cunning enough To circumvent us in riddles. 40
BOSOLA	Will you reject that noble and free league Of amity and love which I present you?
DUCHESS	Their league is like that of some politic kings Only to make themselves of strength and power To be our after-ruin: tell them so. 45
BOSOLA	And what from you?
ANTONIO	Thus tell him: I will not come.
BOSOLA	And what of this?
ANTONIO	My brothers have dispersed Bloodhounds abroad; which till I hear are muzzled, No truce, though hatched with ne'er such politic skill, Is safe, that hangs upon our enemies' will. 50 I'll not come at them.
BOSOLA	This proclaims your breeding. Every small thing draws a base mind to fear As the adamant draws iron. Fare you well sir, You shall shortly hear from's.

Exit.

DUCHESS	I suspect some ambush: Therefore by all my love I do conjure you 55 To take your eldest son and fly towards Milan; Let us not venture all this poor remainder In one unlucky bottom.
ANTONIO	You counsel safely: Best of my life, farewell; since we must part Heaven hath a hand in't; but no otherwise 60 Than as some curious artist takes in sunder A clock, or watch, when it is out of frame, To bring't in better order.

The Duchess and Antonio part – he leaves with their eldest son, she stays behind with Cariola and the two youngest children

64 **boy** *her eldest son*

66 **wit** *faculty of thinking; understanding*

68 **eternal Church** *Christian community in heaven*

70 **fortitude** *moral strength (one of the four 'cardinal virtues' – justice, prudence, temperance are the others; distinguished since the medieval period from the 'theological virtues': faith, hope and charity)*

71–72 **And...bruised** *the second line is a version of a proverb*

71 **unkindly** *much stronger than today:* (1) with unnatural cruelty; (2) 'unrestrained by natural bonds of kindred' *(Oxford English Dictionary)*

72 **cassia** *a fragrant herb similar to cinnamon*

proved *established as genuine; made trial of*

bruised (1) *injured;* (2) *ground (with idea that you need to rub the leaf between your fingers to establish by smell that it is the genuine herb)*

73–74 **Must...tyranny?** *from the second sonnet in Sidney's sequence of sonnets and songs about unhappy love: Astrophel and Stella (Webster changed 'Muscovite' to* **Russian***)*

76, 78 **scourge, scourge-stick** *whip; wordplay:* (1) *the top is a child's toy spun with a whip or stick;* (2) *religious idea, used of God in the Old Testament: to scourge = to punish*

81 **thy...armful** *the baby – the youngest child; there would also be a daughter with them*

86–87 **anchorite...skull** *see note to 2.4.4; the skull was an aid to meditation. English rulers often sought advice from anchorites, but Henry VIII ended a long tradition of English anchoritism in 1539. There were numerous hermits in Italy in the seventeenth century.*

88–89 **lead...sound** *nautical image: depth of water was measured ('sounded') by a piece of lead attached to a line*

s.d. **vizards** *masks (this original stage direction is ambiguous: see note about Bosola on page 128)*

Duchess

75–78 What is the guilt the Duchess feels needs heaven's *scourge-stick*? Is she referring to keeping her marriage secret? 'This acceptance of her fate as a necessary "scourge-stick" marks an important change in her response, a coming to terms with her deeds' (Lee Bliss).

Language

79–80 Webster took this from a poem written in 1611 by John Donne on the death of a fourteen-year-old girl: 'We seem ambitious, God's whole work t'undo; / Of nothing he made us, and we strive too, / To bring ourselves to nothing back' (*The First Anniversary: An Anatomy of the World*). Rupert Brooke said: 'Webster improved even Donne...The metrical skill is astounding...the line ending with "and we strive too," to the simpler easier cadence more suited to speech and to pathos, "...; and we strive"; and the repetition of "nothing" in the same place in the two lines.'

85–87 Michael Neill says that the earlier image where the Duchess describes herself as *a holy relic* (3.2.138) 'springs to grotesque life' in her speech here.

90 Victorious Roman generals were crowned with a wreath of laurel (bay), and Roman emperors were portrayed wearing one, as King James was on the commemorative medal for his accession in 1603. It was said to protect against lightning; Muriel Bradbrook adds that it was also an emblem of their good fame. The withering of the evergreen bay tree was an omen of evil or death; Shakespeare refers to it in *Richard II* 2.4 and *Antony and Cleopatra* 4.15.

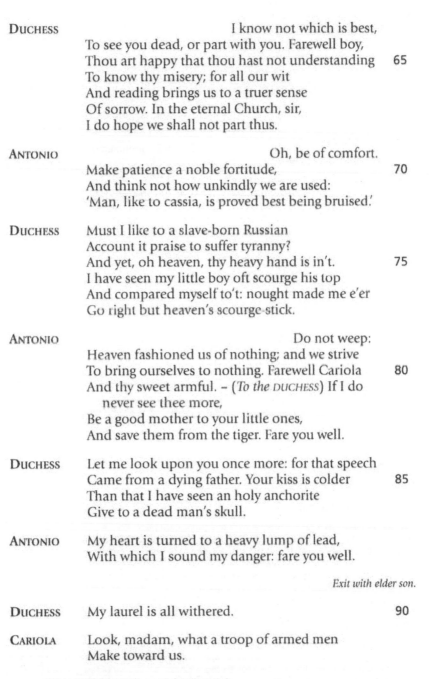

DUCHESS   I know not which is best,
To see you dead, or part with you. Farewell boy,
Thou art happy that thou hast not understanding   65
To know thy misery; for all our wit
And reading brings us to a truer sense
Of sorrow. In the eternal Church, sir,
I do hope we shall not part thus.

ANTONIO   Oh, be of comfort.
Make patience a noble fortitude,   70
And think not how unkindly we are used:
'Man, like to cassia, is proved best being bruised.'

DUCHESS   Must I like to a slave-born Russian
Account it praise to suffer tyranny?
And yet, oh heaven, thy heavy hand is in't.   75
I have seen my little boy oft scourge his top
And compared myself to't: nought made me e'er
Go right but heaven's scourge-stick.

ANTONIO   Do not weep:
Heaven fashioned us of nothing; and we strive
To bring ourselves to nothing. Farewell Cariola   80
And thy sweet armful. – (*To the* DUCHESS) If I do
    never see thee more,
Be a good mother to your little ones,
And save them from the tiger. Fare you well.

DUCHESS   Let me look upon you once more: for that speech
Came from a dying father. Your kiss is colder   85
Than that I have seen an holy anchorite
Give to a dead man's skull.

ANTONIO   My heart is turned to a heavy lump of lead,
With which I sound my danger: fare you well.

                                        Exit with elder son.

DUCHESS   My laurel is all withered.   90

CARIOLA   Look, madam, what a troop of armed men
Make toward us.

    Enter BOSOLA with a guard with vizards.

93   **Fortune's wheel** *an ancient metaphor of fortune and disaster following each other cyclically; there were particularly numerous depictions of the wheel in literature and art in the Middle Ages*

     overcharged overburdened; weighted down

95   **adventure** quarry

97   **counterfeits** imitates

102   **o'ercharged** filled with too much gunpowder

104   **To none...palace** *These three speeches make up only one line, which would be said quickly by the actors: with 'palace' at the end in the same place as 'prison' on the previous line (see note below).*

105–106   **Charon's...again** *In Greek mythology, Charon (pronounced 'Care-ron') was* the boatman who rowed the dead across the River Styx to the underworld.

107–110   **pity...eaten** *see notes to 4.1.134 and 4.2.236*

110   **prattle** chatter idly; talk at length in a childish way

111   **accursed** under a curse

112   **Curses...language** *This may deliberately echo Caliban in* The Tempest, *premiered by the King's Men about two years before: 'You taught me language, and my profit on't / Is I know how to curse' (1.2). This was very serious in this society, e.g. a witch's curse was believed to be very powerful.*

Bosola in performance

The stage direction for his entrance with the guard (see page 127) is ambiguous about who, if anyone, is masked (vizarded). Some productions have Bosola masked or disguised from now until the Duchess's death. In the 1995 Greenwich/Wyndham's Theatres production Bosola wore a hood from this scene onwards, until in 4.2 the Duchess (Juliet Stevenson) suddenly pulled it back from his face – showing she had known it was him throughout. In the 2003 National Theatre production he wasn't disguised until 4.2, when he put on a wig and clergyman's collar (see page 259).

Plot

103–104 In Webster's source (see page 237) the Duchess is also told she is being taken to her house, 'But she was greatly deceived, and knew within short space after the good will her brethren bare unto her. For so soon as these gallants had conducted her into the kingdom of Naples, to one of the castles of her son, she was committed to prison with her children, and she also that was the secretary of her unfortunate marriage [i.e. Cariola].'

DUCHESS	Oh they are very welcome: When Fortune's wheel is overcharged with princes The weight makes it move swift. I would have my ruin Be sudden. (*To* BOSOLA) I am your adventure, am I not? 95
BOSOLA	You are. You must see your husband no more.
DUCHESS	What devil art thou that counterfeits heaven's thunder?
BOSOLA	Is that terrible? I would have you tell me Whether is that note worse that frights the silly birds Out of the corn, or that which doth allure them 100 To the nets? You have harkened to the last too much.
DUCHESS	Oh misery: like to a rusty o'ercharged cannon, Shall I never fly in pieces? Come: to what prison?
BOSOLA	To none.
DUCHESS	Whither then?
BOSOLA	To your palace.
DUCHESS	I have heard that Charon's boat serves to convey 105 All o'er the dismal lake, but brings none back again.
BOSOLA	Your brothers mean you safety and pity.
DUCHESS	Pity? With such a pity men preserve alive Pheasants and quails, when they are not fat enough To be eaten.
BOSOLA	These are your children?
DUCHESS	Yes.
BOSOLA	Can they prattle?
DUCHESS	No: 110 But I intend, since they were born accursed, Curses shall be their first language.
BOSOLA	Fie, madam, Forget this base, low fellow.

114   **counterfeit** false; deceitful *(this either indicates that Bosola is wearing a mask, or she has just realised that he has betrayed her)*

115–117   **Say...virtue** *see Webster's dedication (page 233)*

115   **mean** *see note to 3.4.25*

122   **dog-fish** (1) small shark, mud-fish etc. (2) *scornful term of abuse (see also note to 1.1.39)*

128   **silly** humble

139   **bent** *perhaps:* levelled like a weapon *(continuing the image of line 138)*

   sways *wordplay:* (1) swings; (2) sovereign power; rule

140   **There's no...hill** *Perhaps this means the same as 4.1.75: 'Things...mend'. But since it's a proverbial expression and part of a rhymed couplet it seems ambiguous.*

Bosola and Duchess

113–118 Bosola's lines about Antonio: *base, low fellow...of no birth,* are a direct contradiction to his comments in 3.2. Michael Neill suggests he denigrates Antonio 'in the bitterness of his already divided emotions'. Likewise the Duchess's remarks are the reverse of 3.2, and her speech here (115–117) echoes what Bosola said in 3.2.256–257.

Duchess's parable

119–140 Contrasting opinions:
• Rupert Brooke (1916): 'The Duchess mars the end of a lovely and terrible scene by a would-be funny moral tale about a dogfish and a salmon. Here there is a sort of pathetic suitability in the Duchess, half broken with sorrow, almost unconsciously babbling childish tales to her enemies. But...one finds it hard to believe Webster meant this. If he did, he did not bring his effect off. The tale is too incongruous with the rest of the scene.'
• Muriel Bradbrook (1980): 'The very curious fable that she tells Bosola on her capture implies that good fame cannot be discerned till death; only a complete life may be measured, when those who seem to have few claims may be found to have most.'
• Kathleen McLuskie (1985): 'Her clear insult to Bosola in implying that he is a mere dog-fish with temporary power over the more naturally aristocratic salmon – herself and Antonio – is her last wry joke before the darkness of Act IV.'
• Michael Neill (1997): this parable, 'though offered as a defence of Antonio's low birth...looks forward to her own death as the master day by which her life will be judged...In fact her moral is precisely that with which Delio, confronted with the "great ruin" of the house of Aragon, will end the play.'

| DUCHESS | Were I a man |
| | I'd beat that counterfeit face into thy other. |

| BOSOLA | One of no birth. |

DUCHESS	Say that he was born mean:	115
	Man is most happy when's own actions
	Be arguments and examples of his virtue.

| BOSOLA | A barren, beggarly virtue. |

DUCHESS	I prithee who is greatest, can you tell?
	Sad tales befit my woe: I'll tell you one.	120
	A salmon as she swam unto the sea
	Met with a dog-fish, who encounters her
	With this rough language: 'Why art thou so bold
	To mix thyself with our high state of floods,
	Being no eminent courtier, but one	125
	That for the calmest and fresh time o'th'year
	Dost live in shallow rivers, rank'st thyself
	With silly smelts and shrimps? And darest thou
	Pass by our dog-ship without reverence?'
	'Oh', quoth the salmon, 'sister be at peace:	130
	Thank Jupiter we both have passed the net,
	Our value never can be truly known
	Till in the fisher's basket we be shown.
	I'th'market then my price may be the higher,
	Even when I am nearest to the cook, and fire.'	135
	So to great men the moral may be stretched:
	'Men oft are valued high, when th'are most wretched.'
	But come, whither you please: I am armed 'gainst
	misery,
	Bent to all sways of the oppressor's will.
	'There's no deep valley, but near some great hill.'	140

Exeunt.

4.1 *It is night-time, several days or weeks later, presumably in the Duchess's palace at Malfi, where she is imprisoned. Bosola tells her that Ferdinand has come to visit her*

2 **imprisonment** *see notes below and to 3.5.103–104*

3–5 **She's...shun it** *from Sidney's* Arcadia *about Queen Erona (see also note below)*

5–6 **a behaviour...adversity** *from Sidney's* Arcadia *about Musidorus, one of the heroes (Webster occasionally changed what was originally a reference to a man, to the Duchess)*

9 **four** *several*

12 **restraint** *imprisonment*

13 **mastiffs...tying** *powerful watch-dogs that are fiercer when they are tied up*

14 **apprehend** *feel; imagine*

16–17 **I will...you** *Perhaps this means he no longer wants news of his sister at second-hand and Bosola is to inform her that Ferdinand is coming to visit her.*

s.d. ***Enter...CARIOLA*** *In many productions she will not appear, especially as she has no lines.*

19–20 **wrap..sugar** *a proverbial expression*

21 **elder brother** *We learn later (4.2.266) that they are twins, though he is older in Webster's source, so this may be a mistake.*

23–24 **'Cause...more** *see 3.2.140*

25 **taper** *candle*

Performance

On the Jacobean stage there was little or no scenery: props and language tell the audience where the scene is set, so Webster did not need to specify where the Duchess is being held. She may be locked into various rooms in her palace (see lines 26, 124), perhaps in her bedchamber. In the 2003 National Theatre production (see photograph on page 134) the central position of the screen in this scene, with no other furniture, suggested the Duchess was in a small room or cell. Ferdinand watched her, sitting at a desk on top of the bleachers (steps), wearing headphones, i.e. obviously listening to the Duchess in her cell. The set of the 1995 Cheek by Jowl production was also bare – just black drapes around the acting area – but the few items of furniture were the same as for the bedroom scene (3.2), and the Duchess had a constant supply of drink as well as cigarettes, so it suggested that she was locked in her bedroom.

Language

7–8 This is taken from Sidney's *Arcadia* Book 2, describing Queen Erona who also suffered because she married beneath her; Sidney says that in her sorrow one could 'perceive the shape of loveliness more perfectly in woe, than in joyfulness'. The poet Rupert Brooke comments: 'Webster turned this, with a touch, to poetry in its sheerest beauty. It is just this substitution of the concrete for the abstract – which is the nearest one could get to a definition of the difference between a thought in good prose and the same thought in good poetry – that Webster excels in.'

Act 4

Scene 1

Enter FERDINAND, BOSOLA and servants with torches.

FERDINAND   How doth our sister Duchess bear herself
In her imprisonment?

BOSOLA   Nobly; I'll describe her:
She's sad, as one long used to't, and she seems
Rather to welcome the end of misery
Than shun it: a behaviour so noble   5
As gives a majesty to adversity:
You may discern the shape of loveliness
More perfect in her tears than in her smiles;
She will muse four hours together, and her silence,
Methinks, expresseth more than if she spake.   10

FERDINAND   Her melancholy seems to be fortified
With a strange disdain.

BOSOLA   'Tis so: and this restraint,
Like English mastiffs that grow fierce with tying,
Makes her too passionately apprehend
Those pleasures she's kept from.

FERDINAND   Curse upon her: 15
I will no longer study in the book
Of another's heart: inform her what I told you.

Exit.

Enter DUCHESS and CARIOLA.

BOSOLA   All comfort to your grace.

DUCHESS   I will have none:
Pray thee, why dost thou wrap thy poisoned pills
In gold and sugar?   20

BOSOLA   Your elder brother the Lord Ferdinand
Is come to visit you, and sends you word,
'Cause once he rashly made a solemn vow
Never to see you more, he comes i'th'night:
And prays you, gently, neither torch nor taper   25
Shine in your chamber. He will kiss your hand

The lights are taken away and Ferdinand appears, saying he wishes to be reconciled with his sister. In the dark, he gives her a 'dead man's hand' to kiss, which she thinks is his hand

27   **for his vow** because of his vow

32–33   **For I...pardon** because even though I am entitled to kill, I consider it a more noble type of revenge to pardon instead

33   **cubs** *Perhaps Ferdinand calls her children cubs because his lycanthropy has started (see 5.2.6–10 and 4.2.257–258) or it may simply be a disparaging term for the children.*

38   **sacrament** *i.e. marriage. In Christianity, a sacrament is the outward sign of an*

inward grace as ordained by Christ; Catholics see marriage as one of the sacraments, along with baptism etc. The Duchess insists that her marriage was valid.

40   **thus** in the dark

41   **too...light** too exposed to the public *(with wordplay on* **light** = unchaste; promiscuous)*

46   **ring** *This is a significant emblem throughout the play: see note to 1.1.90.*

'She's sad, as one long used to't' (4.1.3): Bosola watches the Duchess from behind a glass screen, as Ferdinand listens in at the top of the bleachers (National Theatre, 2003)

Performance

29 In the 2003 National Theatre and 1995 Greenwich/Wyndham's Theatres productions all the lights went out, so there was total darkness. In the 1995 Cheek by Jowl production, however, there was some light so the audience could see the actors and the hand, but the actors played it as if they were in total darkness – and the audience saw Ferdinand (Scott Handy) fall clumsily over a chair as he tried to get near the Duchess. When first performed at the Globe, the scene would have been in daylight, with the audience having to imagine it was in the dark; at the Blackfriars it is probable that some of the stage candles were extinguished or removed, making the stage darker (see Martin White in Further reading).

And reconcile himself, but, for his vow,
He dares not see you.

DUCHESS   At his pleasure:
Take hence the lights. He's come.

Exeunt SERVANTS with torches.

Enter FERDINAND.

FERDINAND   Where are you?

DUCHESS   Here, sir.

FERDINAND   This darkness suits you well.   30

DUCHESS   I would ask you pardon.

FERDINAND   You have it;
For I account it the honorabl'st revenge,
Where I may kill, to pardon. Where are your cubs?

DUCHESS   Whom?

FERDINAND   Call them your children;
For though our national law distinguish bastards   35
From true legitimate issue, compassionate nature
Makes them all equal.

DUCHESS   Do you visit me for this?
You violate a sacrament o'th'Church
Shall make you howl in hell for't.

FERDINAND   It had been well
Could you have lived thus always, for indeed   40
You were too much i'th'light. But no more.
I come to seal my peace with you. Here's a hand
To which you have vowed much love: the ring
      upon't
You gave.

Gives her a dead man's hand.

DUCHESS   I affectionately kiss it.

FERDINAND   Pray do, and bury the print of it in your heart.   45
I will leave this ring with you for a love token,

The Duchess discovers that the hand is not her brother's and is shown what seem to be the dead bodies of her husband and children

49 **it** the ring

53 **witchcraft** *note the further allusions to witchcraft here and in lines 61–64*

s.d. ***traverse*** *curtain; screen*

artificial figures *Later Ferdinand says these are made of wax (lines 109–112).*

children *This is the stage direction in the 1623 quarto and may be by Webster, but 'children' seems to be an error for 'elder son' – unless the Duchess forgets the other two children are 'dead' at 4.2.203–205.*

57 **directly** *either at first hand or immediately*

58–59 **cease...recovered** *from lines by the Italian poet Petrarch (1304–74) translated 1579*

61 **wastes** consumes *(as if by disease); destroys*

62 **picture** statue; monumental effigy *(dramatic irony since the figures are made out of wax just like effigies on coffins)*

64 **yond's** that is

property *either* attribute *or* tool; device

66–67 **bind me...death** *This was 'the ritual punishment for an ill-matched marriage' (Muriel Bradbrook).*

Performance

53–54 In the 1995 Cheek by Jowl production, when the Duchess (Anastasia Hille) realised it was a dead man's hand, she was annoyed at yet another prank by her twin brother, and threw it in the bin.

s.d. after 54 The King's Men may have had waxwork/wooden figures made or have used the actual actors 'hanging' in the discovery space behind the curtain in front of the tiring house. In the 2003 National Theatre production, models of Antonio and the boy, wearing identical clothes, descended from the flies to behind the glass screen.

Ideas and interpretations

48–50 *When you need a friend...*: There is a legend, curiously it seems first recorded by Webster in *The Devil's Law-Case* 3.3, that while awaiting execution in the Tower of London after the failed coup in 1601, Elizabeth I's favourite, the Earl of Essex, tried to send her the ring she had given him when she had said similar words to Ferdinand's. The legend goes that the boy he gave it to handed it to the wrong person and it never reached the Queen. For those in the audience who knew the legend, Ferdinand's speech would add to the horror.

s.d. after 54 Webster's father may have provided the funeral coach for Prince Henry in 1612 when the prince's wax effigy was placed on top of the coffin and then displayed in Westminster Abbey. This may have given Webster the idea. Similar effigies were made of every English monarch from Henry V until about 1700; some are still on display in the Abbey.

And the hand, as sure as the ring; and do not doubt
But you shall have the heart too. When you need a
    friend
Send it to him that owned it: you shall see
Whether he can aid you.

DUCHESS   You are very cold.   50
I fear you are not well after your travel –
Ha? Lights! – Oh horrible!

FERDINAND   Let her have lights enough.

Exit.

Enter servants with torches.

DUCHESS   What witchcraft doth he practise, that he hath left
A dead man's hand here?

*Here is discovered behind a traverse the artificial figures of ANTONIO and his
children, appearing as if they were dead.*

BOSOLA   Look you, here's the piece from which 'twas ta'en.   55
He doth present you this sad spectacle,
That now you know directly they are dead.
Hereafter you may, wisely, cease to grieve
For that which cannot be recovered.

DUCHESS   There is not between heaven and earth one wish   60
I stay for after this: it wastes me more
Than were't my picture, fashioned out of wax,
Stuck with a magical needle, and then buried
In some foul dunghill; and yond's an excellent
    property
For a tyrant, which I would account mercy.

BOSOLA   What's that?   65

DUCHESS   If they would bind me to that lifeless trunk
And let me freeze to death.

BOSOLA   Come, you must live.

DUCHESS   That's the greatest torture souls feel in hell,
In hell: that they must live, and cannot die.

70   **Portia** *see note below*

72   **Oh fie: despair?** *To despair of God's help was a mortal sin. Bosola is also shocked when Ferdinand tells him he intends his sister to despair (line 113).*

73   **enjoins** imposes as a penalty

74   **vain** of no use

76–77   **bee...eyelid** *i.e. after the bee has stung once, it can't again, and is harmless (taken from Whetstone: see note to 3.2.23–31)*

77   **fellow** *Some say this indicates that Bosola is in disguise; productions differ, but 4.1.129–132 suggests he is not yet.*

78   **wheel** horrific instrument of torture

81–87   **I...pity itself** *from Sidney's* Arcadia *(as are lines 89–90)*

87–88   **daggers – Puff...vipers** *Some editors find these mixed metaphors puzzling, but it's a graphic illustration of her temporary mental derangement.*

Duchess

70–72 Portia killed herself c. 42 BC by putting hot coals in her mouth and suffocating. She was the wife of Brutus, one of the conspirators who assassinated Julius Caesar, and seems to have become ill through worry for her husband, whom she loved. The Roman writer Plutarch (whom Shakespeare used as a source) says he doesn't know if she killed herself before or after Brutus died, but he heard there was a letter from Brutus mourning her fate. In Shakespeare's *Julius Caesar* (1599), news of her death reaches Brutus before his final battle (4.3); he says: 'Impatient of my absence...she died distract' (i.e. mad). She is therefore not a role model a sane woman might choose, which suggests the Duchess is here verging on madness.

Performance

85 In the 1995 Cheek by Jowl production, the Duchess (Anastasia Hille) was curt and contemptuous when offered Bosola's pity. He turned away quite devastated.

| | Portia, I'll new kindle thy coals again | 70 |

Portia, I'll new kindle thy coals again   70
And revive the rare and almost dead example
Of a loving wife.

BOSOLA   Oh fie: despair? Remember
You are a Christian.

DUCHESS   The Church enjoins fasting:
I'll starve myself to death.

BOSOLA   Leave this vain sorrow.
Things being at the worst, begin to mend: 75
The bee, when he hath shot his sting into your hand,
May then play with your eyelid.

DUCHESS   Good comfortable fellow,
Persuade a wretch that's broke upon the wheel
To have all his bones new set: entreat him live,
To be executed again. Who must dispatch me?   80
I account this world a tedious theatre,
For I do play a part in't 'gainst my will.

BOSOLA   Come, be of comfort, I will save your life.

DUCHESS   Indeed I have not leisure to tend so small a
        business.

BOSOLA   Now, by my life, I pity you.

DUCHESS   Thou art a fool then,   85
To waste thy pity on a thing so wretched
As cannot pity itself. I am full of daggers –
Puff – let me blow these vipers from me.
(*To a* SERVANT) What are you?

SERVANT   One that wishes you long life.

DUCHESS   I would thou wert hanged for the horrible curse   90
Thou hast given me! I shall shortly grow one
Of the miracles of pity. I'll go pray – no,
I'll go curse.

BOSOLA   Oh fie.

4.1 *In a rage, the Duchess curses instead of praying. Ferdinand is delighted; Bosola asks him to stop punishing her in this way*

99 **plagues** *Plague killed tens of thousands in London in the sixteenth and seventeenth centuries.*

make lanes *a metaphor used by Webster's fellow playwright George Chapman for a huge number of people killed, e.g. by one cannon shot*

100 **them** her brothers

tyrants *'tyrant' and 'tyranny' occur almost a dozen times in the play, e.g. 3.5.74*

102–103 **mortified Churchmen** monks who mortified their flesh through austere living and/or inflicting pain on themselves *(see also 4.2.176)*

107 **'It is...speed'** *The second line of the couplet is a commonplace expression.*

108 **plagued in art** tormented by human skill

110 **curious** skilful

quality profession; craft

111 **Vincentio Lauriola** *Webster seems to have made this name up, but his family probably knew people in London who made funeral effigies.*

113 **despair** *this was the goal of the devil; see notes to 4.1.72 and 2.5.66–70*

Bosola

97 This can be read in different ways: for example, Bosola may be at his most cynical – heaven is indifferent to sorrow or joy; or, 'whether or not Bosola intends it so, the line can also be read as reassuring the Duchess that despite the disorder and disintegration in her own life, the divine order still stands' (1995 Cambridge edition).

Act 4 Scene 1

DUCHESS	I could curse the stars.
BOSOLA	Oh fearful!
DUCHESS	And those three smiling seasons of the year Into a Russian winter, nay the world 95 To its first chaos.
BOSOLA	Look you, the stars shine still.
DUCHESS	Oh, but you must Remember, my curse hath a great way to go. Plagues, that make lanes through largest families, Consume them.
BOSOLA	Fie, lady!
DUCHESS	Let them like tyrants 100 Never be remembered but for the ill they have done: Let all the zealous prayers of mortified Churchmen forget them.
BOSOLA	Oh uncharitable.
DUCHESS	Let heaven a little while cease crowning martyrs To punish them. 105 Go howl them this and say I long to bleed: 'It is some mercy, when men kill with speed.'

Exeunt DUCHESS and CARIOLA.

Enter FERDINAND.

FERDINAND	Excellent, as I would wish, she's plagued in art. These presentations are but framed in wax By the curious master in that quality, 110 Vincentio Lauriola, and she takes them For true substantial bodies.
BOSOLA	Why do you do this?
FERDINAND	To bring her to despair.
BOSOLA	Faith, end here And go no farther in your cruelty.

Ferdinand decides to surround the Duchess with mad people. Bosola refuses to see her again except in disguise

115 **penitential garment** *In Catholicism, penance is confessing sins to a priest and showing repentance by praying or fasting. In the past the penitent sometimes wore special clothes.*

117 **beads** rosary beads *(an aid to prayer)*

120 **masques** theatrical entertainments at court, with music and dancing, written for the courtiers to perform *(usually Queen Anne and her ladies)*

courtesans prostitutes

121 **bawds** pimps

ruffians another term for pimps

122 **she'll needs be** it is necessary that she is

123 **forth** out from

common public

125 **practise together** *sexual innuendo*

126 **gambols** leaps in dancing

130–132 **forfeited...lie** that's lost as a result of my acting as an informer and because the dead bodies were fake *(it's not clear what he means, except that he refuses to see her again unless he's disguised)*

134 **Thy pity...thee** pity is not part of your character *(Ferdinand misunderstands him)*

138 **'Intemperate...cruel'** *a proverb:* 'severe fevers make doctors cruel' *(Ferdinand is saying he has to be cruel to cure her, but it can also mean that he is the one that is sick)*

Bosola

130–132 Whether, in 3.5, Bosola appeared to the Duchess as himself or in disguise (see note on page 128), here he demands that he will never appear to her again except in disguise. Indeed, when he next visits her, he enters *like an old man* (s.d. after 4.2.112). Muriel Bradbrook comments that 'with all his many roles, Bosola is never permitted the luxury of being a self. He is the masquer.'

Language

134 The word *pity*, Muriel Bradbrook says, is 'a key word towards the end of the play, but almost always used ironically'. Is it? It is used by Antonio of Bosola (1.1.76), Cariola of the Duchess (1.1.506), Julia of her husband (2.4.57). In 2.5 Ferdinand gets rid of his pity for his sister in his handkerchief (27–28). In 3.5 Bosola tells the Duchess: *Your brothers mean you safety and pity*, which the Duchess dismisses with contempt (107–110). Earlier in 4.1 Bosola tells the Duchess: *I pity you*, but she tells him his pity is *wasted* (84–87). And then in 4.2 Ferdinand, on seeing the dead Duchess, demands of Bosola: *Why didst not thou pity her?* (272) (See also the note to 4.2.346.)

Send her a penitential garment to put on   115
Next to her delicate skin, and furnish her
With beads and prayer books.

FERDINAND   Damn her, that body of hers,
While that my blood ran pure in't, was more worth
Than that which thou wouldst comfort, called a soul.
I will send her masques of common courtesans,   120
Have her meat served up by bawds and ruffians,
And, 'cause she'll needs be mad, I am resolved
To remove forth the common hospital
All the mad folk and place them near her lodging;
There let them practise together, sing and dance   125
And act their gambols to the full o'th'moon.
If she can sleep the better for it, let her.
Your work is almost ended.

BOSOLA   Must I see her again?

FERDINAND   Yes.

BOSOLA   Never.

FERDINAND   You must.

BOSOLA   Never in mine own shape,   130
That's forfeited by my intelligence
And this last cruel lie. When you send me next
The business shall be comfort.

FERDINAND   Very likely,
Thy pity is nothing of kin to thee. Antonio
Lurks about Milan, thou shalt shortly thither   135
To feed a fire as great as my revenge,
Which ne'er will slack till it have spent his fuel:
'Intemperate agues make physicians cruel.'

Exeunt.

4.2 *The location is the same as before, and not much later in time. Cariola tries to comfort the Duchess as the noise of madmen is heard*

1	**consort** company *(Cariola is probably ironic since it also meant: group of musicians)*	12	**durance** imprisonment
		13–14	**robin...cages** *see 3.2.84–85*
11	**This is a prison?** *see note below*		

The madmen scene in the 2003 National Theatre production (see the interview with the director, page 257)

Ideas and interpretations

1–2 The madmen are not in Webster's source (see page 237), but he may have got the idea from it: in Painter's story, when Antonio begins to be aware that the Duchess loves him, Painter compares lovers with 'mad and Bedlam persons' (Bedlam – a corruption of Bethlehem hospital – was the name of the lunatic asylum in London; from the early seventeenth century visitors were allowed to watch the patients chained in their cells).

11 It is not an actual prison cell, since there has been no mention of moving her away from her 'lodging' (see 4.1.124). The 1995 Cambridge edition has changed the question mark to an exclamation mark, believing that the Duchess is making a statement, not asking a question.

Performance

Some critics suggest that 4.2 is structured like a wedding masque (see page 238). The editors of the 1995 Cambridge edition suggest: 'The Duchess may well have her hair unbound now since this was a common stage convention for grief or distraction in Jacobean plays...Unbound hair would also carry the ironic symbolism of a virgin bride preparing for marriage.'

Scene 2

Enter DUCHESS and CARIOLA.

DUCHESS   What hideous noise was that?

CARIOLA   'Tis the wild consort
Of madmen, lady, which your tyrant brother
Hath placed about your lodging; this tyranny
I think was never practised till this hour.

DUCHESS   Indeed I thank him: nothing but noise and folly   5
Can keep me in my right wits, whereas reason
And silence make me stark mad. Sit down,
Discourse to me some dismal tragedy.

CARIOLA   Oh 'twill increase your melancholy.

DUCHESS   Thou art deceived,
To hear of greater grief would lessen mine.   10
This is a prison?

CARIOLA   Yes, but you shall live
To shake this durance off.

DUCHESS   Thou art a fool,
The robin redbreast and the nightingale
Never live long in cages.

CARIOLA   Pray dry your eyes.
What think you of, madam?

DUCHESS   Of nothing: 15
When I muse thus, I sleep.

CARIOLA   Like a madman, with your eyes open?

DUCHESS   Dost thou think we shall know one another
In th'other world?

CARIOLA   Yes, out of question.

DUCHESS   Oh that it were possible we might   20
But hold some two days' conference with the dead,
From them I should learn somewhat I am sure
I never shall know here. I'll tell thee a miracle,

25 **Th'heaven...brass** *from the Bible (Deuteronomy 28.15, 23): Moses tells his people that those who do not obey God's commandments will be cursed: 'And thy heaven that is over thy head shall be brass, and the earth that is under thee shall be iron.'*

26 **sulphur** *associated with hell and devils because it is highly inflammable*

27–30 **I am...easy** *adapted from the French writer Pierre Matthieu; Webster changed the first line from: 'I am inured to my afflictions'*

28 **tanned** *made brown by the sun (added by Webster)*

32 **A deal...practice** *very lifelike in appearance, but not in reality*

33–34 **reverend...pitied** *i.e. not only is the monument worthy of reverence, but it is an object of much pity in a ruined state (and wordplay on **pitied**: pitted = scarred. The image becomes a reality in 5.3 – the echo scene.)*

monument (1) a structure that commemorates a person or an event (e.g. over a grave); (2) statue; effigy

34 **proper** fitting; apt

35–36 **Fortune...tragedy** *Fortuna was an ancient Italian goddess associated with women and the uncertainty of fortune (see note to 3.5.93); this is an ironic echo of 1.1.494–496.*

41 **madmen** *This antimasque of madmen may have drawn on wedding masques (see page 238).*

43 **th'imposthume** the cyst; the abscess

45 **secular priest** a priest who lives in the world, i.e. not a monk (**secular** *here has the negative meaning of 'worldly' =* unlearned; not concerned with religion)

49 **day of doom** Day of Judgement

51 **usher** male attendant on a lady

55 **knave in grain** *wordplay:* (1) thorough rogue; (2) man who grows corn

---

Language

27–28 The image of the *galley-slave* links the Duchess with Bosola (see 1.1.34, 72–73, 220–222); it is also found in Webster's funeral poem for Prince Henry (see pages 233–234). Christy Desmet comments that the 'Duchess's continued sense of alienation can be measured by the persistence of masculine imagery' in the way she refers to herself.

31–32 This reply 'reshaped from *Arcadia,* defines the emblematic and eternalized image or icon which is grief incarnate...As a miniaturist will sparingly touch in pure gold, so Webster kept for the strongest moments the pure gold-on-black of Philip Sidney. Sidney himself (and the images he created) became sacred icons' (Muriel Bradbrook).

Duchess

33–34 Michael Neill says it is as if the Duchess's 'sufferings had already begun her metamorphosis into that effigy of pious widowhood whose cold embrace she had sought to escape in the wooing scene (1.1.458–459) – a metamorphosis which will be symbolically completed at the point of death when she self-consciously mimics the alabaster figure's kneeling posture' (4.2.231–233).

Ferdinand

38–44 'Ferdinand orders the masque of madmen for the Duchess with the ostensible aim of making her sane but with the true aim of making her insane, and yet it is he and not she who becomes mad' (Andrea Henderson).

I am not mad yet, to my cause of sorrow.
Th'heaven o'er my head seems made of molten
    brass,   25
The earth of flaming sulphur, yet I am not mad;
I am acquainted with sad misery
As the tanned galley-slave is with his oar.
Necessity makes me suffer constantly,
And custom makes it easy. Who do I look like now? 30

CARIOLA   Like to your picture in the gallery,
A deal of life in show but none in practice;
Or rather like some reverend monument
Whose ruins are even pitied.

DUCHESS   Very proper:
And Fortune seems only to have her eyesight   35
To behold my tragedy. How now,
What noise is that?

Enter SERVANT.

SERVANT   I am come to tell you
Your brother hath intended you some sport:
A great physician, when the Pope was sick
Of a deep melancholy, presented him   40
With several sorts of madmen, which wild object,
Being full of change and sport, forced him to laugh,
And so th'imposthume broke; the selfsame cure
The Duke intends on you.

DUCHESS   Let them come in.

SERVANT   There's a mad lawyer, and a secular priest,   45
A doctor that hath forfeited his wits
By jealousy, an astrologian
That in his works said such a day o'th'month
Should be the day of doom, and failing of't,
Ran mad; an English tailor crazed i'th'brain   50
With the study of new fashion, a gentleman usher
Quite beside himself with care to keep in mind
The number of his lady's salutations,
Or how do you, she employed him in each
    morning;
A farmer too, an excellent knave in grain,   55

56   **he...transportation** he was banned
     from exporting *(grain was banned from
     export in 1613)*

57   **broker** middleman in business or love
     affairs

61   ***heavy*** sad

74   **perspective** perspective glass: an early
     form of telescope

81   **tithe** decimate: kill one in every ten
     (see also 2.1.119)

82   **pothecary** apothecary: person who
     prepares and sells medicines

     outgo outdo

84   **alum** a compound used in tanning and
     dyeing *(alum manufacture was a papal
     monopoly in the fifteenth century; the
     first mines in England (Guisborough,
     Yorkshire) were discovered and worked
     c. 1600 by Sir Thomas Chaloner – who
     was excommunicated by the Pope)*

     urine *also traditionally used in tanning*

85   **over-straining** *i.e. singing psalms or
     preaching too much*

The music for the madmen's song has survived, written by the composer Robert
Johnson (c. 1583–1633). This is an extract of the vocal part; the full transcription can be
found, for example, in some Revels editions of the play

Ideas and interpretations

• 'Madness was itself thought of as diabolic possession, and the "comic" masque of
madmen prefigures the later madness of Ferdinand' (Muriel Bradbrook).
• The Madmen seem to be divided as nos 1–4 simply to help actors: 1 Madman is only at
first the Astrologer; 2 Madman is perhaps the Lawyer; 3 Madman is sometimes the Priest; 4
Madman is the Doctor.
• 'The masque and its characters provide a grotesque image of the world of the play, and
some of the madmen reflect quite accurately some of the play's central characters'
(Jacqueline Pearson). She suggests 2 Madman recalls Bosola, 3 Madman the Cardinal, and 4
Madman Ferdinand.

Mad 'cause he was hindered transportation;
And let one broker that's mad loose to these,
You'd think the devil were among them.

DUCHESS   Sit, Cariola (*To* SERVANT) – Let them loose when you
                please,
            For I am chained to endure all your tyranny.   60

Enter MADMEN.

Here, by a madman, this song is sung to a dismal kind of music.

Oh let us howl some heavy note,
    some deadly doggèd howl,
Sounding as from the threat'ning throat
    of beasts and fatal fowl.
As ravens, screech owls, bulls and bears,   65
    we'll bill and bawl our parts,
Till irksome noise have cloyed your ears
    and corrosived your hearts.
At last whenas our choir wants breath,
    our bodies being blest,   70
We'll sing like swans to welcome death,
    and die in love and rest.

1 MADMAN   Doomsday not come yet? I'll draw it nearer by a
            perspective, or make a glass that shall set all the
            world on fire upon an instant. I cannot sleep, my   75
            pillow is stuffed with a litter of porcupines.

2 MADMAN   Hell is a mere glass-house, where the devils are
            continually blowing up women's souls on hollow
            irons, and the fire never goes out.

3 MADMAN   I will lie with every woman in my parish the tenth   80
            night: I will tithe them over like haycocks.

4 MADMAN   Shall my pothecary outgo me, because I am a
            cuckold? I have found out his roguery: he makes
            alum of his wife's urine, and sells it to Puritans
            that have sore throats with over-straining.   85

1 MADMAN   I have skill in heraldry.

2 MADMAN   Hast?

149

86–90   **skill in heraldry...gentleman** *One of Webster's main themes is that greatness comes from what a person does and not from a person's lineage; he is mocking the snobbish pastime of acquiring a coat of arms by giving these lines to madmen.*

88   **You do give** if you display

crest *heraldry:* a figure or device on a wreath etc. in a coat of arms

woodcock bird with a long bill that's easy to catch *(thus it is used to mean a fool)*

91   **Greek...Turk** *i.e. Christians have become heathens*

92   **Helvetian** Swiss *(this refers to the popular English translation of the Bible of 1560 which had a Calvinist/Puritan bias; it was published in Geneva)*

93/94   **lay** *wordplay:* (1) expound; (2) apply

94   **corrosive** *wordplay:* (1) acid drug; (2) remedy

96   **He...damned** he who drinks only when he's thirsty is damned *(i.e. drunks are blessed)*

97   **glass** *perhaps:* urinal; *or* perspective glass *(a telescope that shows objects upside down)*

100   **ropemaker** *perhaps:* hangman

101   **snuffling** hypocritical

102   **placket** slit in a skirt; vagina

103–105   **Woe...bed in it** *i.e. he is worried his wife has made him a cuckold (both caroches and masques were used for secret sexual activities)*

103   **caroche** coach *(see also 1.1.229)*

106   **pared** trimmed

107   **agues** fevers

108   **milch bats** bats kept for milking *(as in 'milch-cow'; 'The mad Doctor supposes that bats will, as nocturnal creatures, yield milk suitable for narcotics' John Russell Brown.)*

possets hot drinks of sugared milk with ale or wine and spices

110   **throw...me** agree I am superior

111   **made...costive** made a soapmaker constipated *(difficult because soap was used in suppositories to loosen bowels)*

s.d.   ***Here...thereunto** a stage direction in the 1623 quarto; this describes an antimasque (see page 238)*

Performance

The madmen's speeches need numerous notes because they contained topical, local references that make little sense to us now. Not surprisingly the speeches were not used in the 2003 National Theatre or 1995 Cheek by Jowl or Greenwich/Wyndham's productions. At the National the madmen were replaced by hallucinating screen images; the Cheek by Jowl madmen sang Church phrases in Latin, banged a drum and one mimed giving birth. (See photograph on page 144, and directors' comments on pages 254 and 257.)

Ideas and interpretations

73–112 The madmen's talk denigrates women as sexually unfaithful and lustful. Critics have suggested it shows either Ferdinand's debased view about his sister or his attempt to teach his sister that she is this type of woman.

| 1 MADMAN | You do give for your crest a woodcock's head, with the brains picked out on't: you are a very ancient gentleman. | 90 |

1 MADMAN You do give for your crest a woodcock's head,
with the brains picked out on't: you are a very
ancient gentleman.   90

3 MADMAN Greek is turned Turk, we are only to be saved by
the Helvetian translation.

1 MADMAN Come on sir, I will lay the law to you.

2 MADMAN Oh, rather lay a corrosive, the law will eat to
the bone.   95

3 MADMAN He that drinks but to satisfy nature is damned.

4 MADMAN If I had my glass here, I would show a sight
should make all the women here call me mad
doctor.

1 MADMAN What's he, a ropemaker?   100

2 MADMAN No, no, no, a snuffling knave, that while he shows
the tombs will have his hand in a wench's placket.

3 MADMAN Woe to the caroche that brought home my
wife from the masque at three o'clock in the
morning, it had a large feather bed in it.   105

4 MADMAN I have pared the devil's nails forty times, roasted
them in raven's eggs, and cured agues with them.

3 MADMAN Get me three hundred milch bats, to make possets
to procure sleep.

4 MADMAN All the college may throw their caps at me,   110
I have made a soap-boiler costive. It was my
masterpiece.

*Here the dance consisting of eight madmen, with music answerable thereunto, after
which BOSOLA, like an old man, enters.*

DUCHESS   Is he mad too?

SERVANT   Pray question him: I'll leave you.

Exeunt SERVANT and MADMEN.

118   **insensible** *theological idea:* cannot be detected by the senses

122   **worm-seed** *i.e. food for worms; literally:* dried flower heads of various plants used against intestinal worms

123   **salvatory** box for ointment

     mummy medicine made from embalmed dead bodies (**green** = fresh, *suggesting a living corpse*)

124   **cruded** curdled *(from the Bible, Job 10.1, 9–10: 'My soul is weary of my life...wilt thou bring me into dust again? Hast thou not poured me out as milk, and curdled me like cheese?')*

     fantastical...paste grotesquely designed puff pastry *(a fancy, light, flimsy confection)*

128   **lark...body** *It was proverbial that the body was like a prison; see also 4.2.13–14.*

129   **her** the lark's

131   **compass** (1) circumference; area; (2) circuit of time

134   **riot** (1) violent disorder; (2) loose or wasteful living

136   **merry milkmaid** *One of Overbury's character sketches (see page 234) was of 'A Fair and Happy Milkmaid', who was 'decked in innocency' and went to bed and rose early, since 'too immoderate sleep is rust to the soul' (see note to 1.1.80–82).*

137–138   **mouse...ear** *proverbial expression: see note to 1.1.247*

140   **unquiet bedfellow** *see 3.2.11–13*

141   **still** (1) *the modern meaning:* now as formerly; (2) always

143–144   **Glories...light** *Webster repeated this from* The White Devil *5.1; adapted from the Scottish poet and courtier Sir William Alexander's* The Alexandrean Tragedy *(1607).*

Bosola

122–144 'The only "comfort" he can now bring is the persuasiveness of his own contempt for humanity...a heaven that reflects merely the "small compass of our prison" [131–132] renders meaningless both earthly acts and religious certainty' (Lee Bliss). (See 4.1.132–133.)

Duchess

141 This famous statement may echo Mark Antony's heroical line in Shakespeare's *Antony and Cleopatra:* 'I am Antony yet' (3.13). Some other comments:
• Cambridge edition (1995): 'though admirable as evidence of the Duchess's courage and steadfastness, this reply indicates that she still fails to see Bosola's point: that rank is immaterial in the face of death'.
• Theodora Jankowski (1990): this line 'recalls her political identity and the nobility of her death reinforces it'.
• R S White (1987): 'What strikes us throughout the horrifying events...is the dignity of the Duchess as she firmly resists any recriminations or pleas for mercy. She is "Duchess of Malfi still", revealing patience, stoicism and accepting complete responsibility for her actions.'
• Muriel Bradbrook (1980) implies that if her marriage is genuine, then she is just Giovanna Bologna; i.e. the Duchess's public aristocratic role vanished when she made her secret marriage; she has no right to her title.
• J W Lever (1971): this line 'is an affirmation of reason and an assertion of the Stoic kingship of the mind, undismayed by tyranny'.
• Northrop Frye (1957) comments that the word *still* 'having its full weight of "always", we understand how it is that even after her death her invisible presence continues to be the most vital character in the play'.

BOSOLA	I am come to make thy tomb.

DUCHESS
                                    Ha, my tomb?
Thou speak'st as if I lay upon my deathbed   115
Gasping for breath: dost thou perceive me sick?

BOSOLA   Yes, and the more dangerously since thy sickness
is insensible.

DUCHESS   Thou art not mad, sure; dost know me?

BOSOLA   Yes.   120

DUCHESS   Who am I?

BOSOLA   Thou art a box of worm-seed, at best but a
salvatory of green mummy. What's this flesh?
A little cruded milk, fantastical puff paste: our
bodies are weaker than those paper prisons boys   125
use to keep flies in – more contemptible, since ours
is to preserve earthworms. Didst thou ever see a
lark in a cage? Such is the soul in the body: this
world is like her little turf of grass, and the heaven
o'er our heads like her looking-glass, only gives   130
us a miserable knowledge of the small compass
of our prison.

DUCHESS   Am not I thy Duchess?

BOSOLA   Thou art some great woman, sure, for riot begins
to sit on thy forehead, clad in grey hairs, twenty 135
years sooner than on a merry milkmaid's. Thou
sleep'st worse than if a mouse should be forced to
take up her lodging in a cat's ear; a little infant
that breeds its teeth, should it lie with thee, would
cry out as if thou wert the more unquiet bedfellow. 140

DUCHESS   I am Duchess of Malfi still.

BOSOLA   That makes thy sleeps so broken:
'Glories, like glow-worms, afar off shine bright,
But looked to near, have neither heat nor light.'

DUCHESS   Thou art very plain.   145

4.2   *Bosola prepares the Duchess for death. The executioners bring on her coffin*

152   **resolve me** answer a question for me

153   **fantastical** fanciful; capricious

155–161 **princes'...faces** *a satirical comment on the new fashion of posing on tombs, which arrived in England in the sixteenth century*

162   **effect** meaning; purpose

164   **charnel** cemetery; charnel house *(a vault or other building containing the bones of the dead)*

165   **present** *'The traditional gift of the masquers to the bride here becomes the gift of death' (1995 Cambridge edition).*

167   **benefit** good deed; gift

Bosola (George Anton) disguised as a 'tomb-maker' holds a tape measure in order to measure the Duchess for her coffin; Cariola (Avril Clark) offers her mistress a crucifix (Cheek by Jowl, 1995–6)

Duchess in performance

161 In the unusual 1995 Cheek by Jowl production, the Duchess (Anastasia Hille) threw her whisky in Bosola's face after this line, and lit another cigarette (see photograph above).

Performance

s.d. *Enter EXECUTIONERS with a coffin...:* In the 2003 National Theatre production items were brought in that suggested a modern 'clinical' execution: an operating-theatre light descended over the Duchess, and men wearing see-through masks and aprons pushed hi-tech medical equipment on, as well as the rope to strangle her with, though no coffin. In the 1995 Cheek by Jowl production, at line 170 Bosola (George Anton) pulled away the rug that covered the box-like bench that had been there in 3.2 and Act 4, to reveal a coffin.

BOSOLA	My trade is to flatter the dead, not the living. I am a tomb-maker.
DUCHESS	And thou com'st to make my tomb?
BOSOLA	Yes.
DUCHESS	Let me be a little merry. Of what stuff wilt thou 150 make it?
BOSOLA	Nay, resolve me first, of what fashion?
DUCHESS	Why, do we grow fantastical in our deathbed, do we affect fashion in the grave?
BOSOLA	Most ambitiously: princes' images on their tombs 155 do not lie as they were wont, seeming to pray up to heaven, but with their hands under their cheeks as if they died of the toothache. They are not carved with their eyes fixed upon the stars, but as their minds were wholly bent upon the world the 160 selfsame way they seem to turn their faces.
DUCHESS	Let me know fully therefore the effect Of this thy dismal preparation, This talk fit for a charnel.
BOSOLA	Now I shall.

Enter EXECUTIONERS with a coffin, cords and a bell.

	Here is a present from your princely brothers, 165 And may it arrive welcome, for it brings Last benefit, last sorrow.
DUCHESS	Let me see it, I have so much obedience in my blood I wish it in their veins, to do them good.
BOSOLA	This is your last presence chamber. 170
CARIOLA	Oh my sweet lady!
DUCHESS	Peace, it affrights not me.

172–174   **bellman...suffer** *This custom was set up in 1605 by a gift to Webster's parish church, St Sepulchre's; Webster's father was one of the signatories agreeing to it. A clerk was appointed to ring a handbell outside the dungeon of Newgate prison and exhort those who were about to die at Tyburn to pray and repent.*

176   **By degrees** *gradually*

   mortification *(1) religious practice: killing the lusts of the flesh through pain, fasting etc.; (2) sense of torpor before death*

s.d.   ***Rings the bell** The bellman tolled his bell twelve times.*

177–194   ***Hark...away** This dirge doubles as the bellman's exhortation and as the opposite of an epithalamium (see notes below).*

178   **whistler** *a nocturnal bird (hearing its 'whistle' was an evil omen)*

182   **competent** *sufficient*

184   **your...signed** *an echo of the Duchess's ominous phrase when she courted Antonio (1.1.468)*

187   **mist of error** *see note to 5.5.94*

189   **Strew...sweet** *an echo of the Duchess's comment on her greying hair in happier days (3.2.57–59); ironically this is also what a bride would do*

191   **foul fiend** *the devil*

193   **ull tide...day** *midnight*

198   **Remove...noise** *i.e. Cariola*

199   **last will** *see 1.1.380*

201   **reversion** *bequest*

Bosola

172 'Bosola's weirdly alienated performance is ambivalent, its hallucinatory sequence of transformations, from tomb-maker [147, 175], to bellman, to executioner, reflecting the profound inner conflict of a murderer who has insisted that his last business with his victim "shall be comfort" [4.1.133]' (Michael Neill).

Language

177–194 It seems to have been a custom to recite couplets to prisoners before their execution the next day. Charles Forker gives one example: 'Examine well yourselves, in time repent, / That you may not to eternal flames be sent. / And when St Sepulchre's bell tomorrow tolls, / The Lord above have mercy on your souls.'

178 'The dirge is antithetical to [i.e. the opposite of] an epithalamium, which customarily bade such creatures be silent on the wedding night' (John Russell Brown). In ancient Greece, an epithalamion – the Latin spelling is epithalamium – was a song or poem sung outside a bride's room on her wedding night; it was a literary form revived by poets such as Spenser, Sidney and Donne. The end of the dirge (193–194) also echoes the form, but instead of being brought to the bridegroom, the Duchess is summoned to death.

BOSOLA   I am the common bellman,
That usually is sent to condemned persons
The night before they suffer.

DUCHESS   Even now thou said'st
Thou wast a tomb-maker.

BOSOLA   'Twas to bring you   175
By degrees to mortification. Listen:

Rings the bell.

> *Hark now everything is still,*
> *The screech owl and the whistler shrill*
> *Call upon our dame, aloud,*
> *And bid her quickly don her shroud.* 180
> *Much you had of land and rent,*
> *Your length in clay's now competent;*
> *A long war disturbed your mind,*
> *Here your perfect peace is signed.*
> *Of what is't fools make such vain keeping?* 185
> *Sin their conception, their birth, weeping;*
> *Their life a general mist of error,*
> *Their death a hideous storm of terror.*
> *Strew your hair with powders sweet,*
> *Don clean linen, bathe your feet,* 190
> *And, the foul fiend more to check,*
> *A crucifix let bless your neck.*
> *'Tis now full tide 'tween night and day,*
> *End your groan and come away.*

CARIOLA   Hence villains, tyrants, murderers! Alas, 195
What will you do with my lady? Call for help!

DUCHESS   To whom? To our next neighbours? They are
                mad folks.

BOSOLA   Remove that noise.

EXECUTIONERS seize CARIOLA, who struggles.

DUCHESS   Farewell Cariola,
In my last will I have not much to give:
A many hungry guests have fed upon me, 200
Thine will be a poor reversion.

The Duchess instructs Cariola about her children and tells the disguised Bosola that she is not frightened of death

207 **I forgive them** *It was normal for Christians to forgive their executioners, following Jesus' example (see the Bible, Luke 23.34).*

208 **apoplexy** stroke

catarrh *e.g. influenza; pneumonia etc.*

cough o'th'lungs *e.g. bronchitis; emphysema; tuberculosis*

211–212 **Knowing...world** *see 4.2.18–19 where she wasn't so sure*

216–217 **smothered with cassia** suffocated with the smoke of fragrant burning cassia *(see also 2.4.64 and 3.5.72)*

218–219 **death...exits** *a proverbial and classical Roman idea*

220–221 **strange...ways** *through suicide, murder etc.*

225–226 **last...tedious** *it is proverbial that women talk too much*

Duchess

203–205 Mary Beth Rose says that the Duchess 'dies thinking of her children's welfare, thus dissolving the distinction between "woman" and "greatness" that...Cariola makes after her marriage' (see 1.1.504–506). Judith Haber says about these lines that 'not enough attention is given to the disruptive force of their extraordinary ordinariness. For it is surely remarkable for a "tragic heroine" to die...concerned...with the mundane comforts of her children; and it necessarily unsettles our notions of "tragedy" and of "heroism" when she does so.'

218–222 Philip Franks, who directed the play in 1995, commented: 'Webster articulates a fear of death that's to do with there perhaps not being an afterlife. Whereas with Marlowe the notion of atheism is somehow grandiose, with Webster it's skin-crawlingly terrifying. A lot of his characters die without knowing where they are going. The fantastic thing about the Duchess is the courage she can summon up in the face of that – like those extraordinary lines: *I know death... / any way, for heaven' sake, / So I were out of your whispering.* That is so brave, because she doesn't say: "I commend myself to God; I am going to rest secure in the arms of the Virgin Mary". She just says: I want out of here and anywhere is better than you. And that's fantastic. That's her courage. She finds her moral centre in love, not in religion.'

CARIOLA   I will die with her.

DUCHESS   I pray thee look thou giv'st my little boy
Some syrup for his cold, and let the girl
Say her prayers ere she sleep.

EXECUTIONERS force CARIOLA off.

                         Now what you please: 205
What death?

BOSOLA   Strangling. Here are your executioners.

DUCHESS   I forgive them.
The apoplexy, catarrh, or cough o'th'lungs
Would do as much as they do.

BOSOLA   Doth not death fright you?

DUCHESS   Who would be afraid on't, 210
Knowing to meet such excellent company
In th'other world?

BOSOLA   Yet, methinks,
The manner of your death should much afflict you:
This cord should terrify you?

DUCHESS   Not a whit.
What would it pleasure me to have my throat cut   215
With diamonds, or to be smothered
With cassia, or to be shot to death with pearls?
I know death hath ten thousand several doors
For men to take their exits; and 'tis found
They go on such strange geometrical hinges,   220
You may open them both ways – any way, for
    heaven' sake,
So I were out of your whispering. Tell my brothers
That I perceive death, now I am well awake,
Best gift is they can give, or I can take.
I would fain put off my last woman's fault,   225
I'd not be tedious to you.

EXECUTIONER   We are ready.

228   **Bestow** (1) dispose of; confer (as a
      gift); (2) *ironic wordplay:* give in
      marriage

      will you *This is the Duchess's last
      'will' (see e.g. 1.1.380).*

231   **heaven gates** (1) the gates of the
      tomb; (2) the gates of heaven

233   **upon their knees** *see notes to
      1.1.455–459 and 4.2.33–34*

234   **mandragora** the mandrake plant *(see
      2.5.1):* a narcotic *(a word used also by
      Iago in* Othello *3.3)*

235   **laid out** (1) prepared for burial; (2)
      *wordplay connected with next line on
      laying a table*

236   **feed in quiet** *There is a hint of
      cannibalism in this image, which
      perhaps deliberately refers back to her
      comment about pheasants and quails
      (3.5.108–110).*

244   **answer** *legal language:* reply made to
      a charge; defence

247   **contracted** betrothed

249   **discover** reveal; make known

Ideas and interpretations

231–233 Michael Neill comments on the symbolism of her kneeling: 'By its exact and
ceremonious reversal of the earlier ritual [when the Duchess raises Antonio from kneeling:
1.1.419–422], her dying gesture becomes more than a sign of simple Christian humility; it is
an emblematic recapitulation of one of the play's most insistent themes, the opposition of the
monuments of true fame to the ephemeral architecture of worldly greatness.' Her kneeling
also echoes Bosola's description of how the images of pious princes used to be sculpted on
their tombs (4.2.155–161), and imitates the sculpture of her at her first husband's tomb
(1.1.458–459): 'The Duchess faces her martyrdom in the kneeling posture of the obedient
wife...but converts that image of domestic piety into a martyr's gesture of heroic singularity.
It is a gesture whose full meaning...will be disclosed in the monumental apotheosis of the
Echo scene.'

Duchess and Cariola

242–254 'The desperate attempts of the maid Cariola to avoid death are presented as rather
frenetic and undignified, in contrast to the Duchess's dying moments. Not that we can blame
Cariola, of course, for this, but the dramatic contrast is rather set up to enforce a sense of the
Duchess's courage and open-eyed maturity. In short, everything in the scene is designed to
startle us into a firm and fundamental recognition of the innocence of the Duchess, to make
us reassess any suspicion of her own collusion, and to highlight the injustice. Justice and
injustice, innocence and guilt, are the central terms of the scene, as of the play as a whole'
(R S White).

DUCHESS   Dispose my breath how please you, but my body
           Bestow upon my women: will you?

EXECUTIONER   Yes.

DUCHESS   Pull, and pull strongly, for your able strength
           Must pull down heaven upon me –   230
           Yet stay, heaven gates are not so highly arched
           As princes' palaces: they that enter there
           Must go upon their knees. (*Kneels*) Come violent
               death,
           Serve for mandragora, to make me sleep.
           Go tell my brothers when I am laid out,   235
           They then may feed in quiet.

           They strangle her.

BOSOLA   Where's the waiting woman?
           Fetch her. Some other strangle the children.

                       Exeunt EXECUTIONERS. Enter one with CARIOLA.

           Look you, there sleeps your mistress.

CARIOLA   Oh you are damned
           Perpetually for this! My turn is next,   240
           Is't not so ordered?

BOSOLA   Yes, and I am glad
           You are so well prepared for't.

CARIOLA   You are deceived sir,
           I am not prepared for't! I will not die!
           I will first come to my answer and know
           How I have offended.

BOSOLA   Come, dispatch her.   245
           You kept her counsel, now you shall keep ours.

CARIOLA   I will not die, I must not, I am contracted
           To a young gentleman!

EXECUTIONER   (*Showing the noose*) Here's your wedding ring.

CARIOLA   Let me but speak with the Duke: I'll discover
           Treason to his person.

252   **confession** *In Roman Catholicism, confession of sins to a priest should be made at least once a year.*

253   **When!** when will my orders be obeyed?!

quick with child pregnant *(i.e. when the foetus can be felt)*

254   **Your...saved** *mocking: i.e. you won't have the shame of bearing an illegitimate child* (**credit** = reputation) *(Cariola is strangled after this line)*

Bear her carry Cariola

255   **this** the Duchess's body

259   **here** the Duchess

263   **Cover...young** *This famous line has been called 'a miniature three-act play' (F W Bateson).*

dazzle *perhaps because of the Duchess's identification with light, e.g. 1.1.217; he may also have tears in his eyes (and see 5.2.64)*

264–265   **her infelicity...many** her unhappiness made her life seem much too long

Ferdinand

263 'When Fedinand looks down into his dead sister's dazzling eyes, he sees himself, faces his own death too' (Frank Whigham). Muriel Bradbrook says the sight of her face 'awakens' Ferdinand to what he has done: 'In the darkness of the prison this suggests a halo of glory; sex, violence and religion are fused in nine short words.'

Ideas and interpretations

263 *She died young:* Audiences at the first performances of the play might have thought of Prince Henry, the heir to the throne, who had died aged only 18 in the winter of 1612, especially as the first Duchess was played by a young man of his age. 'In this play Webster transmuted the sorrow that rose from the failure of national hope in one who, like the Duchess, "died young", into a sorrow that could not be defined, that resisted comfort' (Muriel Bradbrook).

Ferdinand in performance

266 *twins:* Delio had wondered if the Cardinal and Ferdinand were twins (1.1.180), but was told they were only similar in *quality*. Some productions have cast actors for the brothers and sister who look like one another, but this couldn't have happened in the original production in 1613/14: the Duchess was played by a young man in his teens, while Ferdinand and the Cardinal were played by two experienced actors: Richard Burbage (the first Ferdinand) was about 46.

BOSOLA	Delays: throttle her.

250

EXECUTIONER She bites and scratches!

CARIOLA   If you kill me now
I am damned! I have not been at confession
This two years.

BOSOLA   When!

CARIOLA   I am quick with child.

BOSOLA   Why then,
Your credit's saved. Bear her into th'next room.
Let this lie still.

         EXECUTIONERS strangle CARIOLA and exeunt with her body.

     Enter FERDINAND.

FERDINAND   Is she dead?

BOSOLA   She is what   255
You'd have her. But here begin your pity.

     BOSOLA shows the children strangled.

         Alas, how have these offended?

FERDINAND   The death
Of young wolves is never to be pitied.

BOSOLA   Fix your eye here.

FERDINAND   Constantly.

BOSOLA   Do you not weep?
Other sins only speak; murder shrieks out.   260
The element of water moistens the earth,
But blood flies upwards and bedews the heavens.

FERDINAND   Cover her face. Mine eyes dazzle. She died young.

BOSOLA   I think not so; her infelicity
Seemed to have years too many.   265

FERDINAND   She and I were twins,
And should I die this instant I had lived
Her time to a minute.

Ferdinand asks Bosola why he didn't pity the Duchess, and for reward gives him only a pardon for the murder

269 **approved** confirmed; demonstrated

273 **Honest** honourable

276 **advanced** raised

282–285 **I had...cause** *It is generally accepted that Ferdinand has made this up. Is he trying to deceive Bosola, or himself?*

285 **that** *could refer either to* **mass of treasure** *or to* **Her marriage**

286 **gall** bitterness

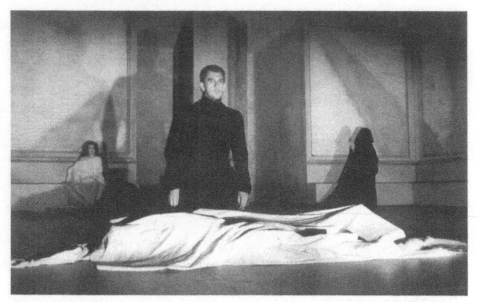

Bosola (Ian McKellen) in the production directed and designed by Philip Prowse, who added a silent, hooded figure of Death (played by Laurance Rudic: right). The critic Sheridan Morley wrote that in this production 'there is the constant sense of brooding, atmospheric evil and of religion in decay which essentially has to be what this political melodrama is all about' (National Theatre, 1985)

Ferdinand in performance

Will Keen, who played Ferdinand in the 2003 National Theatre production, said this scene was the most difficult to play 'because if the whole of the play is a seesaw for him [Ferdinand], then this is the absolute centre – the moment of recognising what he's done – between the frenzy of the sexual jealousy, the destructiveness and the violence. Afterwards he's deranged in a completely different way – his derangement is to do with self-knowledge rather than lack of self-knowledge. He's so frightened of himself, of the shadow which is himself. He cannot deal with the person who has done these things. *Why didst thou not pity her* [272] is the still centre – the moment of realising that he's actually done something.'

Ferdinand

294–295 'In "pardoning" his henchman, he schizophrenically enacts revenge and forgiveness at once' (Frank Whigham).

BOSOLA   It seems she was born first:
               You have bloodily approved the ancient truth
               That kindred commonly do worse agree   270
               Than remote strangers.

FERDINAND   Let me see her face again.
               Why didst not thou pity her? What an excellent
               Honest man might'st thou have been
               If thou hadst borne her to some sanctuary
               Or, bold in a good cause, opposed thyself   275
               With thy advanced sword above thy head
               Between her innocence and my revenge!
               I bade thee, when I was distracted of my wits,
               Go kill my dearest friend, and thou hast done't!
               For let me but examine well the cause: 280
               What was the meanness of her match to me?
               Only, I must confess, I had a hope –
               Had she continued widow – to have gained
               An infinite mass of treasure by her death:
               And that was the main cause. Her marriage,   285
               That drew a stream of gall quite through my heart.
               For thee – as we observe in tragedies
               That a good actor many times is cursed
               For playing a villain's part – I hate thee for't;
               And for my sake say, thou hast done much ill, well. 290

BOSOLA   Let me quicken your memory, for I perceive
               You are falling into ingratitude: I challenge
               The reward due to my service.

FERDINAND   I'll tell thee
               What I'll give thee.

BOSOLA   Do.

FERDINAND   I'll give thee a pardon
               For this murder.

BOSOLA   Ha?

FERDINAND   Yes: and 'tis   295
               The largest bounty I can study to do thee.
               By what authority didst thou execute
               This bloody sentence?

Ferdinand asks by what authority Bosola killed his sister, and tells him to go; Bosola refuses, and demands his payment

300   **Doom** pass sentence on; condemn

308–310   **The wolf...murder** *There was a superstition that wolves dug up murder victims (see also 5.2.8–12).*

311   **pension** payment *(usually at this time a regular payment to someone connected to the court)*

314   **him** God

315   **Can...obedience** can make man obedient

316   **thee** *This is the only time in the play where Bosola addresses Ferdinand as* **thee** *(often used when addressing an inferior – see note to 3.2.140).*

320   **chained bullets** cannonballs linked by a chain *(used in naval warfare for destroying ships' masts)*

     still always

321   **You may** you must

322   **take...blood** strike at whole families

Ideas and interpretations

297–303 'In this play, uniquely among Webster's works, there is no trial; tyranny is condemned by Ferdinand's self-accusation. The only form of sentence we have witnessed was that of her banishment from Ancona, carried out in dumb show' (Muriel Bradbrook).

308–310 'The wolf is to be none other than the demented Ferdinand himself' (Michael Neill; see notes on page 178).

Ferdinand

R S White comments: 'the fact of the Duchess's corpse causes a change in Ferdinand's attitude. He does not exactly repent, but rather he refuses to take any responsibility for the murder he has commissioned...his future degeneration into the form of madness of lycanthropia can be seen as a mental refuge from accepting responsibility for his own actions – a way of avoiding conscience and remorse by entering madness.'

Bosola

317–319 Bosola's image of the brothers' hearts as *hollow graves* echoes Ferdinand's image of his own heart encased in lead as a reaction to the news of his sister's remarriage (3.2.112–114). At last Bosola is beginning to discover what the brothers really are: he is now awake (4.2.324).

BOSOLA   By yours.

FERDINAND   Mine? Was I her judge?
Did any ceremonial form of law
Doom her to not-being? Did a complete jury   300
Deliver her conviction up i'th'court?
Where shalt thou find this judgment registered
Unless in hell? See, like a bloody fool
Th'hast forfeited thy life, and thou shalt die for't.

BOSOLA   The office of justice is perverted quite   305
When one thief hangs another. Who shall dare
To reveal this?

FERDINAND   Oh, I'll tell thee:
The wolf shall find her grave and scrape it up,
Not to devour the corpse but to discover
The horrid murder.

BOSOLA   You, not I, shall quake for't.   310

FERDINAND   Leave me.

BOSOLA   I will first receive my pension.

FERDINAND   You are a villain.

BOSOLA   When your ingratitude
Is judge, I am so.

FERDINAND   Oh horror,
That not the fear of him which binds the devils
Can prescribe man obedience.   315
Never look upon me more.

BOSOLA   Why fare thee well.
Your brother and yourself are worthy men,
You have a pair of hearts are hollow graves,
Rotten, and rotting others: and your vengeance,
Like two chained bullets, still goes arm in arm.   320
You may be brothers: for treason, like the plague,
Doth take much in a blood. I stand like one
That long hath ta'en a sweet and golden dream:
I am angry with myself now that I wake.

4.2 *Ferdinand leaves, showing signs of madness; Bosola now wishes he had never murdered the Duchess, who momentarily comes back to life before dying*

327 **neglected** *see note to 1.1.76–77*

328–332 **I...man** *adapted from Sidney's Arcadia, about a villain's assistants; Sidney has 'and rather to be good friends, than good men' for lines 331–332*

333 **owl-light** dusk *(the Duchess was twice compared to an owl: see note to 2.3.1–9)*

335 **distracted** troubled in mind; mad

painted false; feigned *(see 3.2.276)*

336 **While...tire** while we exhaust our abilities by uselessly hoping for a reward *(it recalls Bosola's line at 1.1.58–59)*

tire *perhaps wordplay connected to* **painted**: (1) exhaust; wear down; (2) dress; attire

342 **sensible** that can be felt; palpable

344 **store** supply

Who's there – *calling out for assistance*

345 **cordial** reviving

346 **So pity...pity** *i.e. if Ferdinand heard and came back to kill her properly; there may be wordplay here:* **pity** = (1) compassion; (2) piety: 'faithfulness to the duties naturally owed to...superiors' *(Oxford English Dictionary)*

opes opens

347 **late** recently; not long ago

352 **atonement** (1) reconciliation; (2) *theological meaning:* restoration of friendly relations between God and sinners

353 **cords of life** nerves; heart-strings

Performance

343–344 In the 2003 National Theatre production, Bosola (Lorcan Cranitch) bent over her about to give her the kiss of life, but broke off when the Duchess spoke.

Bosola

327–332 Frank Whigham says that Bosola had longed for personal service with his prince (see note to 1.1.269–272) and that this explains why he carried on working for Ferdinand: 'Compulsively seeking to be paid, recognized, acknowledged, identified'. Robert Ornstein agrees: Bosola 'seeks to give meaning to his life by loyal service'.

335 *Off my painted honour:* Muriel Bradbrook says 'the Duchess's death converts Bosola, the expected miracle', but another explanation for his change of heart is that he finally realises he will get no reward from Ferdinand – Jacqueline Pearson says that his change 'has a strong undercurrent of personal spite'.

341–342 Theodora Jankowski says that here Bosola views her as a saint, and his 'conviction that the Duchess has the power to lead his soul out of hell recalls Antonio's earlier boast to Delio...[see 1.1.204–205]. Yet there is something profoundly ironic in this scene.'

351–352 This is not true: 'However kindly his motives this deliberate falsehood suggests that Bosola's dependence on fiction and deception is to shape his actions even now that he has rejected "painted honour"' (Jacqueline Pearson).

FERDINAND   Get thee into some unknown part o'th'world   325
             That I may never see thee.

BOSOLA   Let me know
             Wherefore I should be thus neglected. Sir,
             I served your tyranny, and rather strove
             To satisfy yourself than all the world;
             And though I loathed the evil yet I loved   330
             You, that did counsel it, and rather sought
             To appear a true servant than an honest man.

FERDINAND   I'll go hunt the badger by owl-light:
             'Tis a deed of darkness.

                                                               Exit.

BOSOLA   He's much distracted. Off, my painted honour;   335
             While with vain hopes our faculties we tire,
             We seem to sweat in ice, and freeze in fire;
             What would I do, were this to do again?
             I would not change my peace of conscience
             For all the wealth of Europe – She stirs! Here's life! 340
             Return fair soul from darkness, and lead mine
             Out of this sensible hell! She's warm, she breathes:
             Upon thy pale lips I will melt my heart
             To store them with fresh colour. Who's there –
             Some cordial drink! – Alas, I dare not call;   345
             So pity would destroy pity. Her eye opes,
             And heaven in it seems to ope, that late was shut,
             To take me up to mercy.

DUCHESS   Antonio.

BOSOLA   Yes, madam, he is living,
             The dead bodies you saw were but feigned statues; 350
             He's reconciled to your brothers, the Pope hath
                 wrought
             The atonement.

DUCHESS   Mercy.

             She dies.

BOSOLA   Oh, she's gone again: there the cords of life broke.
             Oh sacred innocence that sweetly sleeps

354–358 **Oh sacred...hell** *The remorse that Bosola feels shows him the deep gulf between her saint-like innocence and his inner hell. His* **guilty conscience** *is like a record book in which he sees, as through a distorting mirror or lens* (**perspective**), *his bad deeds far outweigh his good deeds.*

355 **turtles' feathers** turtle-doves' feathers *(this dove was especially noted for the affection it showed its mate, and was often used in poetry as an image for the poet's beloved)*

358 **suffered** allowed

362–363 **My estate...fear** *from Sidney's* Arcadia; **estate** = condition

370 **dispose** disposal; direction

372 **Milan** *presumably to look for Antonio: see 4.1.134–135*

374 **dejection** (1) abasement; (2) depression of spirits

'This is manly sorrow' (4.2.360): Bosola (Lorcan Cranitch) holds the dead Duchess in his arms (National Theatre, 2003)

Bosola

360–362 'Bosola recognizes that in manhood he has learnt to shed the tears of penitence which were not his by nurture or by nature' (1995 Cambridge edition).

360–365 Bosola weeps, and suddenly no longer has any fear. 'Fear' and 'fearful' are words used frequently in this play – by Bosola, the Duchess and Antonio; only the Cardinal seems *fearless* (see 5.2.335).

374 The Duchess's death is not the end of the play. Bosola 'turns away from the Duchess's corpse to point the course of his own future action, anticipating his emergence as the tragedy's second protagonist. Not for nothing is his speech left prosodically suspended on a half-line' (Michael Neill).

On turtles' feathers, whilst a guilty conscience   355
Is a black register wherein is writ
All our good deeds and bad, a perspective
That shows us hell – that we cannot be suffered
To do good when we have a mind to it!
This is manly sorrow: 360
These tears, I am very certain, never grew
In my mother's milk. My estate is sunk
Below the degree of fear: where were
These penitent fountains while she was living?
Oh, they were frozen up. Here is a sight   365
As direful to my soul as is the sword
Unto a wretch hath slain his father.
Come, I'll bear thee hence
And execute thy last will; that's deliver
Thy body to the reverend dispose   370
Of some good women: that the cruel tyrant
Shall not deny me: then I'll post to Milan,
Where somewhat I will speedily enact
Worth my dejection.

Exit carrying the body.

5.1 *Several days later in Milan. Antonio, ignorant of his wife's death, asks Delio about the chances of his being reconciled with the Cardinal and Ferdinand*

2 **misdoubt** have doubts; am suspicious

3 **letters...conduct** documents guaranteeing protection from arrest

4 **repair** going

5 **nets to entrap** *see also 3.5.100–101 and 131*

Pescara *see note on page 174*

6 **in cheat** subject to escheat *(i.e. Antonio's land has somehow returned*

to Pescara, his feudal lord – see lines 41–43)

13–14 **You...To** you always disagree with

19 **Bennet** Benedict *(in Naples: see 5.2.322–324)*

20 **demesnes** lands *(pronounced 'demeans')*

23 **Nor...nor** neither...nor

Performance

This scene is often cut, apart from Antonio and Delio's exchange at 60–76.

Plot

3–5 Antonio fled to Milan just before the Duchess was caught (3.5.56); Ferdinand then knew he *Lurks about Milan* (4.1.135), so possibly Webster means that the brothers gave him safe conduct to actually enter the city. Milan had been an independent city state ruled by powerful ducal families, but during the Italian Wars (1494–1559), Milan was ruled by the French, then the Swiss and the original ducal family (1512–16), then the French again, until finally the city was formally given to Spain in 1559.

Act 5

Scene 1

Enter ANTONIO and DELIO.

ANTONIO   What think you of my hope of reconcilement
To the Aragonian brethren?

DELIO   I misdoubt it;
For though they have sent their letters of safe
    conduct
For your repair to Milan, they appear
But nets to entrap you. The Marquis of Pescara,   5
Under whom you hold certain land in cheat,
Much 'gainst his noble nature hath been moved
To seize those lands, and some of his dependants
Are at this instant making it their suit
To be invested in your revenues.   10
I cannot think they mean well to your life
That do deprive you of your means of life –
Your living.

ANTONIO   You are still an heretic
To any safety I can shape myself.

DELIO   Here comes the Marquis: I will make myself   15
Petitioner for some part of your land,
To know whither it is flying.

ANTONIO   I pray do. (*Withdraws*)

    Enter PESCARA.

DELIO   Sir, I have a suit to you.

PESCARA   To me?

DELIO   An easy one:
There is the citadel of Saint Bennet,
With some demesnes, of late in the possession   20
Of Antonio Bologna; please you bestow them
    on me?

PESCARA   You are my friend. But this is such a suit
Nor fit for me to give nor you to take.

DELIO   No sir?

32–33   **I…with it** *an ironic comment – see lines 49–52*

34–35   **doubly…giving** *referring to the old Roman proverb: 'he gives twice who gives quickly'*

34   **engaged** obliged

42   **ravished…throat** seized by violence

44   **so main…wrong** such a large portion of what has been illegally seized

---

Ideas and interpretations

46 *it is injustice:* 'After the murder of the Duchess, we learn of the "injustice"…of the violent forfeit of Antonio's lands and money by the Cardinal, confirmation for us that it was essentially property which lay at the root of the brothers' objections to their sister's remarrying, and not solicitude for her welfare' (R S White).

Pescara

The Marquis of Pescara appears in the Rome scene in 3.3 and in most scenes in Act 5. Historically he was Ferdinando Francesco d'Avalos (1489–1525), a Spanish-Neapolitan general in the Italian Wars serving Charles V (see note to 3.3.1), responsible for the brilliant Spanish victory against the French at the Battle of Pavia, Italy, in 1525. His wife was the famous poet Vittoria Colonna, a friend of Michelangelo (see 3.3.52).

PESCARA   I will give you ample reason for't
        Soon in private. Here's the Cardinal's mistress. 25

Enter JULIA.

JULIA   My lord, I am grown your poor petitioner,
        And should be an ill beggar, had I not
        A great man's letter here, the Cardinal's,
        To court you in my favour.

She gives him a letter which he reads.

PESCARA   He entreats for you
        The citadel of Saint Bennet, that belonged 30
        To the banished Bologna.

JULIA   Yes.

PESCARA   I could not have thought of a friend I could
        Rather pleasure with it: 'tis yours.

JULIA   Sir, I thank you,
        And he shall know how doubly I am engaged
        Both in your gift and speediness of giving, 35
        Which makes your grant the greater.

                      Exit.

ANTONIO   (*Aside*)   How they fortify
        Themselves with my ruin!

DELIO   Sir, I am
        Little bound to you.

PESCARA   Why?

DELIO   Because you denied this suit to me, and gave't
        To such a creature.

PESCARA   Do you know what it was? 40
        It was Antonio's land: not forfeited
        By course of law but ravished from his throat
        By the Cardinal's entreaty: it were not fit
        I should bestow so main a piece of wrong
        Upon my friend, 'tis a gratification 45
        Only due to a strumpet, for it is injustice.

5.1 *Pescara says he is going to visit the sick Ferdinand, who has arrived in Milan. Antonio decides to visit the Cardinal later that night*

49 **ruddier** *wordplay:* (1) more favourably; (2) more bloodily

52 **his lust** the Cardinal's lust

56 **sauciest** most insolent

57 **they give out** people report

apoplexy *see 4.2.208*

58 **frenzy** mental derangement *('said to be an inflammation of the brain due to an invasion of choler: its symptoms were like those of melancholic madness' John Russell Brown; see note to 2.5.66–70)*

59 **old fellow** *The real Marquis of Pescara died aged only 36 (see note on page 174).*

63 **malice** (1) power to do harm; (2) hatred

66 **As once...Duchess** *see 3.2*

68 **for...shape** *i.e. not in disguise*

69 **fraught** filled

72 **infamous calling** shameful life *(but see note below)*

73 **For...falling** *from Montaigne's Essays*

74 **second** *military metaphor:* support

howe'er in whatever manner; whatever happens

75 **rank** *military metaphor:* abreast; in line

Pescara

This scene, Lee Bliss says, shows that 'good men exist at all social levels and even, like Pescara, function successfully in positions of power. Though Bosola may betray the Duchess's trust, Delio and Cariola remain faithful...Some courtiers, or a Julia, seek to "fortify themselves" with others' ruin, but Pescara displays an innate sense of justice that the play suggests men may either ignore or follow.'

Language

72 *calling* also meant 'station in life', that is, whether a servant or a master, as in St Paul's first letter to the Corinthians 7.20–21, who talks about those who are 'called' to Jesus: 'Let every man abide in the same calling wherein he was called. Art thou called being a servant?...' (Authorised Version, 1611). The same chapter also has the highly relevant point that it is better to let widows marry 'than to burn' (verse 9), so Webster may well have been thinking of these connotations of *calling*. And in a play so concerned with fame and reputation, Antonio's *infamous* is a highly charged adjective for him to use.

Shall I sprinkle the pure blood of innocents
To make those followers I call my friends
Look ruddier upon me? I am glad
This land, ta'en from the owner by such wrong,   50
Returns again unto so foul an use
As salary for his lust. Learn, good Delio,
To ask noble things of me, and you shall find
I'll be a noble giver.

DELIO   You instruct me well.

ANTONIO   (*Aside*) Why, here's a man, now, would fright
                    impudence   55
                From sauciest beggars.

PESCARA   Prince Ferdinand's come to Milan
                Sick, as they give out, of an apoplexy;
                But some say 'tis a frenzy. I am going
                To visit him.

                                                    Exit.

ANTONIO   'Tis a noble old fellow.

DELIO   What course do you mean to take, Antonio?   60

ANTONIO   This night I mean to venture all my fortune,
                Which is no more than a poor lingering life,
                To the Cardinal's worst of malice. I have got
                Private access to his chamber and intend
                To visit him about the mid of night   65
                As once his brother did our noble Duchess.
                It may be that the sudden apprehension
                Of danger – for I'll go in mine own shape –
                When he shall see it fraught with love and duty,
                May draw the poison out of him, and work   70
                A friendly reconcilement. If it fail,
                Yet it shall rid me of this infamous calling:
                For better fall once than be ever falling.

DELIO   I'll second you in all danger, and howe'er,
                My life keeps rank with yours.   75

ANTONIO   You are still my loved and best friend.

                                                    Exeunt.

The gallery of a palace in Milan. The Marquis of Pescara has arrived to visit Ferdinand; the doctor describes Ferdinand's strange disease

3   **air...gallery** *see note to 1.1.218*

6   **lycanthropia** lycanthropy: a delusion that one has become a wolf *(this mental disorder was thought to be due to witchcraft in the Middle Ages, and today is linked to schizophrenia)*

6–19 **lycanthropia...try** *Webster's source was* Admirable and Memorable Histories *by the French theologian and historian Simon Goulart (died 1628), translated into English in 1607 (see also note below).*

10–12 **wolves...bodies up** *This recalls Ferdinand's speech at 4.2.307–310.*

12   **since** ago

13   **One** someone

14   **leg of a man** *This may recall the Duchess's line at 4.2.236.*

18   **bad** bade: commanded

23   **fit** sudden attack of madness

24   **nearer** more intimate

25   **Paracelsus** *Swiss physician and alchemist, also known as Theophrastus von Hohenheim (1493–1541), influential in using chemicals in medicine and importance of personal observation; he recognised that madness was an illness and not the work of the devil.*

26   **buffet** beat with the hands

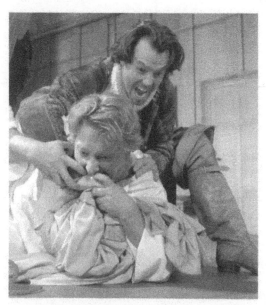

Ferdinand (Simon Russell Beale) bites the hand of a courtier (Bobby Goodale) trying to restrain him (Greenwich/Wyndham's Theatres, 1995)

Ferdinand

6–19 Webster has prefigured this disease (see 2.1.63, 3.2.88, 4.1.33, 4.2.257–258 and 308–310). The editors of the 1995 Cambridge edition say: 'Lycanthropy was regarded by contemporary writers as an extreme manifestation of jealousy.' J W Lever comments: 'Ferdinand's lycanthropia – his delusion that he is a wolf – results from the murder of his humanity and reduces him to the level of a predatory beast.'

16–18 'The inverted wolfskin is an image both of secret viciousness and (in its recollection of the penitent's hair shirt) of the inward suffering that ensues from it' (Michael Neill).

Scene 2

Enter PESCARA and DOCTOR.

PESCARA   Now Doctor, may I visit your patient?

DOCTOR   If't please your lordship: but he's instantly
To take the air here in the gallery,
By my direction.

PESCARA   Pray thee, what's his disease?

DOCTOR   A very pestilent disease, my lord,   5
They call lycanthropia.

PESCARA   What's that?
I need a dictionary to't.

DOCTOR   I'll tell you:
In those that are possessed with't there o'erflows
Such melancholy humour they imagine
Themselves to be transformed into wolves: 10
Steal forth to churchyards in the dead of night
And dig dead bodies up: as two nights since
One met the Duke 'bout midnight in a lane
Behind St Mark's church, with the leg of a man
Upon his shoulder; and he howled fearfully;   15
Said he was a wolf, only the difference
Was, a wolf's skin was hairy on the outside,
His on the inside; bad them take their swords,
Rip up his flesh, and try. Straight I was sent for,
And having ministered to him, found his grace   20
Very well recovered.

PESCARA   I am glad on't.

DOCTOR   Yet not without some fear of a relapse:
If he grow to his fit again I'll go
A nearer way to work with him than ever
Paracelsus dreamed of: if they'll give me   25
Leave I'll buffet his madness out of him.
Stand aside, he comes.

*Enter CARDINAL, FERDINAND, MALATESTE and BOSOLA, who remains in
the background.*

29 **solitariness** *It was said that those affected with melancholy should not be on their own.*

30–31 **Eagles...together** *There is a similar idea in Sidney's* Arcadia: *'Eagles we see fly alone; and they are but sheep which always herd together.'*

30 **daws** jackdaws

36 **Stay it** stop it

41 **shadow...hell** *If there is any logical connection in what Ferdinand says in his madness, perhaps one meaning of* **shadow** *as 'phantom' links to* **hell**.

42–43 **good...persons** *an allusion either to the practice of paying gaolers, or to the sale of knighthoods and other titles by King James (see page 233); if latter, Pescara's line (44) adds to the satire*

45–48 **patience...Moscow** *This strangely recalls the Duchess at 3.5.70–74.*

48 **Moscow** *The English and Russians had made diplomatic contact at the beginning of Elizabeth I's reign. In April 1613 Sir Thomas Overbury was imprisoned in the Tower because he refused to be sent as ambassador to Moscow (see page 234.*

49–51 **the patientest...after** if the most patient man in the world were to compare with me in a trial, I would crawl after the snails

51 **sheep-biter** dog that bites or worries sheep

Ferdinand's shadow

• J W Lever (1971): 'The darkness of his deed is expressed in the shadow his own shape casts on the ground, which in his insanity he tries to throttle.'
• R S White (1987): 'The degeneration of Ferdinand into one who is afraid of his own shadow, and mimics wolves in digging up graves, is a signal that at last, and at least, he is besieged by some kind of conscience about his malicious deeds. There is some part of his personality still independent of the corrupting power of his office and power, which turns upon him destructively.'
• Michael Neill (1997) calls the shadow Ferdinand's 'dark shadow self': 'Ferdinand's incestuous desire for his sister issues in a...wolfish frenzy of self-cancellation, enacted for the audience in a bizarre stage action, when he throws himself upon his own shadow in the conviction that it is following him with malign intent.'

Performance

In the 1985 National Theatre production directed by Philip Prowse, an actor played a hooded figure of Death (see photograph on page 164); in this scene Ferdinand took him for his shadow and tried to throttle him.

Language

39 *nothing*: Jacqueline Pearson says that Act 5 is very different in style, imagery and language from the other Acts, and that the end of Act 4 and Act 5 are full of negatives: *silence, never, no, not-being* and especially *nothing* – which echoes through the last Act: 'After the affirmation of the Duchess's life and death the society she leaves behind her is negative and sterile.'

FERDINAND   Leave me.

MALATESTE   Why doth your lordship love this solitariness?

FERDINAND   Eagles commonly fly alone: they are crows, daws   30
            and starlings that flock together. – Look, what's that
            follows me?

MALATESTE   Nothing, my lord.

FERDINAND   Yes.

MALATESTE   'Tis your shadow.   35

FERDINAND   Stay it, let it not haunt me.

MALATESTE   Impossible, if you move, and the sun shine.

FERDINAND   I will throttle it.

Throws himself upon his shadow.

MALATESTE   Oh, my lord, you are angry with nothing.

FERDINAND   You are a fool. How is't possible I should catch   40
            my shadow unless I fall upon't? When I go to hell,
            I mean to carry a bribe, for look you, good gifts
            evermore make way for the worst persons.

PESCARA   Rise, good my lord.

FERDINAND   I am studying the art of patience.   45

PESCARA   'Tis a noble virtue.

FERDINAND   To drive six snails before me, from this town to
            Moscow – neither use goad nor whip to them, but
            let them take their own time – the patientest man
            i'th'world match me for an experiment – and I'll   50
            crawl after like a sheep-biter.

CARDINAL   Force him up.

They get FERDINAND to his feet.

FERDINAND   Use me well, you were best: what I have done,
            I have done, I'll confess nothing.

59–60 **beard...civil** *see note below*

60 **civil** decently

61 **mad tricks** a *'recommended cure for madness, but of disputed worth'* (John Russell Brown)

63 **salamander's skin** *see note to 3.3.49*

64 **cruel...eyes** *this recalls 3.3.48–50 and 4.2.263*

65 **white...egg** *The Old Testament prophet Isaiah wrote of wicked men: 'None calleth for justice...They hatch cockatrice' eggs...he that eateth of their eggs dieth' (59.4–5: Authorised Version, 1611).*

cockatrice basilisk *(see note to 3.2.87)*

present taking immediate effect

67 **brook** enjoy; put up with

71 **put...gown?** *addressed to the doctor: see note below*

72 **urinals** glass vessels used by doctors for the examination of urine

73 **rose water** *used in medicines, particularly as an eye lotion for red and inflamed eyes*

74–75 **fetch a frisk** cut a caper; perform a brisk dance *(perhaps Ferdinand is being held and is trying to free himself)*

75 **upon my peril** at my risk

77 **tame...dormouse** *The other references to dormice (1.1.288–291 and 3.1.21–22) suggest the doctor will fail.*

79 **cullis** meat broth

79–81 **flay...Hall** *see pages 236–237;* **anatomies** = skeletons; corpses for dissection

82–84 **beasts...lechery** *A corrupt Athenian in old age, as described by Plutarch (died c. AD 126), 'lived so insolently, and governed so lewdly...that there was nothing left of him, no more than of a beast sacrificed, but the tongue and belly' (translation by Thomas North who died c. 1601).*

85 **throughly** thoroughly

Ideas and interpretations

'Ferdinand's confused babble and the comic exchange with the buffoon doctor which breaks down in fisticuffs form an interlude of low comedy' (Lee Bliss). Bliss adds that this is one of a number of examples in Act 5 where 'comic, even farcical intrusions...block our sympathies' – i.e. there's a kind of comic distancing after the Duchess's death.

59–60 The editors of the 1995 Cambridge edition suggest it is likely that 'given the Doctor's bizarre language and actions, the business with removing his gown, and his humiliation by Ferdinand...we have here an accurate indication of comedy makeup. If the role was doubled by a boy actor playing Cariola...the disguise of false beard and eyebrows would be especially welcome.'

Doctor

71 A character who is seldom noticed, let alone produce laughs, in modern productions, but who seems to have been recognised as a comic role by 1708: the fourth quarto printing of the play notes that the doctor removes *four* gowns at line 71. This reflects a theatrical practice of the early eighteenth century, but may also indicate that Webster intended him to be funny.

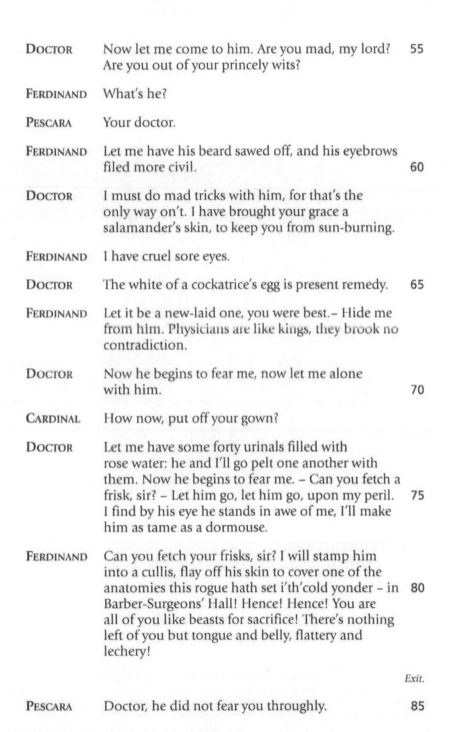

DOCTOR	Now let me come to him. Are you mad, my lord?	55
	Are you out of your princely wits?	
FERDINAND	What's he?	
PESCARA	Your doctor.	
FERDINAND	Let me have his beard sawed off, and his eyebrows	
	filed more civil.	60
DOCTOR	I must do mad tricks with him, for that's the	
	only way on't. I have brought your grace a	
	salamander's skin, to keep you from sun-burning.	
FERDINAND	I have cruel sore eyes.	
DOCTOR	The white of a cockatrice's egg is present remedy.	65
FERDINAND	Let it be a new-laid one, you were best.– Hide me	
	from him. Physicians are like kings, they brook no	
	contradiction.	
DOCTOR	Now he begins to fear me, now let me alone	
	with him.	70
CARDINAL	How now, put off your gown?	
DOCTOR	Let me have some forty urinals filled with	
	rose water: he and I'll go pelt one another with	
	them. Now he begins to fear me. – Can you fetch a	
	frisk, sir? – Let him go, let him go, upon my peril.	75
	I find by his eye he stands in awe of me, I'll make	
	him as tame as a dormouse.	
FERDINAND	Can you fetch your frisks, sir? I will stamp him	
	into a cullis, flay off his skin to cover one of the	
	anatomies this rogue hath set i'th'cold yonder – in	80
	Barber-Surgeons' Hall! Hence! Hence! You are	
	all of you like beasts for sacrifice! There's nothing	
	left of you but tongue and belly, flattery and	
	lechery!	

Exit.

PESCARA	Doctor, he did not fear you throughly.	85

5.2 The Cardinal makes up a story to account for Ferdinand's madness and pretends to Bosola that the Duchess is still alive

86 **forward** bold; aggressive

89 **accident** event; circumstance

90 **distraction** insanity

93–96 **None...riches** *This was taken from the* Histories *by Simon Goulart (see note to 5.2.6–19) about a noble Italian family.*

110 **full...engagement** entire undertaking

112 **I do not...sorrow** I think sorrow

113 **oft-dyed garment** *i.e. a muddy colour: see note below*

The Doctor (Julien Bell) tries to cure Ferdinand (Will Keen) (National Theatre, 2003)

Ideas and interpretations

92–96 . 'This fabrication is a parody of the story of the Duchess: we are reminded of Ferdinand's claim that he had hoped to gain "infinite mass of treasure by her death" [4.2.284]' (Jacqueline Pearson).

102–103 *I much...live:* 'By inventing a "tradition" that implies that his brother is incurable, the Cardinal tries to frighten off his hearers and prevent any attempt to help his brother. He may also be preparing them for a death that he is thinking of bringing about himself' (John Russell Brown).

112–113 *sorrow...garment:* taken from Donne's poem on the death of a girl, *Anatomy of the World* (see note to 3.5.79–80): 'And colour is decayed: summer's robe grows / Dusky, and like an oft dyed garment shows. / ...Perchance the world might have recovered, / If she whom we lament had not been dead'. That the murderous Cardinal quotes from it is somehow shocking, and also suggests he won't be able to keep the secret.

DOCTOR True, I was somewhat too forward.

Exit.

BOSOLA (*Aside*) Mercy upon me, what a fatal judgement
        Hath fallen upon this Ferdinand.

PESCARA   Knows your grace
        What accident hath brought unto the Prince
        This strange distraction?   90

CARDINAL (*Aside*) I must feign somewhat. (*Aloud*) Thus they
          say it grew:
          You have heard it rumoured for these many years,
          None of our family dies but there is seen
          The shape of an old woman, which is given
          By tradition to us, to have been murdered   95
          By her nephews for her riches. Such a figure
          One night, as the Prince sat up late at's book,
          Appeared to him: when crying out for help,
          The gentlemen of's chamber found his grace
          All on a cold sweat, altered much in face   100
          And language; since which apparition
          He hath grown worse and worse, and I much fear
          He cannot live.

BOSOLA (*To* CARDINAL) Sir, I would speak with you.

PESCARA   We'll leave your grace,
        Wishing to the sick Prince, our noble lord,   105
        All health of mind and body.

CARDINAL   You are most welcome.

Exeunt all except CARDINAL and BOSOLA.

        Are you come? (*Aside*) So: this fellow must not
          know
        By any means I had intelligence
        In our Duchess' death, for though I counselled it,
        The full of all th'engagement seemed to grow   110
        From Ferdinand. (*To* BOSOLA) Now sir, how fares
          our sister?
        I do not think but sorrow makes her look
        Like to an oft-dyed garment: she shall now
        Taste comfort from me. Why do you look so wildly?

5.2 *The Cardinal asks Bosola to find Antonio and kill him, and he will get whatever reward he wants*

117–119   **If you'll...be** *see note below*

121–122   **They...begin** *the opposite of Delio's moralising couplet at 2.5.82–83*

128–129   **style...advancement** name your price

131   **camp** *This is a reminder that there is a military campaign going on (e.g. see note to 5.1.3–5), and that the Cardinal is dressed as a soldier.*

  approved confirmed

133   **follow...Mass** *In Webster's source (see page 237), Daniel de Bozola ambushed and killed Antonio at the church where he had gone for Mass.*

135   **school-name** *refers to schoolmen, i.e. medieval academics; the Cardinal is implying that their learning is now seen as old-fashioned and without substance, and that this may be Antonio's view of **religion***

(presumably this is instead what the Cardinal thinks of religion)

for fashion...world as a fashionable thing to do

140–141   **Jews...money** *Jews were often in the money-lending business since for a long time Christians were forbidden to charge interest.*

142–143   **Or...picture** *This detail may come from Webster's own experience – see page 228, note to 3.2.48–51 and 4.2.31–32. He used the motif of portraiture even more in* The Devil's Law-Case.

143   **brought** *Some editions change this spelling – which is in the first 1623 quarto printing – to 'bought', which perhaps makes more sense.*

144   **Happily may take** perhaps may succeed

Ideas and interpretations

117–119 The meaning depends on whether the comma after *me* is a mistake or not. The Revels edition has instead the comma after *entreat*: 'If you'll do one thing that I'll ask you, even if my brother were dead I'd make sure you have the reward you want', but the original placing of the comma, as opposite, gives the meaning: 'I'll plead for you with Ferdinand, and even if...'.

Cardinal

136–138 It is an extremely serious matter if a Catholic priest reveals, even indirectly, what is said to him in secret in a confession: in those days the priest might be excommunicated or sent for life to an enclosed monastery. For a cardinal to actually suggest it is even more serious. In the aftermath of the Gunpowder Plot of 1605, Webster's Protestant audience would relish a Catholic cardinal sinking as low as this.

Oh, the fortune of your master here, the Prince,   115
Dejects you. But be you of happy comfort.
If you'll do one thing for me, I'll entreat
Though he had a cold tombstone o'er his bones,
I'd make you what you would be.

BOSOLA   Any thing:
Give it me in a breath, and let me fly to't.   120
They that think long, small expedition win,
For musing much o'th'end, cannot begin.

Enter JULIA.

JULIA   Sir, will you come in to supper?

CARDINAL   I am busy, leave me.

JULIA   (*Aside*) What an excellent shape hath that fellow!

                                                          Exit.

CARDINAL   'Tis thus: Antonio lurks here in Milan,   125
               Enquire him out, and kill him. While he lives
               Our sister cannot marry, and I have thought
               Of an excellent match for her. Do this, and style me
               Thy advancement.

BOSOLA   But by what means shall I find him out?

CARDINAL   There is a gentleman called Delio   130
               Here in the camp, that hath been long approved
               His loyal friend: set eye upon that fellow,
               Follow him to Mass; may be Antonio,
               Although he do account religion
               But a school-name, for fashion of the world   135
               May accompany him; or else go enquire out
               Delio's confessor, and see if you can bribe
               Him to reveal it. There are a thousand ways
               A man might find to trace him, as to know
               What fellows haunt the Jews for taking up   140
               Great sums of money – for sure he's in want –
               Or else go to th'picture-makers and learn
               Who brought her picture lately – some of these
               Happily may take.

5.2 *Bosola pretends to agree to kill Antonio. The Cardinal's mistress, Julia,*
enters with a pistol and declares her love for Bosola

147 **basilisks** *see note to 3.2.87*

150 **I must...example** *i.e. be cunning* (**his**
= the Cardinal's)

151–152 **There...fox** *i.e. because it's the safest*
thing to do

151 **trace** follow the footprints of

152 **fox** crafty man

157 **Love-powder** *Bosola told Ferdinand*
that he believes in these (3.1.66–69).

163 **kissing comfits** perfumed
sweetmeats *(e.g. sugared fruit)* for
sweetening the breath

164 **discover** show; make known

Bosola

Lorcan Cranitch, who played Bosola in the 2003 National Theatre production, wondered why
Bosola doesn't kill the Cardinal in this scene. The critic Mary Beth Rose says simply that
Bosola is 'isolated, perplexed...alienated, paralysed'.

145–146 *I...world:* The audience know that Bosola means one thing and that the Cardinal
thinks he means another, but the dramatic irony is that Bosola will fail to see Antonio and kill
him by mistake: see 5.4.45–53 and 5.5.93–94.

Julia

This scene parallels the Duchess's wooing of Antonio in 1.1. Muriel Bradbrook describes it as
a 'parody' of the Duchess's wooing. Frank Whigham comments on Julia's role as
'Renaissance court strumpet': 'Julia reaches out to two sources of power in the play, the
Cardinal and Bosola...By rejecting her decrepit husband Julia also testifies to her ruthless
erotic vigour and so makes herself especially alluring to such men. But her achievement is
finally self-wasting: Bosola merely employs her, and the Cardinal tires of her and kills her.'

BOSOLA	Well, I'll not freeze i'th'business,
	I would see that wretched thing Antonio 145
	Above all sights i'th'world.

CARDINAL	Do, and be happy.

Exit.

BOSOLA	This fellow doth breed basilisks in's eyes,
	He's nothing else but murder; yet he seems
	Not to have notice of the Duchess' death.
	'Tis his cunning: I must follow his example, 150
	There cannot be a surer way to trace
	Than that of an old fox.

Enter JULIA pointing a pistol at him.

JULIA	So, sir, you are well met.

BOSOLA	How now?

JULIA	Nay, the doors are fast enough.
	Now sir, I will make you confess your treachery.

BOSOLA	Treachery?

JULIA	Yes, confess to me 155
	Which of my women 'twas you hired, to put
	Love-powder into my drink?

BOSOLA	Love-powder?

JULIA	Yes, when I was at Malfi,
	Why should I fall in love with such a face else?
	I have already suffered for thee so much pain, 160
	The only remedy to do me good
	Is to kill my longing.

BOSOLA	Sure your pistol holds
	Nothing but perfumes or kissing comfits; excellent
	lady,
	You have a pretty way on't to discover
	Your longing: come, come, I'll disarm you, 165
	And arm you thus. (*Embraces her*) Yet this is
	wondrous strange.

168–171 **Now...them** *Compare this speech with the Duchess's at 1.1.445–463.*

169 **nice** coy; shy

170 **familiar** familiar spirit *(see note to 1.1.265)*

173–176 **There wants...well** *from Sidney's* Arcadia

173 **wants** lacks

174 **I...compliment** *i.e. I'm no good at the language of courtship*

177–178 **if...unguilty** if you accuse me of beauty I must plead innocent *(from Sidney's* Arcadia*)*

178–180 **Your bright...sunbeams** *two clichéd ideas*

188 **scruple** very small part

191 **sudden** abrupt; impetuous

192 **use to** are accustomed to

Ideas and interpretations

'The comic associations of love-at-first-sight, coupled with a woman's bold and witty wooing, become shockingly misplaced both in the context of death and madness and when the principals are not young lovers but murderers and adulterers' (Lee Bliss).

Language

177–178 *charge...unguilty:* 'The first of a series of references to crime and punishment in the next forty lines, anticipating the *justice* [5.2.279] of Julia's death' (1995 Cambridge edition).

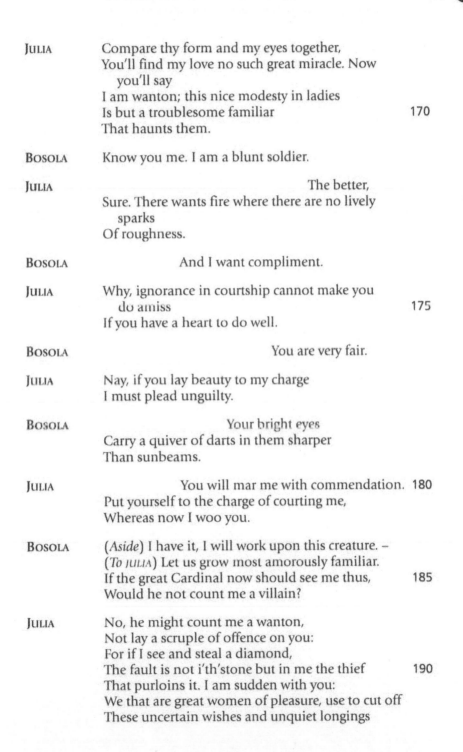

JULIA   Compare thy form and my eyes together,
             You'll find my love no such great miracle. Now
                 you'll say
             I am wanton; this nice modesty in ladies
             Is but a troublesome familiar   170
             That haunts them.

BOSOLA   Know you me. I am a blunt soldier.

JULIA   The better,
             Sure. There wants fire where there are no lively
                 sparks
             Of roughness.

BOSOLA   And I want compliment.

JULIA   Why, ignorance in courtship cannot make you
                 do amiss   175
             If you have a heart to do well.

BOSOLA   You are very fair.

JULIA   Nay, if you lay beauty to my charge
             I must plead unguilty.

BOSOLA   Your bright eyes
             Carry a quiver of darts in them sharper
             Than sunbeams.

JULIA   You will mar me with commendation. 180
             Put yourself to the charge of courting me,
             Whereas now I woo you.

BOSOLA   (Aside) I have it, I will work upon this creature. –
             (To JULIA) Let us grow most amorously familiar.
             If the great Cardinal now should see me thus,   185
             Would he not count me a villain?

JULIA   No, he might count me a wanton,
             Not lay a scruple of offence on you:
             For if I see and steal a diamond,
             The fault is not i'th'stone but in me the thief   190
             That purloins it. I am sudden with you:
             We that are great women of pleasure, use to cut off
             These uncertain wishes and unquiet longings

5.2 *To prove her love, Bosola asks Julia to find out why the Cardinal is melancholy; Julia tells Bosola to hide and she will do it immediately*

194–195 **in...excuse** *from Sidney's* Arcadia: *'in one instant to join a dear delight with a just excuse'*

198 **presently** immediately

206 **Emperor** *see note to 3.3.1*

206–207 **mice...houses** *proverbial expression*

210 **calling** occupation

212 **some** some who

215 **cabinet** private room; boudoir

216 **have...you** take it away with you

And in an instant join the sweet delight
And the pretty excuse together. Had you been in
   th'street,   195
Under my chamber window, even there
I should have courted you.

BOSOLA   Oh, you are an excellent lady.

JULIA   Bid me do somewhat for you presently
To express I love you.

BOSOLA   I will; and if you love me,
Fail not to effect it.   200
The Cardinal is grown wondrous melancholy:
Demand the cause, let him not put you off
With feigned excuse; discover the main ground on't.

JULIA   Why would you know this?

BOSOLA   I have depended on him,
And I hear that he is fallen in some disgrace   205
With the Emperor. If he be, like the mice
That forsake falling houses, I would shift
To other dependence.

JULIA   You shall not need follow the wars,
I'll be your maintenance.

BOSOLA   And I your loyal servant;
But I cannot leave my calling.

JULIA   Not leave an   210
Ungrateful general, for the love of a sweet lady?
You are like some cannot sleep in feather beds,
But must have blocks for their pillows.

BOSOLA   Will you do this?

JULIA   Cunningly.

BOSOLA   Tomorrow I'll expect th'intelligence.

JULIA   Tomorrow? Get you into my cabinet,   215
You shall have it with you. Do not delay me,
No more than I do you. I am like one

5.2 *The Cardinal tells his servants that no one is allowed to talk to Ferdinand. Julia tries to get the Cardinal to reveal why he is sad*

217–219 **I am...sealed** *from Sidney's* Arcadia; *this prefigures her death and also recalls Bosola's lines at 1.1.59–60*

221 **skein** quantity of thread wound on a reel

226 **consumption** wasting disease

228 **quit off** rid of

230 **secretary** *the original meaning:* one privy to a secret; confidante

230–231 **remove...bosom** *this recalls 3.2.112–114: the lead of the secret will become the lead of her tomb*

232–238 **Are...tongue** *based on lines in Sidney's* Arcadia

That is condemned: I have my pardon promised,
But I would see it sealed. Go, get you in,
You shall see me wind my tongue about his heart   220
Like a skein of silk.

Exit BOSOLA.

Enter CARDINAL followed by SERVANTS.

CARDINAL   Where are you?

SERVANT   Here.

CARDINAL   Let none upon your lives
I Iave conference with the Prince Ferdinand
Unless I know it. (*Aside*) In this distraction
He may reveal the murder.   225

Exeunt SERVANTS.

Yond's my lingering consumption:
I am weary of her and by any means
Would be quit off.

JULIA   How now, my lord,
What ails you?

CARDINAL   Nothing.

JULIA   Oh, you are much altered.
Come, I must be your secretary and remove   230
This lead from off your bosom. What's the matter?

CARDINAL   I may not tell you.

JULIA   Are you so far in love with sorrow
You cannot part with part of it? Or think you
I cannot love your grace when you are sad,
As well as merry? Or do you suspect   235
I, that have been a secret to your heart
These many winters, cannot be the same
Unto your tongue?

CARDINAL   Satisfy thy longing,
The only way to make thee keep my counsel
Is not to tell thee.

5.2 *The Cardinal warns Julia about the danger of knowing his secret, and begins to tell her what it is*

241 **still** always

243–244 **if...know** *i.e. if you are true to me – your other self – you'll tell me*

251–252 **as great...adultery** *In Roman Catholicism adultery is a mortal sin and those who don't repent are damned.*

253 **perfect...constancy** *this echoes 2.4.11–19*

258 **breasts** heart; place for private thoughts

hooped with adamant ringed with the hardest iron *(i.e. like a barrel; this was a commonplace phrase)*

264 **dally** play

Julia kisses the book (5.2.273) (Nicola Redmond; Paul Brennen as the Cardinal) (Cheek by Jowl, 1995–6)

Performance

251–252 In the 2003 National Theatre production, the Cardinal (Ray Stevenson) was angry with Julia for reminding him of this; in the 1995 Cheek by Jowl production the Cardinal (Paul Brennen) laughed.

JULIA   Tell your echo this –   240
Or flatterers, that like echoes still report
What they hear, though most imperfect – and not
        me:
For if that you be true unto yourself,
I'll know.

CARDINAL   Will you rack me?

JULIA   No, judgement shall
Draw it from you. It is an equal fault,   245
To tell one's secrets unto all, or none.

CARDINAL   The first argues folly.

JULIA   But the last tyranny.

CARDINAL   Very well – why, imagine I have committed
Some secret deed which I desire the world
May never hear of.

JULIA   Therefore may not I know it?   250
You have concealed for me as great a sin
As adultery: sir, never was occasion
For perfect trial of my constancy
Till now: sir, I beseech you.

CARDINAL   You'll repent it.

JULIA   Never.

CARDINAL   It hurries thee to ruin. I'll not tell thee.   255
Be well advised, and think what danger 'tis
To receive a prince's secrets: they that do,
Had need have their breasts hooped with adamant
To contain them. I pray thee yet be satisfied,
Examine thine own frailty; 'tis more easy   260
To tie knots than unloose them: 'tis a secret
That like a ling'ring poison may chance lie
Spread in thy veins, and kill thee seven year hence.

JULIA   Now you dally with me.

CARDINAL   No more: thou shalt know it.
By my appointment the great Duchess of Malfi   265

5.2 *The Cardinal tells Julia that his sister and her children were recently murdered on his orders. He makes Julia kiss a poisoned book, and she dies as Bosola comes out of hiding*

266 **four nights since** *several nights ago (e.g. see 4.1.9)*

268 **settles** *image of a liquid settling and gradually becoming clear after being shaken*

268–270 **bosom...secret** *recalls 4.2.318–319*

272 **book** *perhaps a Bible*

278 **I forgive you** *echoes the Duchess's forgiveness of her executioners (4.2.207)*

283–284 **'Tis...done** *from Sidney's* Arcadia

Language

269–270 Julia's bosom as a *grave* is another example of the insistent imagery of monuments, graves and tombs in this play (see also, for example, Bosola's lines at 4.2.318–319 and 5.5.97–98).

Julia

279–280 She betrayed only a 'murderer's confidence', says Lee Bliss, so her death 'hardly seems the "equal piece of justice" she claims'.

Performance

271 In the 1995 Cheek by Jowl production, the Cardinal started weeping after *It lies not in me to conceal it*, and laid his head on her lap.

285 In the 2003 National Theatre production, as at the death of other characters (see page 256), Julia stood up to say her last line to the audience, and then went to sit on the steps to watch the rest of the play.

And two of her young children, four nights since
Were strangled.

JULIA   Oh heaven! Sir, what have you done?

CARDINAL   How now, how settles this? Think you your bosom
Will be a grave dark and obscure enough
For such a secret?

JULIA   You have undone yourself, sir.   270

CARDINAL   Why?

JULIA   It lies not in me to conceal it.

CARDINAL   No? Come, I will swear you to't upon this book.

JULIA   Most religiously.

CARDINAL   Kiss it.

She kisses the book.

Now you shall never utter it. Thy curiosity
Hath undone thee. Thou'rt poisoned with that book; 275
Because I knew thou couldst not keep my counsel,
I have bound thee to't by death.

Enter BOSOLA.

BOSOLA   For pity sake, hold!

CARDINAL   Ha, Bosola!

JULIA   I forgive you
This equal piece of justice you have done,
For I betrayed your counsel to that fellow,   280
He overheard it: that was the cause I said
It lay not in me to conceal it.

BOSOLA   Oh foolish woman,
Couldst not thou have poisoned him?

JULIA   'Tis weakness
Too much to think what should have been done.
I go I know not whither. (*Dies*)   285

Bosola tells the Cardinal that Julia hid him because of her lust for him. He agrees again to kill Antonio

290–291   **Make...dispose of** *i.e. I'm not that easy to get rid of*

294–295   **wherefore...purposes** *Wood was often painted to look like marble, for example the timber columns on the Globe stage that held up the 'heavens' (see photograph on page vi). (This is also another metaphor from painting, and appearance and reality.)*

297–298   **go hide...in't** *i.e. kill the people they hired to do treasonous acts*

303   **conduct** lead

308   **smother** suffocating smoke

309   **Yes** *Although this is what will happen, Bosola might not intend to lie here – he could be thinking that telling Antonio that his wife and two other children are dead will kill him.*

      that body Julia

310   **common bier** public stretcher for dead bodies *(i.e. Bosola is saying that he is becoming a stretcher-bearer for corpses)*

Cardinal

293 The Cardinal's 'cool, unemotional detachment is more terrifying than Ferdinand's impassioned raving', he seems 'rather an automaton than a trickster villain...When Bosola discovers him to be a "fellow murderer", the Cardinal still expects proffered fortune and honors to ensure his tool's loyalty. The smug certainty of psychological penetration and control no longer adequately corresponds to reality' (Lee Bliss).

CARDINAL	Wherefore com'st thou hither?
BOSOLA	That I might find a great man like yourself, Not out of his wits as the Lord Ferdinand, To remember my service.
CARDINAL	I'll have thee hewed in pieces!
BOSOLA	Make not yourself such a promise of that life 290 Which is not yours to dispose of.
CARDINAL	Who placed thee here?
BOSOLA	Her lust, as she intended.
CARDINAL	Very well, now you know me for your fellow murderer.
BOSOLA	And wherefore should you lay fair marble colours Upon your rotten purposes to me, 295 Unless you imitate some that do plot great treasons And, when they have done, go hide themselves i'th' graves Of those were actors in't?
CARDINAL	No more, There is a fortune attends thee.
BOSOLA	Shall I go sue to Fortune any longer? 300 'Tis the fool's pilgrimage.
CARDINAL	I have honours in store for thee.
BOSOLA	There are a many ways that conduct to seeming Honour, and some of them very dirty ones.
CARDINAL	Throw to the devil 305 Thy melancholy. The fire burns well, What need we keep a stirring of it, and make A greater smother? Thou wilt kill Antonio?
BOSOLA	Yes.
CARDINAL	Take up that body.
BOSOLA	I think I shall Shortly grow the common bier for churchyards. 310

5.2 *The Cardinal tells Bosola to return after midnight to move Julia's body, but Bosola also plans to find Antonio and join him to revenge the Duchess's death*

313   **horse-leeches** *see 1.1.55*

       rank *see note to 1.1.312*

314   **use to** usually

316   **train** attendants

318–319   **help...lodging** *Bosola carries the body offstage at the end of the scene.*

322–324   **Castruchio...citadel** *see 5.1.26–36 and note to 1.1.114–118*

325   **turn** (1) act of good will; (2) trick

329–331   **though...dangerous** *from Sidney's* Arcadia

330   **estate** condition

333   **frost-nailed** nails on shoes to prevent people from slipping on ice

334   **The precedent...me** the example is here in front of me *(Julia's body)*

335   **Bears...blood** *perhaps:* keeps his spirits up while shedding blood

336   **Security** confidence that one is secure

       Security...hell *This follows on from Bosola's comment that the Cardinal* **seems fearless***: it is a vice to have theological certainty that stems from pride and self-centredness.*

       suburbs of hell *a phrase often used by preachers*

337   **dead wall** *architectural term for a blank wall unbroken by windows or other openings: the kind of wall that encircles a cemetery*

340   **biters** blood-suckers *(e.g. horse-leeches: line 313)*

341   **Some...blood** *i.e. his children*

Bosola

342 *in a most just revenge:* 'This spy, who repents and institutes a counter-vengeance for the murder which he himself had executed on command, reaffirms the tragic fate of the servant' (Muriel Bradbrook).

CARDINAL	I will allow thee some dozen of attendants To aid thee in the murder.

BOSOLA	Oh, by no means. Physicians that apply horse-leeches to any rank swelling, use to cut off their tails, that the blood may run through them the faster: let me have no 315 train when I go to shed blood, lest it make me have a greater when I ride to the gallows.

CARDINAL	Come to me after midnight to help remove that body to her own lodging: I'll give out she died o'th'plague, 'twill breed the less enquiry after 320 her death.

BOSOLA	Where's Castruchio, her husband?

CARDINAL	He's rode to Naples to take possession of Antonio's citadel.

BOSOLA	Believe me, you have done a very happy turn. 325

CARDINAL	Fail not to come. There is the master key Of our lodgings, and by that you may conceive What trust I plant in you.

Exit.

BOSOLA	You shall find me ready. Oh poor Antonio, though nothing be so needful To thy estate as pity, yet I find 330 Nothing so dangerous. I must look to my footing; In such slippery ice-pavements men had need To be frost-nailed well, they may break their necks else. The precedent's here afore me: how this man Bears up in blood, seems fearless! Why, 'tis well: 335 Security some men call the suburbs of hell, Only a dead wall between. Well, good Antonio, I'll seek thee out, and all my care shall be To put thee into safety from the reach Of these most cruel biters that have got 340 Some of thy blood already. It may be I'll join with thee in a most just revenge:

5.3 After Bosola exits with Julia's body, the location moves to the ruined cloister of the old abbey, outside the Cardinal's window

343–344 **The...justice** *from Sidney's* Arcadia

344 **Still methinks** I constantly think

346 **Oh...cup** *i.e. experience the pain of repentance (see the Bible: Matthew 20.22)*

1 **Yond's...window** *This at once tells the audience that the location is outside the room of the previous scene.*

1–2 **This...abbey** *After the dissolution of the monasteries by Henry VIII, many religious houses were partly pulled down and replaced with mansions – such as at the Blackfriars friary where this play was first performed.*

3 **to yond...river** *perhaps:* up to the bank of the river over there *(at the Blackfriars the Thames riverbank was very near)*

4 **cloister** *The Blackfriars playhouse was next to the old cloister of the friary.*

7 **distinction** pronunciation

11 **reverend** worthy of deep respect *(with idea of something sacred)*

12 **questionless** without doubt

12–17 **open court...doomsday** *Abbots and other important religious men were often buried in the cloister of a monastery or other religious house, a practice that ended in England at the Reformation when monasteries were dissolved.*

18 **diseases** (1) disturbances *(dis-ease)*; (2) illnesses

21 **accent** tone

Language

343–344 *The weakest...justice:* Rupert Brooke commented: 'Webster wanted to make Bosola say fine things. He had many in his mind or his note-book: some were borrowed, some his own. He put them down, and they answer their purpose splendidly...Webster reset other people's jewels and redoubled their lustre.'

Duchess

344–345 'In a significant, almost indeed in a literal, sense the dead Duchess haunts the final act, a constant poignant reminder of a better way of living' (Jacqueline Pearson).

Performance

344–345 In the 2003 National Theatre production the Duchess (Janet McTeer) sat on the steps, centre stage, watching the action behind a glass screen. Just for a moment Bosola (Lorcan Cranitch) looked straight at her, and she at him.

Ideas and interpretations

9–19 In the 1530s King Henry VIII broke England's allegiance to the Roman Catholic Church, and from then onwards England gradually became a Protestant nation. Many other European states also changed to follow Protestant Christianity in this period called the 'Reformation'. Monks, friars and nuns were no longer allowed to continue their life of prayer or service; abbeys and friaries were taken over by the state: many were destroyed, some still survive as ruins. A thousand years of England's religious history came to an end. Michael Neill comments: 'The full meaning of the Echo scene is shaped by Antonio's moralization on the ruined abbey – a setting whose poignant spectacle of violated glories and defaced memorials belongs not to the play's nominal Italian setting, but to a peculiarly English post-Reformation context.'

The weakest arm is strong enough that strikes
With the sword of justice. – Still methinks the
    Duchess
Haunts me! There, there, 'tis nothing but my
    melancholy.   345
Oh penitence, let me truly taste thy cup,
That throws men down, only to raise them up.

Exit.

Scene 3

Enter ANTONIO and DELIO.

DELIO   Yond's the Cardinal's window. This fortification
Grew from the ruins of an ancient abbey,
And to yond side o'th'river lies a wall,
Piece of a cloister, which in my opinion
Gives the best echo that you ever heard,   5
So hollow and so dismal, and withal
So plain in the distinction of our words
That many have supposed it is a spirit
That answers.

ANTONIO   I do love these ancient ruins.
We never tread upon them but we set   10
Our foot upon some reverend history,
And questionless, here in this open court
Which now lies naked to the injuries
Of stormy weather, some men lie interred
Loved the church so well, and gave so largely to't, 15
They thought it should have canopied their bones
Till doomsday; but all things have their end:
Churches and cities, which have diseases like to
    men,
Must have like death that we have.

ECHO   *Like death that we have.*

DELIO   Now the echo hath caught you.

ANTONIO   It groaned, methought, and gave 20
A very deadly accent.

5.3   *The echo seems to be advising Antonio not to visit the Cardinal that night*

22	**pretty one** fine echo	33	**passes** events
22–23	**you...musician** *see note below*	41	**never...more** *see 3.5.81*
30–31	**Wisdom...Than time** time lessens great grief more than wisdom does		

Structure

Act 5 scene 3 has been seen as a symbolic contrast to Ferdinand's desecration of a churchyard (see 5.2.8–19) and also as a reflective pause before the slaughter at the end of the tragedy, similar to the beginning of the churchyard scene in Shakespeare's *Hamlet* (5.1).

Ideas and interpretations

For Michael Neill, 5.3 is a crucial scene in order to understand the 'full significance' of the Duchess's death. The scene has been neglected or often regarded as just a 'Gothic' extravagance, but Neill says it yields its meaning if you study the imagery, which 'reveals the play as a dramatized pageant of Fame'.

Performance

22–23 In the 2003 National Theatre production, Delio (Jonathan Slinger) made the sound of a huntsman's trumpet after *huntsman*, whistled after *falconer*, then hummed a few notes after *musician*. After each sound he made there was an amplified echo of it.

24 In the 1995 Cheek by Jowl production, the Duchess (Anastasia Hille) watched Act 5 sitting at the back of the stage. In this scene she stood up and said all the echo lines to Antonio (Matthew Macfadyen), but he couldn't see her. In the 2003 National Theatre production, the Duchess (Janet McTeer) spoke the echo, from line 24 onwards, into a microphone – which had the resonance of an echo.

ECHO	*Deadly accent.*
DELIO	I told you 'twas a pretty one: you may make it A huntsman, or a falconer, a musician, Or a thing of sorrow.
ECHO	*A thing of sorrow.*
ANTONIO	Ay sure, that suits it best.
ECHO	*That suits it best.* 25
ANTONIO	'Tis very like my wife's voice.
ECHO	*Ay, wife's voice.*
DELIO	Come: let's walk farther from't. I would not have you go to th'Cardinal's tonight: Do not.
ECHO	*Do not.*
DELIO	Wisdom doth not more moderate wasting sorrow 30 Than time: take time for't, be mindful of thy safety.
ECHO	*Be mindful of thy safety.*
ANTONIO	Necessity compels me. Make scrutiny throughout the passes Of your own life; you'll find it impossible To fly your fate.
ECHO	*O fly your fate.* 35
DELIO	Hark: the dead stones seem to have pity on you And give you good counsel.
ANTONIO	Echo, I will not talk with thee, For thou art a dead thing.
ECHO	*Thou art a dead thing.*
ANTONIO	My Duchess is asleep now, And her little ones, I hope sweetly: oh heaven 40 Shall I never see her more?
ECHO	*Never see her more.*

5.4 Antonio hears the echo for the last time and thinks he sees a face of sorrow, which Delio says he imagined. Delio goes to fetch Antonio's eldest son to confront the Cardinal. The location changes to inside the palace just before midnight

42–43 **I marked...that** I paid attention only to that echo

43 **on the sudden** suddenly

45 **fancy** imagination

ague fever *(see 5.4.67–69)*

46–47 **For...life** *adapted from the French writer Pierre Matthieu*

48 **save...halves** *from Montaigne's Essays*

50 **second** *see 5.1.74*

51 **his** the Cardinal's

53 **How ever** *see 5.1.74*

54–55 **Though...none** *based on lines in* The Alexandrean Tragedy *(see note to 4.2.143–144)*

56 **Contempt...own** *i.e. the most courageous attitude to life and suffering comes from within us*

3 **suffer us** allow us

Performance

42–45 In the first printing of this play (1623 quarto) the stage direction at the beginning of 5.3 adds: 'Echo, from the Duchess's grave'. This could be to help the reader: there is no reference to a specific stage effect or prop and Delio says it's Antonio's imagination (45), so the echo presumably just came from offstage. But John Russell Brown notes it as odd that Antonio thinks the echo is visible *(a face folded in sorrow)* and suggests that Webster had the King's Men reuse a stage property from an earlier play consisting of a tombstone whose doors fly open to reveal a great light and the Duchess. But there is nothing in Webster's source, nor in the play, to suggest that the Duchess's body was moved from Malfi and buried in Milan.

43–44 Philip Franks, director (1995): 'The echo scene works amazingly well in performance, the audience wants the Duchess back, and the hopelessness of her trying to send a message from beyond the grave that doesn't get through is heartbeaking. We are so schooled in Jacobean and Elizabethan drama to ghosts appearing and saying things and people going: "OK then", but here the message doesn't get heard, except for his extraordinary: *on the sudden a clear light / Presented me a face folded in sorrow*, which is like – "I thought I saw something. No I didn't." Juliet Stevenson said the lines offstage and then she walked on at the end of it. Antonio was right down the front, it was very dark, but there was a huge power surge and she walked across the back and looked at him. And he went, "Oh, God, what...?" He didn't see her. But she saw him. He saw her face only in his mind's eye. But the audience saw her.'

Ideas and interpretations

The location for 5.4 moves back to inside the fortification/palace. Roderigo and Grisolan are very minor characters who appear in 1.1 and 2.2, serving the Duchess. It's possible that Webster deliberately intended their appearance here as courtiers of the Cardinal/Ferdinand to show that they had deserted the Duchess; they certainly have no redeeming characteristics.

ANTONIO   I marked not one repetition of the echo
But that: and on the sudden a clear light
Presented me a face folded in sorrow.

DELIO   Your fancy, merely.

ANTONIO   Come, I'll be out of this ague;   45
For to live thus is not indeed to live:
It is a mockery and abuse of life.
I will not henceforth save myself by halves,
Lose all, or nothing.

DELIO   Your own virtue save you.
I'll fetch your eldest son and second you: 50
It may be that the sight of his own blood
Spread in so sweet a figure may beget
The more compassion.

ANTONIO   How ever, fare you well.
Though in our miseries Fortune hath a part,
Yet in our noble suff'rings she hath none.   55
Contempt of pain — that we may call our own.

Exeunt.

Scene 4

*Enter CARDINAL, PESCARA, MALATESTE, RODERIGO,
GRISOLAN.*

CARDINAL   You shall not watch tonight by the sick Prince,
His grace is very well recovered.

MALATESTE   Good my lord, suffer us.

CARDINAL   Oh, by no means.
The noise, and change of object in his eye,
Doth more distract him. I pray, all to bed,   5
And though you hear him in his violent fit,
Do not rise, I entreat you.

PESCARA   So sir, we shall not.

CARDINAL   Nay, I must have your promise

5.4 *The Cardinal tells his courtiers not to get out of bed if they hear Ferdinand or himself calling. In a soliloquy he reveals he will kill Bosola – which Bosola overhears*

10 **sensibly** with good sense

11 **Let...trifle** 'let us bind ourselves by oath to honour this small request' *(John Russell Brown)*

16 **cutting** being cut

17 **protested** vowed

19 **osier** willow tree

20–21 **kindness...child** *very clearly linking Ferdinand with the devil (see also 3.5.39)*

25 **Julia's body** *This is the first time she is given a name by a character in the play – after her death.*

27–28 **I...prayer** *from Sidney's* Arcadia *(Webster added:* **the devil***)*

28 **For** from

30 **turn** purpose

Plot

13–18 The Cardinal's bizarre instructions are Webster's way of explaining why no one comes to his aid in scene 5.

Cardinal

1–18 'The carefully, even comically elaborated instructions to his courtiers set up a practical joke on the world which kills him...If earlier commentary portrayed him as a center of evil and corruption, act 5 defines him as a fool' (Lee Bliss).

26–28 'In so reticent a character, this revelation of the pangs of conscience comes as a shock' (1995 Cambridge edition).

Upon your honours, for I was enjoined to't
By himself; and he seemed to urge it sensibly.   10

PESCARA   Let our honours bind this trifle.

CARDINAL   Nor any of your followers.

MALATESTE   Neither.

CARDINAL   It may be, to make trial of your promise
When he's asleep, myself will rise and feign
Some of his mad tricks, and cry out for help,   15
And feign myself in danger.

MALATESTE   If your throat were cutting
I'd not come at you, now I have protested
      against it.

CARDINAL   Why, I thank you.

Withdraws.

GRISOLAN   'Twas a foul storm tonight.

RODERIGO   The Lord Ferdinand's chamber shook like an osier.

MALATESTE   'Twas nothing but pure kindness in the devil,   20
To rock his own child.

Exeunt all but CARDINAL.

CARDINAL   The reason why I would not suffer these
About my brother, is because at midnight
I may with better privacy convey
Julia's body to her own lodging.   25
Oh, my conscience!
I would pray now, but the devil takes away my
      heart
For having any confidence in prayer.
About this hour I appointed Bosola
To fetch the body: when he hath served my turn,   30
He dies.

Exit.

Enter BOSOLA.

5.4 *In the dark in the Cardinal's chamber, Bosola mistakenly thinks Ferdinand is talking about killing him, and thinks Antonio is the hired killer sent to do the murder – so Bosola attacks him with his sword*

33   **one's footing** someone's footsteps

34   **Strangling...death** *In this and his next speech Ferdinand is obviously deranged and thinking of the Duchess – not of Bosola.*

36–38   **What...see it** *The editors of the 1995 Cambridge edition suggest this should be in prose even though it is in verse in the 1623 quarto.*

40   **desert** merit; deserving a reward

      breath life

41   **black...death** *a commonplace idea*

43   **dark lantern** *see note on page 60*

44   **take him** find the Cardinal *(but Bosola hears instead:* kill Bosola)

47   **suit** (1) redress of a wrong; (2) petition to a prince

49–50   **That...myself** *perhaps:* who can only be my true self because of the death you have given me

49   **benefit** good deed; gift

Performance

s.d. after 46 In the 2003 National Theatre production there was light enough for the audience to see Antonio enter. Then Bosola fired a pistol from offstage as if he had heard someone mentioning his death but it was too dark for him to see who it was. All the killings in this scene and 5.5 were done realistically, with much blood, but the actors said their last lines standing up, straight to the audience (see page 256). In a different way, but perhaps with a similar intention of not attempting to portray these deaths too realistically, the 1995 Cheek by Jowl killings were done by mime – with none of the actors touching each other or even looking at each other.

Antonio

'Antonio's final action, the desperately naive journey to the Cardinal for reconciliation, freezes him for us, as one whose unsought elevation never brought much sense of how to navigate the webs of alliance and enmity' (Frank Whigham). Mary Beth Rose dismisses Antonio's attempt at reconciliation as 'futile'.

BOSOLA   Ha? 'Twas the Cardinal's voice: I heard him name
          Bosola, and my death. – Listen, I hear one's footing.

Enter FERDINAND.

FERDINAND   Strangling is a very quiet death.

BOSOLA   (*Aside*) Nay then, I see I must stand upon my guard. 35

FERDINAND   What say to that? Whisper, softly: do you agree to't?
          So. It must be done i'th'dark – the Cardinal
          Would not for a thousand pounds the Doctor
             should see it.

                                                    Exit.

BOSOLA   My death is plotted. Here's the consequence of
             murder.
          'We value not desert, nor Christian breath,   40
          When we know black deeds must be cured with
             death.'

Withdraws. Enter ANTONIO and a SERVANT.

SERVANT   Here stay sir, and be confident, I pray.
          I'll fetch you a dark lantern.

                                                    Exit.

ANTONIO   Could I take him at his prayers,
          There were hope of pardon.

BOSOLA   Fall right my sword: 45
          I'll not give thee so much leisure as to pray.

BOSOLA wounds ANTONIO.

ANTONIO   Oh, I am gone! Thou hast ended a long suit
          In a minute.

BOSOLA   What art thou?

ANTONIO   A most wretched thing,
          That only have thy benefit in death,
          To appear myself.

Enter SERVANT with a lantern.

5.4

The servant's lantern reveals that Bosola has fatally wounded Antonio by mistake. Bosola tells Antonio that his wife has been murdered; Antonio hopes that his remaining son will never live in a prince's court

51 **my home** death; my grave

53 **'bove** above: more than

54–55 **stars'...them** *see note below*

54 **banded** bandied *(literally:* to strike a ball to and fro in real tennis; *there may also be wordplay with 'banded' – the balls were made of strips of cloth/bands wound together)*

60–62 **Some...sadness** some people are so upset when they hear sad news that they hope to die; I am glad that I will die in earnest *(with wordplay on* **sad** *in line 61)*

63 **balmed** soothed/healed with an ointment

65–66 **Like...air** *an idea also found in other authors of the time*

65 **wanton** (1) undisciplined; (2) spoiled; self-indulgent

whose...care who only care about being entertained

66 **We...air** we pursue what is worthless

67–68 **Pleasure...ague** *i.e. pleasure is merely that time when we are not suffering*

68 **preparative** serving to prepare us

70 **process** story *(i.e. what led to my death)*

72 **And...princes** *similar to the last words of Vittoria in* The White Devil *5.6; see also about King James's court on pages 233–235*

Bosola

53 Bosola has killed Antonio by mistake, the man he would have saved *'bove mine own life.* Perhaps this is symbolic of his whole inability to distinguish between good and evil, between enemies and friends.

Language

54–55 *stars' tennis balls...them:* This image occurs quite often in literature of the time, e.g. in Sidney's *Arcadia.* Real (or royal) tennis is an ancient game that was especially popular with English and French monarchs in the sixteenth and seventeenth centuries. It was played in a walled and roofed court; one side of the net was the 'service' side; the other was the 'hazard' side (see 1.1.62 for Bosola's wordplay). Henry VIII's tennis court at Hampton Court Palace survives, as does part of his tennis court wall at Whitehall Palace in central London.

65–66 The poet Rupert Brooke commented that the use of couplets was old-fashioned, but when most authors used it, 'they did it with grace; using it almost as a musical device, to bring the continued melody of their verse to a close. And in the earlier plays, where one or more rhyming couplets end most scenes and many speeches, and even, especially in the more lyrical parts, come into the middle of passages, the rest of the versification is of a simple, rhythmical end-stopped kind; and so the couplets seem scarcely different from the rest, a deeper shade of the same colour. Webster's couplets are electric green on crimson, a violent contrast with the rough, jerky, sketchy blank verse he generally uses.'

Ideas and interpretations

72 Jacqueline Pearson comments on Antonio: 'At the beginning of the play he praised the "fixed order" [1.1.6] of the French court. Now he dies with a profound distrust of the ambiguous "order" imposed by great men, wishing that his son should "fly the courts of princes". Tragedy is replaced by horrifying accident and a disturbing pessimism.' She adds: 'This painfully ironic scene casts doubts on the whole possibility of just action in a post-tragic world.'

SERVANT	Where are you sir?	50
ANTONIO	Very near my home. – Bosola?	
SERVANT	Oh misfortune!	
BOSOLA	(*To* SERVANT) Smother thy pity, thou art dead else. –	

BOSOLA (*To* SERVANT) Smother thy pity, thou art dead else. –
    Antonio?
The man I would have saved 'bove mine own life!
We are merely the stars' tennis balls, struck and
    banded
Which way please them. Oh good Antonio,   55
I'll whisper one thing in thy dying ear
Shall make thy heart break quickly: thy fair
    Duchess
And two sweet children –

ANTONIO   Their very names
Kindle a little life in me –

BOSOLA   Are murdered!

ANTONIO Some men have wished to die   60
At the hearing of sad tidings. I am glad
That I shall do't in sadness. I would not now
Wish my wounds balmed, nor healed, for I have no
    use
To put my life to: in all our quest of greatness,
Like wanton boys whose pastime is their care,   65
We follow after bubbles blown in the air.
Pleasure of life, what is't? Only the good hours
Of an ague; merely a preparative to rest,
To endure vexation. I do not ask
The process of my death: only commend me   70
To Delio.

BOSOLA   Break heart.

ANTONIO And let my son fly the courts of princes. (*Dies*)

BOSOLA Thou seem'st to have loved Antonio?

SERVANT   I brought him hither
To have reconciled him to the Cardinal.

5.5 *The servant carries Antonio's body off, so when he and Bosola appear again it is presumably at or near Julia's lodging. Bosola tells the Cardinal he is going to kill him*

75 **I...that** I do not ask you to do that

76 **tender** care for

80 **misprision** *i.e. his killing of Antonio:* (1) *legal language:* wrong action; (2) mistaking one thing for another; (3) failure to appreciate or recognise someone or something as valuable

83–84 **look...bear'st** *i.e. do not say a word about this*

s.d. **with a book** *a stage convention to show melancholy*

2 **He says** *i.e. the author of the book he is carrying*

 material (1) real; actual; (2) important; significant

2–3 **in hell...alike** *Various devotional works have been suggested as a source for this.*

4 **Lay him by** *put that book/author aside (echoed later at 89–90)*

 tedious (1) wearisome and long in extent; (2) annoying; painful

5 **fishponds** *Ponds for freshwater fish were a common feature on the estates of bishops and other rich men.*

6 **a thing...a rake** *Here this farming tool is perhaps a parody of a bishop's crosier; but this is also an image of Death – who carries a rake in some contemporary illustrations.*

8 **ghastly** (1) ghost-like, death-like; (2) terrifying; (3) full of fear *(the first meaning echoes Bosola's first line in the play, see 1.1.29)*

10 **lightens into action** *see note to 1.1.82*

13 **Hold** stop

14 **prayers and proffers** *The alliteration emphasises Bosola's scorn.*

Language

79–80 *I...hammer:* This recalls Bosola's previous image of blacksmithing (3.3.319–320), but now the Cardinal is the metal about to go in the fire and under the blows of the hammer, and Bosola is the blacksmith/devil – whereas before Bosola was the anvil on which the devil worked (the Cardinal is associated with the devil by Bosola at 1.1.45–48): their roles are reversed.

1–7 Rupert Brooke described this as a 'legitimate and superb use of soliloquy...The words and thought are mysteriously thrilling. They sharpen the agony of the spectator's mind to a tense expectation; which is broken by the contrast of the swift purpose of Bosola's entry, with the servant and the body, and the violent progression of events ensuing. The whole is in tone together; and the effect bites deep.'

Cardinal

5–7 Muriel Bradbrook: 'The Cardinal knows already that he is in Hell; looking in his fish-ponds for his own image, he has seen "a thing arm'd with a rake" that seems to strike at him. (It is an echo of the scene where the Duchess sees the face of Ferdinand instead of Antonio's.)'

| BOSOLA | I do not ask thee that: | 75 |

BOSOLA   I do not ask thee that: 75
Take him up, if thou tender thine own life,
And bear him where the Lady Julia
Was wont to lodge. Oh, my fate moves swift.
I have this Cardinal in the forge already,
Now I'll bring him to th'hammer. Oh direful
     misprision,   80
I will not imitate things glorious
No more than base; I'll be mine own example.
(*To* SERVANT) On, on, and look thou represent, for
     silence,
The thing thou bear'st.

Exeunt.

Scene 5

Enter CARDINAL with a book.

CARDINAL   I am puzzled in a question about hell:
He says, in hell there's one material fire,
And yet it shall not burn all men alike.
Lay him by. How tedious is a guilty conscience!
When I look into the fishponds in my garden   5
Methinks I see a thing armed with a rake
That seems to strike at me.

Enter BOSOLA and SERVANT with ANTONIO's body.

Now! Art thou come? Thou look'st ghastly:
There sits in thy face some great determination,
Mixed with some fear.

BOSOLA   Thus it lightens into action: 10
I am come to kill thee.

CARDINAL   Ha? Help! Our guard!

BOSOLA   Thou art deceived, they are out of thy howling.

CARDINAL   Hold: and I will faithfully divide
Revenues with thee.

BOSOLA   Thy prayers and proffers
Are both unseasonable.

217

5.5 *The courtiers hear the Cardinal crying for help but think he is just testing them, as he said he would. The Marquis of Pescara, however, decides to find out what is happening*

16 **confined** restricted

s.d. ***above*** *At the Blackfriars and Globe the courtiers entered on the upper stage – the balcony where the musicians sat.*

19 **My...rescue!** I'll swap my dukedom for rescue! *(see note below)*

24 **But...honour** *see their promise at 5.4.11–12*

28 **accent** tone

29 **howsoever** in any case

engines tools

30 **aloof** at a distance

Cardinal

19 *My...rescue!* This recalls Richard III's famous line at the Battle of Bosworth by Shakespeare (5.4): 'A horse! a horse! my kingdom for a horse!' (the play was published in 1597). In Webster's source the Cardinal had passed on his dukedom to his younger brother, Ferdinand, but perhaps Webster couldn't resist this echo.

Performance

The courtiers' lines are often cut completely or abbreviated, especially as it's difficult to stage if Bosola fails to kill the Cardinal for such a long time. It's worth trying to act out the whole of this final scene to see how it might work, and then to discuss if Webster either is incompetent as regards stagecraft, or was intending it to be inept and maybe deliberately wanted audience laughter – or if 400 years later it's impossible to know what worked then.

CARDINAL	Raise the watch!　　　　　15
	We are betrayed!
BOSOLA	I have confined your flight:
	I'll suffer your retreat to Julia's chamber,
	But no further.
CARDINAL	Help! We are betrayed!

Enter PESCARA, MALATESTE, RODERIGO and GRISOLAN, above.

MALATESTE	Listen.
CARDINAL	My dukedom, for rescue!
RODERIGO	Fie upon his counterfeiting.
MALATESTE	Why, 'tis not the Cardinal.
RODERIGO	Yes, yes, 'tis he:　　　　　20
	But I'll see him hanged ere I'll go down to him.
CARDINAL	Here's a plot upon me! I am assaulted! I am lost
	Unless some rescue!
GRISOLAN	He doth this pretty well,
	But it will not serve to laugh me out of mine
	honour.
CARDINAL	The sword's at my throat!
RODERIGO	You would not bawl so loud then.　25
MALATESTE	Come, come, let's go to bed, he told us thus much
	aforehand.
PESCARA	He wished you should not come at him, but
	believe't,
	The accent of the voice sounds not in jest.
	I'll down to him, howsoever, and with engines
	Force ope the doors.

Exit.

RODERIGO	Let's follow him aloof,　　　30
	And note how the Cardinal will laugh at him.

Exeunt above.

5.5 *Bosola kills the servant and shows the dead body of Antonio to the Cardinal, whom he then wounds with his sword*

36 **Antonio?** *It is surprising that the Cardinal has either not commented on Antonio's dead body until now, or not noticed it until now.*

38–39 **Thou...sword** *The figure of Justice in paintings or sculpture traditionally has a sword in one hand, and a* **balance** *(= pair of scales) in the other, in order to weigh right and wrong.*

39 **Oh mercy!** *He echoes his sister as she died (4.2.352).*

40–42 **thy greatness...thee** *from Sidney's* Arcadia

43 **leveret** young hare *(a feeble animal not worth hunting)*

45 **alarum** alarm: the call to arms

46 **vaunt-guard** vanguard

47 **honour of arms** *perhaps:* privileges granted to the defeated

49–50 **The devil?...party?** *perhaps:* Are you the devil? Because my brother wouldn't fight on the enemy's side.

Bosola

32–34 Bosola kills the servant. He has murdered again, so was there any point in his tears and repentance at the Duchess's death? Is this what he meant at 5.4.81–82: *I'll be mine own example?*

Cardinal

39 Lee Bliss notes that the Cardinal echoes the Duchess 'just before Bosola stabs him. The Cardinal, of course, is selfishly begging for the life he has so thoroughly forfeited, but his cry reminds us of those larger questions of value which the play has raised. Is there a place for mercy or love in this world?'

Ferdinand

45–48 *Give me a fresh horse!* (45) is an echo of 'Give me another horse' (5.3) – the line Shakespeare gives Richard before the Battle of Bosworth when he wakes at midnight from a nightmare, abused by the ghosts of those he has murdered. The first audiences would have felt the echo even more since Ferdinand was played by the same actor who played Richard III – Richard Burbage. Ferdinand's mad belief that he is on a battlefield also ironically recalls his desire in the first scene of the play to fight in a real battle instead of in a courtly game (1.1.93–94).

BOSOLA   There's for you first –

He kills the SERVANT.

              'Cause you shall not unbarricade the door
              To let in rescue.

CARDINAL   What cause hast thou to pursue my life?

BOSOLA   Look there.   35

CARDINAL   Antonio?

BOSOLA   Slain by my hand unwittingly.
              Pray, and be sudden. When thou kill'dst thy sister
              Thou took'st from Justice her most equal balance
              And left her nought but her sword.

CARDINAL   Oh mercy!

BOSOLA   Now it seems thy greatness was only outward,   40
              For thou fall'st faster of thyself than calamity
              Can drive thee. I'll not waste longer time – there!

Wounds the CARDINAL.

CARDINAL   Thou hast hurt me.

BOSOLA   Again!

Wounds him again.

CARDINAL   Shall I die like a leveret
              Without any resistance? Help! Help! Help!
              I am slain!

Enter FERDINAND.

FERDINAND   Th'alarum? Give me a fresh horse!   45
              Rally the vaunt-guard, or the day is lost!
              Yield! Yield! I give you the honour of arms,
              Shake my sword over you. Will you yield?

CARDINAL   Help me! I am your brother.

FERDINAND   The devil?

5.5 *As the Cardinal and Bosola struggle, Ferdinand stabs both of them. Bosola then kills Ferdinand*

51 **ransom** *It was normal to seek ransom money for nobles captured in war.*

55–57 **Caesar's...disgrace** *from Whetstone (see note to 3.2.23–31). Webster's first-known play was about Julius Caesar. Pompey and Caesar ruled Rome from 60 BC but they fell out and Caesar defeated Pompey in 48 BC; the latter fled to Egypt and was murdered. Caesar was assassinated in Rome at the feet of a statue of Pompey.*

60 **barber** *Barbers also performed minor surgery and pulled teeth.*

66 **broken winded** *a disordered breathing in horses (treated with wet hay)*

67 **dog-kennel** *recalls Bosola's* **dog days** *(1.1.39)*

68 **vault credit** leap over my reputation

affect seek

high luxurious

72–73 **'Whether...dust'** *i.e. as diamonds can only be cut by other diamonds, so humans fall because of a fault in their own natures (the rhyme suggests that Ferdinand fell through lust for his sister)*

75 **hold...teeth** *from Montaigne's* Essays

77 **pyramid** *a symbol of pride as well as of a great ruin, in which the Egyptian pharaohs had hoped to live for ever – but they rotted into 'nothing' just as the Cardinal will (see line 90)*

'Oh my sister' (5.5.71): Ferdinand (Will Keen) dies against the glass screen as the ghost of his sister (Janet McTeer) watches (National Theatre, 2003)

Language

72–73 Michael Neill says the word *dust* is 'a metonymy for the sinful nature of humanity' (a metonymy is a figure of speech in which one part of a thing is used to stand for the whole thing, e.g. 'the stage' stands for the theatrical profession). But, Neill adds, 'uttered as Ferdinand's last word it is bound to suggest the dust to which his body is about to be consigned; it signals that same ignoble collapse into the undifferentiation of the grave that Bosola, with grim satisfaction, announces for the Cardinal: *I do glory...nothing* [76–79]'.

My brother fight upon the adverse party? 50
There flies your ransom!

He wounds the CARDINAL and, in the scuffle, gives BOSOLA his death wound.

CARDINAL   Oh justice!
I suffer now for what hath former been:
'Sorrow is held the eldest child of sin.'

FERDINAND   Now you're brave fellows: Caesar's fortune was 55
harder than Pompey's, Caesar died in the arms of
prosperity, Pompey at the feet of disgrace: you both
died in the field. The pain's nothing: pain, many
times, is taken away with the apprehension of
greater – as the toothache with the sight of a barber 60
that comes to pull it out. There's philosophy
for you.

BOSOLA   Now my revenge is perfect: sink, thou main cause
Of my undoing! The last part of my life
Hath done me best service. 65

He kills FERDINAND.

FERDINAND   Give me some wet hay, I am broken winded.
I do account this world but a dog-kennel:
I will vault credit and affect high pleasures
Beyond death.

BOSOLA   He seems to come to himself
Now he's so near the bottom. 70

FERDINAND   My sister! Oh my sister, there's the cause on't!
'Whether we fall by ambition, blood, or lust,
Like diamonds we are cut with our own dust.'

Dies.

CARDINAL   Thou hast thy payment too.

BOSOLA   Yes, I hold my weary soul in my teeth, 75
'Tis ready to part from me. I do glory
That thou, which stood'st like a huge pyramid
Begun upon a large and ample base,
Shalt end in a little point, a kind of nothing.

The courtiers arrive to find the Cardinal dying and Bosola fatally wounded. Bosola tells them what happened, and dies

85 **in the main** in the most important part

89 **rushes** *Fresh rushes were often used as a floor covering (including on the stage) for cleanliness, warmth, cushioning, and to disguise unpleasant smells.*

91 **withstand** resist; oppose

94 **mist** *an important word in this play, punned on in the next line; perhaps it*

sums up Webster's world *(see also 4.2.187)*

97 **dead walls** *see 5.2.337*

103 **stagger in distrust** hesitate; waver with doubts

105 **Mine...voyage** echoes the Duchess's reference to Charon's boat *(3.5.105)*

Bosola

81–87 'Besides the bizarre twist of the killer avenging two of his own victims, there is a risk of bathos here: after listing three murders, there is an anticlimax when he cites his own neglect as the fourth occasion for revenge' (Martin Wiggins).

92 'Bosola's definition of himself as a justified avenger is...cut across by the brutally simple summing up of his career by Malateste' (Jacqueline Pearson). But is Malateste's opinion of any value?

105 'Bosola's departure is seaward, to the galleys, to the pathless wilderness from which he entered the play, a castaway looking for solid ground to call his own' (Frank Whigham).

Language

101–102 Webster took this from Sidney's *Arcadia:* 'in such a shadow, or rather pit of darkness, the wormish mankind lives', and changed 'wormish' to *womanish*. Jacqueline Pearson comments: 'This quotation...seems to have been altered specifically to create ambiguity about the adjective "womanish", when the play's heroine has been anything but "fearful", and has died refusing to see the world as only a "pit of darkness". Bosola's flip pessimism is discredited by our memory of what has gone before: a world that has produced the Duchess and been coloured by her values might seem to be more than simply a pit of darkness.'

Ideas and interpretations

Critics and audiences have often thought the deaths in this Act are messy, almost farcical. In 1887 George Saintsbury wrote that 'the fifth act is a kind of gratuitous appendix of horrors stuck on without art or reason'. The modern critic Michael Neill, however, believes: 'It would be unwise to assume that so painstaking a craftsman arrived at this design [of Act 5] out of dramatic incompetence.' The messy deaths, he says, are instead part of the social and moral teaching of the play, especially in their contrast to the 'ceremonial formality of the Duchess's death'.

Enter PESCARA, MALATESTE, RODERIGO and GRISOLAN.

PESCARA How now, my lord?

MALATESTE Oh sad disaster.

RODERIGO How comes this? 80

BOSOLA Revenge for the Duchess of Malfi, murdered
By th'Aragonian brethren; for Antonio,
Slain by this hand; for lustful Julia,
Poisoned by this man; and lastly, for myself,
That was an actor in the main of all, 85
Much 'gainst mine own good nature, yet i'th'end
Neglected.

PESCARA How now, my lord?

CARDINAL Look to my brother.
He gave us these large wounds as we were
struggling
Here i'th'rushes. And now, I pray, let me
Be laid by, and never thought of. 90

Dies.

PESCARA How fatally, it seems, he did withstand
His own rescue!

MALATESTE Thou wretched thing of blood,
How came Antonio by his death?

BOSOLA In a mist: I know not how;
Such a mistake as I have often seen 95
In a play. Oh I am gone.
We are only like dead walls, or vaulted graves,
That ruined, yields no echo. Fare you well.
It may be pain but no harm to me, to die
In so good a quarrel. Oh this gloomy world! 100
In what a shadow, or deep pit of darkness,
Doth womanish and fearful mankind live!
Let worthy minds ne'er stagger in distrust
To suffer death or shame for what is just.
Mine is another voyage. 105

5.5 *Delio arrives with the eldest son of Antonio and the Duchess and sums up the moral of the play*

110 **armed** prepared *(note that Delio says the first and last lines of the play)*

112–113 **this...right** *This is much discussed, i.e. in Webster's source (and 3.3.70–72) the Duchess had a son by her first husband, so Antonio's son could not inherit the Dukedom, only his mother's property. See also Antonio's wish for his son (5.4.72).*

113–117 **These wretched...matter** *an important addition to Webster's theme of what is true greatness and reputation*

118–119 **Nature...truth** *adapted from Sidney's* Arcadia

120–121 **'Integrity...end'** *perhaps: The Duchess will live on for ever in people's memories because she lived a life of integrity (but there are many different views about the meaning of this couplet, and therefore about the meaning of the play)*

120 **Integrity of life** an upright and uncorrupted life *(see note below)*

121 **crown** give honour to

Ideas and interpretrations

• Lee Bliss: 'Delio's concluding assertions are as wide of the play's mark as Antonio's opening disquisition on the ideal commonwealth...The "young, hopeful gentleman" may inherit only sorrows.'
• J W Lever: The boy 'offers hope of bringing to pass that reformed order his father had longed for in the first scene of the play. In spite of the dread horoscope [2.3.56–65], despite the opposition of the stars, he has survived...A favourite Renaissance maxim declared that reason, or the wise man, overcomes the stars. The unnamed boy standing next to his father's trusted friend may perhaps be taken as a sign, however tenuous, of Webster's trust in the final triumph of reason and his ultimate belief in a better age.'

Language

120 *Integrity of life* are the first words of Ode 1.22 by the Roman poet Horace: *'Integer vitae scelerisque purus...'*: 'The man of upright life and free from sin / requires no Moorish spears nor bow / and quiver laden with poisoned / arrows... / For as I wandered free from care / singing of Lalage in Sabine / woods, unarmed, beyond my bounds, / there fled a wolf' i.e. the poet had integrity of life, so he was not attacked. Andrew Gurr therefore sees irony in the phrase since the Duchess did not escape the wolf Ferdinand: the words might suggest to some in the audience that she did *not* have *integrity of life*.

Performance

The 2003 National Theatre production began with a young boy and Delio entering on a dark stage, the only lighting on people sitting on steps that ran the full length of the stage. Repeating the beginning, Delio and the boy entered at the end. Delio referred with dismissive contempt to *These wretched eminent things* (113) – Ferdinand and the Cardinal. However, in the 1995 Cheek by Jowl production, at line 113 the 'dead' actors stood up and grouped themselves as for a photograph: the Duchess and her brothers sat on chairs, and behind them stood Bosola and Antonio. Delio's line was directed at all five of them. (See also comments about the 1995 Greenwich/Wyndham's production on page 254.)

Dies.

PESCARA   The noble Delio, as I came to th'palace,
                Told me of Antonio's being here, and showed me
                A pretty gentleman, his son and heir.

Enter DELIO with ANTONIO's son.

MALATESTE   Oh sir, you come too late.

DELIO   I heard so, and
                Was armed for't ere I came. Let us make noble use   110
                Of this great ruin; and join all our force
                To establish this young hopeful gentleman
                In's mother's right. These wretched eminent things
                Leave no more fame behind 'em than should one
                Fall in a frost and leave his print in snow: 115
                As soon as the sun shines, it ever melts,
                Both form and matter. I have ever thought
                Nature doth nothing so great, for great men,
                As when she's pleased to make them lords of truth:
                'Integrity of life is fame's best friend,   120
                Which nobly, beyond death, shall crown the end.'

                                                    Exeunt.

Webster's life and career

Almost nothing was known about John Webster until 1976. Research published that year showed that he was from a well-off London family, whose trade was making carts, wagons and the new, highly fashionable, coaches. He was born perhaps in 1578/9, so he was about fifteen years younger than Shakespeare. The family business and home was in Cow Lane (now called Smithfield Street) just outside the city wall (see map on page v). Cow Lane was well known for fortune tellers and near the huge, muddy, stinking marketplace of Smithfield – the horse, pig, sheep and cattle market where executions sometimes took place, and where the ancient and often disorderly St Bartholomew's Fair was held every August. The equally ancient St Bartholomew's Hospital and Newgate prison were nearby. Webster's father also hired out horses and vehicles – particularly for funerals; it makes sense that the family trade of the author of two plays so imbued with images of death was closely involved with funerals. It was also a trade with many dealings with blacksmiths, and Webster's maternal grandfather was a blacksmith. The family were involved in the city pageants put on by the guilds, and mixed with actors, writers and craftsmen. Several portrait painters lived in the district, some of whom were friends of the Websters (e.g. see note to 3.2.48–51), and next door was Shakespeare's printer William White.

At the age of 9 Webster probably went to the day school founded in 1561 by his father's guild, the Merchant Taylors. This was one of the leading craft guilds – known as City livery companies – that ran the City of London. Merchant Taylors' School was near London Bridge and took about 250 boys. School lasted from seven in the morning until five in the evening. Just before Webster's time it was run by a famous headmaster who believed vehemently in the importance of the English language, but boys would also have a solid education in Latin. They put on plays and were encouraged to practise sport – especially football – but tennis was banned. In 1598 Webster went on to the Middle Temple (see photograph on page 232); it was one of the four Inns of Court where students were taught law, but it was not just for those intending to be lawyers: the Inns were the third university in the land, along with Oxford and Cambridge. The critic Charles Forker calls the Middle Temple: 'an enclave of intellectual and social privilege in Renaissance London'. Young men also made useful contacts and friends. Webster's fellow playwrights John Marston and John Ford were Middle Templars, and an exact contemporary was Thomas Overbury, whose murder in 1613 was the great scandal of the day (see page 234).

Webster is known today as the sole author of three plays (*The White Devil, The Duchess of Malfi* and *The Devil's Law-Case*) and as a collaborator on about seven plays that survive (critics disagree about the plays he had a hand in). He is first heard of as a playwright in the 'Diary' (accounts book) of the theatre owner Philip Henslowe: in May 1602 Webster is listed as collaborating on a (lost) play about Julius Caesar. But two popular farces about sexual intrigues which he wrote with his friend Thomas Dekker in 1604/5 survive: *Westward Ho* and *Northward Ho*. These were performed by the fashionable boys' company at the small indoor theatre at St Paul's.

After the bad plague year of 1603, plague closed the playhouses for months every year from 1605 to 1610, which may explain why nothing is recorded as written by Webster until 1612 when *The White Devil* appeared, but he was a slow writer, and this was the first play he had written on his own. He had also got married in 1606 to Sara, the daughter of a prominent member of the Saddlers' Company, and she was pregnant – a son was born two months later; other children followed over the years. He started writing *The Duchess of Malfi* probably in 1612; it was performed in 1613/14, and, unlike his earlier play, it was a success. Charles Forker sees Bosola as 'in some respects a reworking of Flamineo' – the main male character in *The White Devil* – and says: 'Webster's fascination with such malcontent figures, impoverished intellectuals forced to degrade their talents and corrupt their integrity in the service of naked power or courtly values they despise, may have had its foundation to some extent in Webster's own life.'

At the same time as Webster's twin tragedies on murder at a royal court, two unexpected deaths occurred: the heir to the throne – later rumoured to be due to poison – and Webster's friend Sir Thomas Overbury in the Tower of London, who was later found to have been poisoned. The funeral lament that Webster wrote on Prince Henry's death was dedicated to Robert Carr, the King's 'favourite'; ironically it was later rumoured that Carr had poisoned Henry, and three years later he and his wife were found guilty of Overbury's murder (see page 234). Real life was not so very different from that in Webster's two tragedies.

Webster's other surviving play that he wrote unaided, *The Devil's Law-Case* (c. 1617), is a tragicomedy that is rarely performed. In the same year he was lampooned in a poem as 'Crabbed Websterio / The playwright, cartwright', although the cartmaking business seems to have been run by his brother after their father's death. 'Crabbed' may imply he had some deformity, or more likely that he was bad-tempered. In 1624 a Merchant Taylor was chosen as Lord Mayor and Webster was invited to write the pageant, a prestigious commission in which he at last followed playwrights such as Dekker and Middleton. He died probably in the 1630s.

An engraving of Robert Carr and Frances Howard, the Earl and Countess of Somerset, around the time of their trials for the murder of Sir Thomas Overbury in 1616

Key dates

1564 Shakespeare and Marlowe born.

1567 Mary Queen of Scots forced to abdicate in favour of her year-old son, James VI.

1576 James Burbage opens the Theatre.

c. 1578 John Webster born in London.

1587 Mary Queen of Scots executed for a treasonous plot against Elizabeth.

1601 Earl of Essex attempts coup, executed for high treason.

1602 First record of Webster as a playwright.

1603 Elizabeth I dies, aged 69, and is succeeded by her cousin James VI of Scotland as James I of England; plague: closure of the theatres.

1604 Coronation of James, who declares himself 'King of Great Britain, France and Ireland', even though England and Scotland were not a united kingdom; large number of knighthoods sold; peace treaty with Spain; Webster writes *Westward Ho* with Dekker for the Children of Paul's and expands Marston's *The Malcontent* for the King's Men.

1605 Gunpowder Plot: Catholics try to blow up Parliament and King James; Webster writes *Northward Ho* with Dekker for the Children of Paul's.

1606 First Union flag adopted; Shakespeare's *Macbeth* at the Globe.

1607 The 'flight of the earls' from Ireland: all Ireland now governed by the English.

1610 King James's cousin Lady Arbella Stuart marries secretly and is imprisoned (she dies, it is said insane, in the Tower in 1615); in Italy Galileo looks at the stars through his telescope.

1611 Authorised Version of the Bible published; new title of baronet created by James and sold to anyone who could afford it.

1612 ?January: Webster's *The White Devil* a failure at the Red Bull theatre and published; 7 November: Prince Henry dies at age of 18.

1613 February: Masques in celebration of the marriage of James's daughter Elizabeth; 29 June: Globe theatre burns down; 15 September: Sir Thomas Overbury dies in the Tower of London; 26 December: Robert Carr (now Earl of Somerset) – Overbury's friend and James's favourite – marries the newly divorced former Countess of Essex, Lady Frances Howard.

1614 Globe rebuilding completed by June; James finds new favourite: George Villiers, later made Duke of Buckingham; the only parliament called between 1610 and 1621 ('the Addled Parliament') dissolved after two months; 31 October: Ben Jonson's comedy *Bartholomew Fair* opens the Hope theatre on Bankside; first performances of *The Duchess of Malfi* at Blackfriars theatre (or late 1613).

1615 Murder trials begin for Overbury's death by poisoning; James starts selling peerages.

1616 Shakespeare dies; Earl and Countess of Somerset tried for murder of Overbury and found guilty (released from prison in 1622); Villiers made Master of the Horse.

1620 Pilgrim Fathers sail from Plymouth in the *Mayflower* to colonise America.

1623 The First Folio of Shakespeare's plays and Webster's *The Duchess of Malfi* and *The Devil's Law-Case* published.

1625   James I dies and is succeeded by Charles I; a bad plague year.
1628   Villiers' astrologer stoned to death by a London mob outside the Fortune
       theatre; Villiers assassinated a few months later.
1632   John Webster dies around this time; Countess of Somerset dies of cancer.
1642   Beginning of the First Civil War (until 1646).
1649   Charles I executed and England declared a Commonwealth.

The Blackfriars theatre

In 1614 there were six open-air amphitheatres in London – including the Red Bull in Islington some distance north of the Thames, and the Globe on the south bank of the Thames – but there was perhaps only one indoor theatre, the Blackfriars. This fashionable 'hall' theatre was just inside the city wall on the north bank of the river, a few hundred metres south-west of St Paul's Cathedral.

Webster's earlier play *The White Devil* had been performed in the winter of 1611/12 by Queen Anne's Men at the Red Bull; it was a failure. According to Webster, it was performed 'in so dull a time of winter, presented in so open and black a theatre', and the audience were 'ignorant asses'. So Webster may deliberately have written *The Duchess* for the King's Men to perform at the more exclusive Blackfriars. The King's Men (the company to which Shakespeare and the actor Richard Burbage – the first Ferdinand – belonged) also owned the Globe, where it was performed later.

Richard Burbage's father James had built the first successful open-air playhouse in London: the Theatre. Twenty years later, in 1596, James Burbage leased rooms in the old Blackfriars friary to turn into a theatre, but the residents objected, so it had been let to boy players instead. In 1609 the King's Men were at last able to use it as their winter playhouse. Apart from Burbage and Shakespeare, the partners in the Blackfriars included Henry Condell – the first Cardinal, and William Ostler – Antonio. Blackfriars attracted a wealthier and better-educated audience, as well as law students from Middle Temple – an audience who would recognise Webster's quotations from Montaigne and Sidney's *Arcadia*.

There are no contemporary drawings, but the lease suggests the theatre was in a large hall, 14 metres wide and 30 metres long, about the size of a basketball court, and a similar size to Middle Temple Hall (see photograph on page 232). The stage was at one end, and the audience sat on wooden benches in the 'pit' in front of it, and in two or three tiers of curved galleries. The theatre was all-seating and held about 600 people compared to over 2000 at the Globe, and seats cost more: the most expensive were the boxes flanking each side of the stage, and hiring a stool to sit on the stage itself. It had a different atmosphere from the Globe since both actors and audience were lit by candles; men in the audience smoked their pipes; and the need to trim the candles meant there were pauses between the acts. Plays were performed six days a week on winter afternoons. The theatre entrance may have been in the street that is still today called Playhouse Yard, and there were complaints about traffic jams from the large number of coaches!

The Blackfriars theatre

The Blackfriars theatre was remodelled out of the upper floor of a stone building, 'the Parliament Chamber', in the friary that had belonged to the Dominican friars since the thirteenth century (they were preaching friars who wore black robes). They had been forced to surrender it to Henry VIII in 1538 at the dissolution of the monasteries, when England turned towards Protestantism and away from Roman Catholicism, which had been England's faith for a thousand years. Some of the friars' buildings had been demolished; others were turned into residences or offices. The echo scene (5.3) must have had a particular resonance here – especially to those in the audience who had not given up their Catholic faith – because on one side of the theatre was the friars' cloister, and on the other side the river. Also, the friary was the burial site of distinguished people, and in 1529 this great hall was the courtroom for the divorce case against Henry VIII's first queen, the Spanish Catholic Catherine of Aragon, where she made a dramatic appeal for justice on her knees before the King.

The success of the King's Men at the Blackfriars marked the end of the open-air 'amphitheatres' and began a new tradition of theatre building that has lasted for over three hundred years.

The sixteenth-century Middle Temple Hall in 2002 during a performance of Twelfth Night by Shakespeare's Globe company. This was the 400th anniversary of the play performed here by Shakespeare and his company. Webster may well have been in the original audience; the Hall was his schoolroom and where he dined. It also gives an idea of the type of hall the Blackfriars theatre used, though the actors would instead have acted on a raised stage at one end of the hall, and not in the round

Social, historical and literary context

James I and his court

The peaceful accession of a Protestant family man as King in 1603 – especially after over forty years of one woman's reign – was a matter of celebration (James and Queen Anne had two sons and one daughter). But a backlash followed when English wealth and offices were handed to Scottish favourites. The London playwrights Jonson, Chapman and Marston were imprisoned in 1605 for anti-Scottish jokes in *Eastward Ho*. Elizabeth's court had its fair share of corruption and scandals, but contemporaries believed James's court was worse. In one aspect it was – Elizabeth had kept a tight grip on expenditure, but James and Anne threw money around, as Simon Schama in his *History of Britain* (2001) describes:

> Lands, monopolies, offices, jewels, houses were all showered on favourites, who then took their cue from the king by themselves spending colossally more than they could afford. The entire court culture was drunk on spending, and there was plenty to spend it on: elaborate masques (average cost £1400 a year) devised by Ben Jonson and Inigo Jones... The craze for conspicuous waste was contagious.

James constantly needed money and one successful way of raising it was to sell titles and even create new titles to sell: thus in his reign there were 32 new earls, 19 viscounts, 56 knight baronets (a new title) and 800 new knights (at £30 a head). Cash payment was replacing the old feudal ties; titles were debased – they were no longer a sign of greatness. Webster dedicated the first printing of *The Duchess* in 1623 to Baron Berkeley – the 22-year-old grandson of Lord Hunsdon, patron of the King's Men in Elizabeth's reign – with the significant words: 'My Noble Lord I do not altogether look up at your title, the ancientest nobility being but a relic of time past, and the truest honour indeed being for a man to confer honour on himself, which your learning strives to propagate and shall make you arrive at the dignity of a great example.'

One funeral and a wedding

Henry, Prince of Wales, heir to the throne, died suddenly in November 1612 of typhoid fever. He was 18 – handsome, athletic, patron of scientists and actors, the hope of the nation. It was a devastating blow for many, including his grief-stricken father. The critic Charles Forker believes that Henry was one of Webster's 'special heroes': 'Prince Henry had been an honorary Merchant Taylor, had been feasted by the company at their hall in 1607, and, only a year before his untimely death, had presented "Two brace of fatt bucks" to the fraternity.' Webster probably interrupted his work on *The Duchess* to write his long funeral poem, *A Monumental Column*, published in 1613. The critic Michael Neill says: 'The two [play and poem] are very much companion pieces. Like the play, the poem is a meditation on the transience of worldly pride, and a celebration of the Fame that the memorializing genius of poetry alone can render immortal.' Neill also says that the poem's contempt for worldly greatness is similar to Delio's last speech about 'wretched eminent things' (see 5.5.113–117), and that 'Prince Henry's death…seems to have supplied the emotional impulse for this most elegiac of Jacobean tragedies.'

Three months later, in February 1613, the extravagant marriage celebrations for James's daughter Elizabeth – to the Protestant Elector Palatine of Germany – broke the sombre mood of the court, and there were plays and masques, as well as running at the ring on horseback. King James took the ring upon his lance several times, as did the new heir, 12-year-old Prince Charles, mounted on a Spanish jennet (see note to 1.1.120).

Scandal and poison

James's sexual preferences were for men. His relationship with his former page Robert Carr blossomed in 1607 when the 20-year-old Scot broke his leg at a tournament. James, who was then in his early forties, helped nurse him, and over the next few years heaped money and titles on him – in 1613 Carr was made Earl of Somerset. Unfortunately James also involved the ill-educated Carr in state affairs, but the young man received help in his new administrative duties from a more able friend – and probable lover – Thomas Overbury, who was about five years older. (Perhaps Webster is referring in *The Duchess* to the way England is being ruled: e.g. see the notes to 1.1.4–22 and 11–22.) Overbury was from a Gloucestershire family, and after Oxford had completed his education at Middle Temple Hall at the same time as Webster. A quarrelsome, arrogant man, Overbury was praised for his literary talent by the playwright Ben Jonson – who later quarrelled with him. Overbury wrote several character sketches (such as 'The Courtier' and 'The Virtuous Widow' – who does not think of remarrying), a literary genre popular in the seventeenth century. They were published in 1614 after his death and went through many reprints, with additional 'characters' written by Webster, among others.

Overbury was knighted in 1608 and became the most powerful man at court after Carr – until Carr decided to marry the beautiful Frances Howard, Countess of Essex (see photograph on page 229). In 1613, at the age of 22, she was scandalously granted an annulment from her first husband on the grounds of his impotency due to witchcraft. Overbury was against the marriage: he quarrelled with Carr, refused the post of ambassador to Russia (see note to 5.2.48), was imprisoned in the Tower of London, and died there in agony three months before the sumptuous wedding of Frances to the newly created Earl of Somerset in December 1613. But two years later the Countess was under house arrest at Blackfriars, accused of dabbling in black magic and poison, and in 1616 she was found guilty of murdering Overbury by sending him poisoned tarts and jellies, as well as an enema of mercury sublimate. (There are many references to poison in *The Duchess*, e.g. 1.1.13–14.) She and her husband – who insisted he was innocent – were imprisoned for six years. Mrs Anne Turner, a widow who was the Countess's confidante, was hanged at Tyburn in 1615 as an accessory to the murder. Before her death she blamed the decadence and debauchery of King James's court:

Oh the court, the court! God bless the King and send him better servants about him, for there is no religion in the most of them, but malice, pride, whoredom, swearing and rejoicing in the fall of others. It is so wicked a place as I wonder the earth did not open and swallow it up.

Women

Women were believed to be inferior to men, and female power was generally seen as a deviation from the natural order, but in the sixteenth century there were three female monarchs in Britain: Henry VIII's daughters Mary Tudor and Elizabeth, and in Scotland their cousin, Mary Queen of Scots (James I's mother Mary Stuart). The main problem was if a female ruler married, since a wife was expected to submit to her husband. Elizabeth I had solved this problem by remaining unmarried; Mary Tudor's marriage to the Spanish king Philip II was unpopular but short-lived and without issue; Mary Stuart's liaisons were disastrous – but had produced King James. (See, for example, notes on pages 48 and 88.)

Marriage was a social and economic contract (e.g. see notes to 1.1.303–305 and 5.1.46). Women might be forced into marriage – often because of property and money – but in this period it was beginning to be seen that marriage should instead be for companionship: as a partnership of love (e.g. see note to 2.4.79–83). And, although women were dominated by men, Juliet Dusinberre in her book *Shakespeare and the Nature of Women* (2nd edition 1996) comments:

> The great advances in women's history in the past twenty years have fleshed out a picture which complicates the simple reading of early modern patriarchy as a society in which women were subject to male authority. Of course they were, but they also had their own modes of challenging that authority. Haven't we all?

Witchcraft and astrology

Witches were believed to be in alliance with the Devil and derive their power from him. There was a witch-craze across Europe in this period, but it was on a much smaller scale in England. In Scotland King James became obsessed by witches at the time of the North Berwick witch trials in 1590–1; in 1597 he wrote a tract on the subject, the *Daemonologie*, in which he wrote of witches using wax images and raising storms. The modern historian John Walter says one reason why it was usually women who were accused of witchcraft was because of 'the threat that solitary women were thought to pose to a society in which women were expected to be subordinated to either father or husband'. The white witch – the cunning man or wise woman – was often assisted by a 'familiar' (a spirit in the form of an animal). Witches were asked for charms to find lost goods, for example, or ease toothache. Love potions were especially popular, but the penalty for using witchcraft to provoke unlawful love was one year's imprisonment, and from 1604 the penalty for a second offence was death. In 1612 there was a famous witch trial in Lancashire. The twenty-one defendants were aged between 9 and 80 years, and were mainly female of poor village backgrounds. Ten were hanged. An account of the trial was published by Thomas Potts, the London-based clerk of the court, in 1613. (See, for example, notes on page 40 (Old Lady) and to 2.5.47–48 and 66–70.)

Like the belief in witchcraft, belief in astrology (e.g. see 2.3) was also, in John Walter's words, 'an attempt to master a hostile and unpredictable universe'. Astrology was increasingly under attack in the seventeenth century, but virtually everybody believed in it. When there was an important decision to make, a person would consult an astrologer, not a clergyman, and many people had their children's horoscopes cast at birth. Annual almanacs sold in their thousands: costing one or two pence, they contained lists of lucky and unlucky days and predictions for the future. Astrology also played a large part in medical diagnoses. Gamini Salgado in his book *The Elizabethan Underworld* says that some astrological doctors did not need to even see the patient: 'they could determine what was wrong with him merely by examining a specimen of his urine taken at a specified time'. People from all social classes made appointments with astrologers to find the most auspicious time to do something, to get answers to marital questions (such as whether a woman was a virgin, or would remain faithful, or which man was the father of a child), who would win a lawsuit, and perhaps most often to help catch a thief and retrieve stolen goods. One well-known London astrologer was Simon Forman, who died in 1611. He also practised as a doctor and alchemist and seduced a number of his female clients. Four years after his death he featured in the Overbury murder trial since he had made love potions and magical figures to help Frances Howard attract the love of Robert Carr; she was certainly not the only court lady he had helped with their love affairs. (This is particularly relevant for Ferdinand's question about love potions, see 3.1.59–77.)

Plague and anatomy

The plague had an enormous impact, not only on people's personal lives, but also on how they viewed life and death (e.g. see 4.1.99). In the first quarter of the seventeenth century there were outbreaks of plague in London almost every year, with corpses sometimes carried by the wagonload to burial pits. A particularly bad outbreak in 1603 postponed James I's coronation for a year. In Webster's parish almost 2000 died of plague between July and December. Those who could, fled the capital; most had nowhere to go.

Ferdinand's threat to the doctor, to 'flay off his skin to cover one of the anatomies this rogue hath set i'th'cold yonder – in Barber-Surgeons' Hall' (5.2.79–81) whisks the play from northern Italy to central London, and highlights a rediscovered science that was having a cultural impact beyond medicine: anatomy. Barber-Surgeons' Hall is in Monkwell Square, just north of the city walls and less than half a mile east of the Webster family business. Barbers had performed minor surgery since the Middle Ages and their livery company combined with the surgeons to become the Barber-Surgeons' Company in 1540.

The critic Michael Neill believes that the trauma of plague combined with the science of anatomy 'to produce an entirely new understanding of the human body'.

Medieval anatomy lessons had been largely book-based, but the Flemish physician Andreas Vesalius (1514–64) insisted on dissecting in person. His book, *De Humani Corporis Fabrica*, Neill says: 'is acknowledged as one of the founding masterpieces of modern Western medicine; but, as critics have increasingly begun to recognize, it is also a key document in the larger cultural history of the period.' It had an impact on plays such as *The Duchess*, which 'is haunted by images of grotesque anatomical disclosure', especially in Bosola's meditations and Ferdinand's actions after the Duchess's death. There were public dissections in Europe from the mid sixteenth century onwards which attracted large audiences. Barber-Surgeons' Hall was licensed to conduct four dissections of the bodies of criminals a year, and it seems likely that Webster attended at least one of these.

The sources of *The Duchess of Malfi*

Webster found the story in William Painter's collection of translations into English, *Palace of Pleasure* (1567). Painter translated the story from a French version by Belleforest, who had expanded it from one of Bandello's Italian short stories. And Matteo Bandello (1485–1561), who had fled to France and been made a bishop, wrote about events that had actually happened; he may even have been the real Delio. The real Antonio Bologna, household steward of the Duchess of Amalfi, was murdered in Milan in 1513. A few months earlier, Antonio's wife – Giovanna d'Aragona, Duchess of Amalfi – had mysteriously disappeared with their two children. She had an elder brother, the Cardinal of Aragon, and another brother who had taken his brother's title of Marquis when the former had become Cardinal. In Bandello's account the Duchess's two brothers had their sister and her two children strangled for marrying beneath herself.

Webster made many changes and additions to Painter's story, but perhaps the most important were creating Bosola as a major character, and changes in the character of the Duchess (Painter's version is more or less the same as Belleforest's):
* In Painter's tale, Bosola appears, briefly, only at the end as Antonio's assassin. Webster created his Bosola out of many characters in Painter's story, including unnamed spies in the Duchess's household and her prison tormenter.
* There are many moralising comments by Painter deploring the Duchess's actions (e.g. see note to 3.2.304–315). Even if it is perhaps not clear whether Webster approved or not of the Duchess's marriage, his attitude to the Duchess is not one of moral condemnation. The critic J W Lever, however, believes that Painter's views were perhaps not really that different from Webster's, because the 'short pietistic insertions in Painter's story…are to be found in all this class of *novelle* published with an eye to the new reading public. The object…was to provide a sop for the more strait-laced members of the middle class.'

Webster used another source for Ferdinand's lycanthropy: a translation published in 1607 of *Admirable and Memorable Histories* by the French theologian and historian Simon Goulart who had fled from religious persecution to Geneva. Perhaps Webster had also seen the play about Antonio and the Duchess by the prolific Spanish playwright Lope de Vega. What is certain is that he took many ideas and phrases (for

3.2 onwards) from Sidney's *Arcadia*. Sir Philip Sidney, poet and soldier, died in battle against the Spanish at the age of 31, two years before the English defeat of the Spanish Armada in 1588. He became a national hero. *Arcadia* is a prose pastoral romance, with some poems; it was published after his death in 1593 and reprinted in 1613. About forty 'borrowings' have been noted.

Another author that Webster borrowed from was the French writer Michel de Montaigne, whom he quoted about nineteen times. Montaigne (1533–92) invented essays as a literary form. In the 1580s he published his *Essays* on subjects as diverse as 'On vehicles' and 'On physiognomy' – which were a portrait of himself as he searched for the truth. They were first translated into English by John Florio, an Italian Protestant refugee and friend of Sidney and possibly Shakespeare.

In the Renaissance there were different attitudes to using such quotations, which today we are scrupulous in acknowledging. Rupert Brooke writing a hundred years ago perhaps sums up the general attitude today: 'as a rule he weaves in his quotations extraordinarily well; they become part of the texture of the play, adding richness of hue and strength of fabric'.

Masques and antimasques

It is said that *The Duchess* has many effects that come from masques and antimasques – in particular 4.2, beginning with the entry of the masquers (the madmen). Masques were traditional forms of courtly entertainment involving dancing, singing and poetry, with characters often from classical mythology. In James I's reign they evolved into spectacular presentations with vast amounts of money spent on sets, special effects and costumes. They involved some professional actors, but the stars were the courtiers who took part in them, especially Queen Anne and her ladies. The masques celebrated harmony and order under the reign of the King, and many were a collaboration between Ben Jonson (who wrote the script) and Inigo Jones (who designed the set and costumes).

The antimasque was a recent development and acted as a contrast to what followed in the masque, such as contrasting ugliness with beauty. Jonson's *The Masque of Queens*, devised for Anne in 1609, began with an antimasque of twelve witches (who danced to infernal music) because, Jonson said, they were 'the opposites to good Fame', which was represented by twelve beautiful queens at the start of the masque proper. The antimasque in Thomas Campion's *The Lords' Masque* for the marriage of Princess Elizabeth in 1613 included a troop of madmen led by 'Mania'.

Plays with similar themes

Webster's *The White Devil* (1612), a masterpiece written just before *The Duchess of Malfi*, has been seen as a 'twin tragedy' as it is similar in theme, structure, characterisation and imagery. Set also in Italy, the central characters are the Machiavellian Flamineo and his sister Vittoria, who is tried for adultery and murder. There are deaths, madness, poisonings, a ghost, revenge, and some remorse.

Critics of *The Duchess* often find similarities in Shakespeare's tragedies *Hamlet* (c. 1601), *Troilus and Cressida* (c. 1602), *Othello* (c. 1603) and *Antony and Cleopatra* (c. 1606), all of which Webster probably saw on stage. For example, there are parallels between Desdemona in *Othello* and the Duchess: both defy male relatives to marry a man of their own choosing; both are killed for supposedly sexual crimes. And Michael Neill sees parallels between the deaths of the protagonists in *Antony and Cleopatra* and in *The Duchess* (see Further reading).

John Marston's *The Malcontent* (1603) exposes court corruption, lust and greed, but this time as a tragicomedy, so although it has attempted poisonings and murders, no one dies. The 'malcontent' hero – who believes 'Man is the slime of this dung-pit' – spends much of the play in disguise as an assassin, and wins back his dukedom and wife. The poet Rupert Brooke said of Marston: 'Filth, horror, and wit were his legacy; it was a splendid one.'

The Revenger's Tragedy (1606), by either Cyril Tourneur or Thomas Middleton, shows the rottenness of the court, in which the central character disguised as a malcontent is hired to commit a murder and tricks the Duke into kissing a poisoned skull; most of the characters kill one another.

Middleton's tragedy *Women Beware Women* (c. 1621) is set in Florence and involves incest, forced marriage, corruption at court and poison, and also ends in the death of most of the characters.

The Changeling (1622), by Middleton and William Rowley, has many parallels with *The Duchess*. The 'heroine', Beatrice-Joanna, is also an aristocratic lady but this time she is wooed by her steward (who is also the villain of the piece) after he has killed her intended husband – on her orders. The villain, 'honest De Flores', has parallels with Bosola, and is said to be a deliberate reworking of Shakespeare's Iago.

John Ford, Webster's friend, wrote a famous tragedy involving incestuous love: *'Tis Pity She's a Whore* (c. 1630). In the final scene the brother kills his sister and enters with her heart on his dagger. It is Ford's most famous play. A less well-known play by him, *The Broken Heart*, is another Stuart tragedy which focuses on a woman.

Criticism

In the eighteenth and nineteenth centuries, critics were often hostile to Webster. Although the Duchess herself was admired, critics condemned the horrors of the play, which had 'no conceivable purpose except to make our flesh creep', as the theatre critic William Archer wrote in 1893. In particular, Act 5 was viewed as incompetent. But there were critics, beginning with Charles Lamb, who admired the power of the play and, above all, Webster's language. Since the late nineteenth century, Act 5 has been re-evaluated as an integral part of Webster's purpose, and more recently feminist critics have illuminated Webster's choice of a woman as his main protagonist. In the last few decades, the study of the play against its social, cultural and political background has cast light on such concerns as the status of women, death, religion, social mobility, and corruption and power at King James's court.

Criticism

Charles Lamb, 1808

The London-born writer Charles Lamb was briefly in a mental asylum at the age of 20, and shortly afterwards his sister Mary killed their mother (in 1796). Lamb's influential anthology, *Specimens of English Dramatic Poets who Lived about the Time of Shakespeare*, began a new appreciation of Webster after his neglect in the eighteenth century. In this extract Lamb writes about the suffering and death of the Duchess in Act 4. (His two quotations are from *Othello* 3.3 and Webster's *The White Devil* 3.2.)

> To move a horror skilfully, to touch a soul to the quick, to lay upon fear as much as it can bear, to wean and weary a life till it is ready to drop and then step in with mortal instruments to take its last forfeit: this only a Webster can do. Writers of an inferior genius may 'upon horror's head horrors accumulate' but they cannot do this. They mistake quantity for quality, they 'terrify babes with painted devils' but they know not how a soul is capable of being moved; their terrors want dignity, their affrightments are without decorum.

Rupert Brooke, 1916

The poet Rupert Brooke died in the early years of World War I aged 27. At Cambridge University he helped found the Marlowe Dramatic Society. His dissertation, *John Webster and the Elizabethan Drama*, was written in 1911–12 and won him a fellowship at King's College, Cambridge. It was published after his death.

From Chapter 4:

> It is often discussed if the plots of *The White Devil* and *The Duchess of Malfi* are weak. Webster's method does not really take cognisance of a plot in the ordinary sense of the word. He is too atmospheric...
>
> The end is a maze of death and madness. Webster's supreme gift is the blinding revelation of some intense state of mind at a crisis, by some God-given phrase. All the last half of *The Duchess of Malfi* is full of them. The mad Ferdinand, stealing across the stage in the dark, whispering to himself, with the devastating impersonality of the madman, 'Strangling is a very quiet death,' is a figure one may not forget. And so in the next scene, the too sane Cardinal:
>
>> How tedious is a guilty conscience!
>> When I look into the fish-ponds in my garden
>> Methinks I see a thing armed with a rake
>> That seems to strike at me.
>
> It is one of those pieces of imagination one cannot explain, only admire.
>
> But it is, of course, in or near the moment of death that Webster is most triumphant. He adopts the romantic convention, that men are, in the second of death, most essentially and significantly themselves. ...Webster, more than any man in the world, has caught the soul just in the second of its decomposition in death, when knowledge seems transcended, and the darkness closes in, and boundaries fall away. ...So in this play Ferdinand 'seems to come to himself,' as

Bosola says, 'now he's so near the bottom.' He is still half-mad; but something of the old overweening claim on the universe fires up in the demented brain: 'Give me some wet hay... / I will vault credit and affect high pleasures / Beyond death.'

From Chapter 5:

This essence [the essence of Webster and of his work] generally presents itself more or less in the form of a view of the universe, recognisable rather by its emotional than by its logical content. The world called Webster is a peculiar one. It is inhabited by people driven, like animals, and perhaps like men, only by their instincts, but more blindly and ruinously. Life there seems to flow into its forms and shapes with an irregular abnormal and horrible volume. That is ultimately the most sickly, distressing feature of Webster's characters, their foul and indestructible vitality. It fills one with the repulsion one feels at the unending soulless energy that heaves and pulses through the lowest forms of life. They kill, love, torture one another blindly and without ceasing. A play of Webster's is full of the feverish and ghastly turmoil of a nest of maggots. Maggots are what the inhabitants of this universe most suggest and resemble. The sight of their fever is only alleviated by the permanent calm, unfriendly summits and darknesses of the background of death and doom. For that is equally a part of Webster's universe. Human beings are writhing grubs in an immense night. And the night is without stars or moon. But it has sometimes a certain quietude in its darkness; but not very much.

T S Eliot, 1920

The Anglo-American poet and dramatist T S Eliot was, like Rupert Brooke, an admirer of Webster's language. The extracts below are from an article he wrote after seeing a production of the play and from his poem 'Whispers of Immortality', which he wrote during World War I.

I have not yet spoken of one very important reason why Webster's plays, in spite of their loose construction and incoherences, give a greater effect of unity than those of his contemporaries, and that is his greater gift of language... Webster has a natural overflowing gift for language, conspicuous in a time of rich and surprising phrase... the poet of whom he most reminds us, in this gift of startling phrase, is John Donne. In comparing Webster to a poet who was not a dramatist, I do not mean to suggest that the value of his writing lies in the poetry and *not* in the drama. His verse is essentially dramatic verse, written for the theatre by a man with a very acute sense of the theatre. The later Elizabethan and the Jacobean poetry is forever brooding upon the more terrifying aspect of death, of the death of evil-doers, and of physical mortification and corruption... but in Donne, and to a less degree in the plays of Webster, there is a spiritual terror as well.

From: 'Whispers of Immortality'

Webster was much possessed by death
And saw the skull beneath the skin;
And breastless creatures under ground
Leaned backward with a lipless grin.

Daffodil bulbs instead of balls
Stared from the sockets of the eyes!
He knew that thought clings round dead limbs
Tightening its lusts and luxuries.

Kenneth Tynan, 1960

[Guardian News Service Limited: an extract from *The Duchess of Malfi* by Kenneth Tynan
published in *The Observer* (18th December 1960) © Observer]

Tynan was a drama critic who helped change public taste in the 1950s away from
poetic drama to working-class drama, and championed new playwrights such as
Samuel Beckett; in the 1960s he was also the literary manager of the National
Theatre. The following is from a review in the *Observer* newspaper. (He refers to the
horror of the Nazi concentration camp of Belsen, liberated in 1945; for Bedlam see
note to 4.2.1–2.)

> Webster is not concerned with humanity. He is the poet of bile and brainstorm,
> the sweet singer of apoplexy; ideally, one feels, he would have had all his
> characters drowned in a sea of cold sweat. His muse drew nourishment from
> Bedlam, and might, a few centuries later, have done the same from Belsen. I
> picture him plagued with hypochondria, probably homosexual, and consumed by
> feelings of persecution – an intensely neurotic mind, in short, at large in the
> richest, most teeming vocabulary that any age ever offered to a writer.
> One imagines his contemporaries dismissing him as 'that charnel-house poet',
> much as we nowadays dub Beckett the dramatist of the dustbin. And although
> we cannot call him the inventor of the sick joke (a field in which Kyd, Marlowe
> and Shakespeare were all ahead of him), he certainly rolled back the frontiers of
> the new genre – as witness the scene in which Duke Ferdinand extends a hand
> for his sister to shake, omitting to warn her that it has lately been severed from a
> corpse. In the whole of Webster's work, scarcely an act is committed that is not
> motivated by greed, revenge or sexual rapacity.
> Yet his characters die superbly, asserting their selfhood to the last breath –
> even the least of them, such as the Duchess's maid, who expires with a sudden,
> plaintive cry of: 'I am quick with child!' Webster's people are most themselves
> when the knife, noose or potion is nearest; you might say that his plays come
> alive the closer they get to death.

Bosola

Muriel Bradbrook, 1980

[The Orion Publishing Group Ltd: an extract from *John Webster: Citizen and Dramatist* by M.C.
Bradbrook published by Weidenfeld & Nicolson Ltd (1980) © Orion Publishing Group Ltd]

Professor Bradbrook taught at Cambridge University, and died in her eighties in
1993. This extract is from her book *John Webster: Citizen and Dramatist*. (Masques

are discussed on page 238; 'litotes' = a figure of speech which uses an understatement, often for irony, e.g. 'not bad' for 'very good'.)

Bosola, the chief instrument in the Duchess's betrayal and subjection, also bears the strongest witness to her virtues. In prison he may hope, in some confused way, to save her soul if not her body from Ferdinand's damnable plan to 'bring her to despair'; but there is a collusive relation between the two men that makes the servant in some way an emanation of his lord.

Ferdinand, in such utterance – or, again, when Bosola urges the need for her penance – 'Damn her! that body of hers / While that my blood ran pure in 't was more worth / Than that which thou wouldst comfort, call'd a soul' [4.1.117–119] – and in the constant imagery of fire, blood and tempest that surrounds him, may be considered as diabolically possessed even before his madness takes over. This leaves Bosola also the prisoner of dark powers, tempted by devils in human form (as a 'scholar', he might have been once in holy orders).

Ferdinand has sworn in the bedchamber scene that he will never see the Duchess more. When Bosola meets her it is always in some form of disguise: 'vizarded' at her capture, dressed as an old man (the stage emblem for mortality), then a 'tomb maker', then playing 'the common bellman'. Whether for their effect upon her, or for relief to himself, these disguises enable Bosola to act as a kind of priest, even whilst he conducts the execution. Yet at the end he is still asking for reward from Ferdinand; he expects to be paid the rate for the job – a pension. He is cheated by the two devils who have brought him so low.

Bosola is not the same kind of Protean shape-changer as Flamineo [in *The White Devil*]; his melancholy is not assumed, and his 'antic dispositions' have more than a touch of Hamlet about them; but he is a Hamlet who cannot unpack his heart with words. However, his death speech is firmly orchestrated ('One can almost see the conductor's raised baton,' ejaculates one critic). He begins on a low note, with the unwilling murder of 'his other self', his fellow-servant and the lover of the Duchess, Antonio:

Such a mistake as I have often seen
In a play.   [5.5.95–96]

He recollects 'the dead walls or vaulted graves' where the Duchess's voice had echoed, but he hears none:

O this gloomy world!
In what a shadow or deep pit of darkness
Doth (womanish and fearful) mankind live. [5.5.100–102]

He rises to a brave sentiment, but falls away as he too feels 'Charon's boat' approach:

Let worthy minds ne'er stagger in distrust
To suffer death or shame for what is just –
Mine is another voyage. [5.5.103–105]

Then, 'staggering in distrust', he ends on this faint litotes.

He can mock his own degradation wittily – 'I think I shall shortly grow the common bier for churchyards' [5.2.309–310] – yet, with all his many roles, Bosola is never permitted the luxury of being a self. He is the masquer, in both senses: he comes with ceremony to his captive Duchess; he leads those scenes that have been generally understood as parody or inversion of a Court masque.

Michael Neill, 1997

[Oxford University Press: an extract from *Issues of Death: Mortality and Identity in English Renaissance Tragedy* by Michael Neill (1997)]

Neill is Professor of English at the University of Auckland, New Zealand. This is an extract from his book *Issues of Death: Mortality and Identity in English Renaissance Tragedy.* (For Montaigne and Webster's dedication see pages 238 and 233; Thersites is the scurrilous Greek cynic in Shakespeare's *Troilus and Cressida.*)

At one extreme of its social argument, the play sets the caste pride of the Aragonian brothers, for whom their sister's marriage of disparagement unpardonably taints 'our blood | The royal blood of Aragon and Castile' [2.5.21–23]; at the other extreme it places the sardonic levelling of Bosola, who (like many an alienated Jacobean intellectual) has made his Montaigne into a bible of degraded scepticism:

> a duke was your cousin-german, removed. Say you were descended from King Pippin, or he himself, what of this? Search the heads of the greatest rivers in the world, you shall find them but bubbles of water. Some would think the souls of princes were brought forth by some more weighty causes than those of meaner persons. They are deceived, there's the same hand to them; the like passions sway them; the same reason that makes a vicar go to law for a tithe-pig and undo his neighbours makes them spoil a whole province, and batter down goodly cities with the cannon. [2.1.110–121]

Setting aside its openly contemptuous tone, this is remarkably close to the attitudes of Webster's dedication, but Bosola's cynicism is like Thersites': in its insistence on the sameness of motive behind all human behaviour it threatens a plague of indistinction. It is in part Bosola's activity which brings Antonio to the despairing perception that 'The great are like the base; nay, they are the same' [2.3.52]; just as it is Bosola who undercuts the Duchess's last attempts to proclaim her royal self, with its echo of Anthony's heroical 'I am | Anthony yet' [Shakespeare, *Antony and Cleopatra* 3.13]:

> DUCHESS Am not I thy Duchess?
> BOSOLA Thou art some great woman sure; for riot begins to sit on thy forehead
>   (clad in grey hairs) twenty years sooner than on a merry milkmaid's…
> DUCHESS I am Duchess of Malfi still.
> BOSOLA That makes thy sleeps so broken:
>   Glories, like glow-worms, afar off shine bright,
>   But look'd to near, have neither heat nor light.
>
> [4.2.133–136, 141–144]

Yet it is precisely at this moment that Bosola chooses to cast himself in the ambiguous role of a tomb-maker whose 'trade is to flatter the dead' [4.2.146]. And there is another side to Bosola's satiric malice, which emerges, curiously enough, in the course of his attempt to persuade the Duchess to betray the identity of her husband. When she seeks to parry his effusive praise of Antonio with an evasive 'But he was basely descended' [3.2.255], Bosola comes back with what at first appears to be a piece of stock moralization, culled from the pages of Sidney's *Arcadia:* 'Will you make yourself a mercenary herald, | Rather to examine men's pedigrees than virtues?' [3.2.256–257] But the sentiment answers closely to a rankling sense of neglect in the world of courtly reward which is not at all feigned; and it is this which fuels his subsequent reflections upon Antonio's fate with an emotion powerful enough to overwhelm the Duchess's natural caution. Her confession – 'Oh, you render me excellent music... | This good one that you speak of is my husband' [3.2.271–272] – while it tells the court informer exactly what he wants to know, at the same time deals a crippling blow to his cynical composure. His reply registers genuine wonder, an emotion compounded of astonishment at this profound shock to his habitual construction of the world, as well as the simple excitement of discovery:

> Do I not dream? can this ambitious age
> Have so much goodness in't as to prefer
> A man merely for worth, without these shadows
> Of wealth, and painted honours? possible?

> [3.2.273–276]

It is true that there is a degree of comic exaggeration in what follows, as though the old sardonic Bosola were reasserting his ironic control:

> You have made your private nuptial bed
> The humble and fair seminary of peace. ...
> Should you want
> Soldiers, 'twould make the very Turks and Moors
> Turn Christians, and serve you for this act.

> [3.2.278–279, 285–287]

But it is important, if Bosola's subsequent conversion is to seem convincingly motivated, that the irony be understood for what it is – self-mockery directed at an emotion as dangerous as it is unfamiliar.

Bosola and Antonio

Jacqueline Pearson, 1980

Pearson is Professor of English Literature at the University of Manchester.

Especially interesting...are the unexpected links which are developed between two strikingly unlike characters, Antonio and Bosola. Again we expect an absolute contrast between the Duchess's virtuous husband and the man who tortures and kills her, but again as the play progresses the two come to seem more alike. The two are linked from the first minutes of the play. Antonio first introduces Bosola and helps to control the audience's response to him [1.1.23–28, 76–84]: he is on stage with Delio while Bosola first talks to the Cardinal. Both men have travelled, both have some link with France. They are associated in Ferdinand's mind [1.1.234–235]. Antonio who took the ring oftenest is linked with Bosola who holds the provisorship of the horse and who gives the Duchess apricots ripened in horse-dung. At the end of the play it is Bosola who takes the part which should have been Antonio's, bringing 'comfort' [4.1.133] to the Duchess, rebuking Ferdinand, begging the 'fair soul' [4.2.341] to return to life, imagining himself haunted by the dead woman, and even avenging her murder. Both the plays [*The Duchess* and *The White Devil*] are given coherence by these links between characters, which prevent us from making simple value-judgements. ...Antonio can be no model of virtue: he is too like the equivocal Bosola.

Duchess

R S White, 1987

[Palgrave Macmillan: an extract from 'The Moral Design of *The Duchess of Malfi*', published in *New Casebooks, The Duchess of Malfi: John Webster*, edited by Dympna Callaghan (2000)]

White is Professor of English at the University of Western Australia. Renaissance literature, he says, aimed to teach, as well as give pleasure, and he believes that is just what the play does. He says, just after this extract: 'It is what happens after her death that clinches the moral dimensions of the play.' (The German playwright Brecht wrote an adaptation of the play, which was first performed in New York in 1946.)

The Duchess of Malfi is generically unusual, even unique in Elizabethan and Jacobean tragedy. The norm of tragedy was the fall of an initially heroic man or the rise and fall of a great villain. This play is the tragedy of a virtuous woman who achieves heroism through her death. Not only this, she is inescapably a victim of others' evil and of social attitudes, rather than one undermined by inner weakness or overweening ambition. ...

This uniqueness seems to be the main reason why modern critics have had difficulty in dealing with the play. If one reads the Introduction to the most thorough edition, John Russell Brown's Revels text, we find almost strange contortions, carried out apparently without conscious knowledge, to dislodge the Duchess from centre stage: the theatrical history emphasises the fame of the leading male actors, to the extent that Brown can confidently hypothesise that 'In any reconstruction of the first performance of *The Duchess* the female parts will appear less interesting than the roles played by Lowin and Burbage about whom so much is known'. The section on 'Characters' begins with two pages on Bosola, two on Antonio, and only one half-page paragraph on the Duchess, while 'Structure' deals thoroughly with Bosola and Ferdinand. Even more telling is Brown's treatment of the play's 'Viewpoint', where he mentions only critics who dwell on Ferdinand, Antonio or Bosola. Brown is not unusual in his treatment. Rather, he follows what seems to be a well-worn critical formula or orthodoxy dating from T. S. Eliot. In death as in life the Duchess is a victim, this time of critics who understandably go on to find something distorted and even 'muddled' in the play as a whole. All that they can make of it is 'savage farce'. Immediately, scepticism must be expressed about readings of the play which turn it into an indulgence in cruelty for its own sake, an exercise in 'horrid laughter', an amoral and detached presentation of strange psychological states. Instead, since we can be sure that Webster has as part of his intention, and that the play has as part of its design, the creation of a value-system, it is reasonable and virtually necessary to acknowledge its moral terms and the centrality of the Duchess herself, in order to understand the play as a totality. ...

In fact, the plot could hardly be more emphatic as an example of the tragedy of the innocent victim. (I should stress once again that 'victim' does not require a lack of assertiveness – far from it, in this case.) The Duchess, a young widow who by inheritance of property has suddenly become a potent commodity in the eyes of her family, falls in love with her steward and marries him, thus arousing the ire of her brothers, who succeed in having her murdered. Like the rival families in *Romeo and Juliet* they suffer remorse and penitence, but unlike Shakespeare's families, they meet their deaths in ways which satisfy poetic justice. A whole society is indicted, and the Duchess's integrity and refusal to accept empty social forms fuel a cause that outlasts her mercenary persecutors. When stated so baldly the narrative is self-evidently ethically instructive, powerful in its manipulation of sympathies, and not at all problematical in its tone, which is designed to arouse anger against the Duchess's family and society at large. We can see clearly why Bertolt Brecht...would have been sufficiently attracted to the play, as one about economic alienation and class, to rewrite it, ending with the death scene of the Duchess herself. He, at least, was not distracted from the central narrative line.

Judith Haber, 1999

[Northwestern Univeristy Press: an extract from 'My Body Bestow upon My Women' by Judith Haber published in *The Space of the Feminine in The Duchess of Malfi*, from *Renaissance Drama n.s. 28* edited by Jeffrey Masten and Wendy Wall © Northwestern University Press (1999)]

Haber is an associate professor of English at Tufts University, Massachusetts. Here she discusses the Duchess's use of the word 'gossips' in the bedroom scene, when she thinks she is talking to Antonio but is overheard by Ferdinand: 'I'll assure you / You shall get no more children till my brothers / Consent to be your gossips' (3.2.65–67).

Although this word is usually glossed simply as 'godparents' (which was, indeed, its original meaning), it has resonances in this context that are difficult to ignore. As Adrian Wilson and others have noted, by the seventeenth century, the term 'had acquired a wider meaning that referred specifically to women'...: a woman's gossips were her close female friends, and, especially, those friends who were invited to a pregnant woman's lying-in... In his fascinating discussion, Wilson shows how the ceremony of childbirth, of which the gossips were an essential part, was associated with the creation of a collective female space, from which men were excluded; during the lying-in, conventional roles were reversed, female agency was privileged, and women were placed 'on top'...

One sees this reversal occurring during the Duchess's first pregnancy, when (for reasons other than the usual) all the officers are locked in their rooms, and she is given their keys, reversing the traditional enclosure of the woman that Ferdinand eventually literalizes in this play. ...Finally, of course, one must note that 'gossip' is associated with speech – and with a particular kind of speech, both feared and disdained by men: a chattering, frivolous, 'sportive' speech, rather than 'speech indeed'. In early modern contexts, even more clearly than now, 'to gossip' seems to imply 'to speak as a woman'; loosely flowing like women's bodies, similarly lacking in control and closure, 'gossiping' was the activity of all-female gatherings, and was often connected with explicit hostility to males... Most of the suggestions that I have been outlining here are brought together in the satirical defense of childbirth customs in a 1683 pamphlet, *Fifteen Real Comforts of Matrimony*. This pamphlet, which was purportedly authored by a woman and which ends with a manifesto for government by women, was written in response to an earlier, explicitly misogynist piece that detailed the woes of marriage...; the author replies to the earlier writer's complaints about the gathering of a woman's friends during her pregnancy:

> Then for Gossips to meet, nay to meet at a lying in, and not to talk, you may as well dam up the Arches of *London*-Bridge, as stop their mouths at such a time. 'Tis a time of freedom, when women, like Parliament-men, have a priviledge to talk Petty Treason. ...

In the pamphlet, the lying-in is seen as a form of carnival, a 'time of [allowed] freedom': the topsy-turvy misrule of the gossips is but licensed sport, which is ultimately not threatening to the dominant order. In *The Duchess of Malfi*, however, the sportiveness of the Duchess's circle is inseparable from its subversiveness. When Ferdinand enters (with a visual pun on 'enter'), holding up his phallic poniard to relocate the scene's climax, reassert the terms of patriarchy, and remind the Duchess whose image she 'properly' is, he seems at first not only terrifying, but also ridiculous – as if he had wandered in from another, more melodramatic play.

Ferdinand

Frank Whigham, 1985 (revised 1996)

Whigham is Professor of English at the University of Texas at Austin, USA. He is a literary theorist known as a New Historicist; that is, he believes that a text needs to be studied against its social background (such as questions of rank and gender), and he uses the study of anthropology as well as history in his analysis of a text. It has not always been taken for granted that Ferdinand has incestuous desires for the Duchess. Just before this extract Whigham says that in Jacobean England, the social elite arranged marriages very carefully in order to maintain their group status. But sometimes, for financial or other reasons, a marriage partner had to be sought from an inferior class: this was the fastest way up the social ladder for a man, and was generally treated with contempt by the elite. This social mobility, Whigham argues, has a connection with the taboo of incest. ('ascriptive' = a group in which status is based on, for example, birth and not on achievement.)

First, though, let us review the critical history of Ferdinand's incestuous desires. F. L. Lucas first addressed the possibility in 1927, though he thought it dubious. Clifford Leech presented the view more fully in 1951, in *John Webster: A Critical Study*. Leech's argument occasioned resistance from, for instance, J. R. Mulryne (in 1960), as implying too readily 'the desire to consummate the passion'. In response Leech itemized his evidence in 1963, in *Webster: The Duchess of Malfi*:

> The grossness of his language to her in Act I, the continued violence of his response to the situation, his holding back from identifying her husband and, when that identity is established, from killing him until the Duchess is dead, his momentary identification of himself with her first husband, his necrophily in Act V – all these things…seem to point in one direction.

These items are widely thought to suggest incestuous desires, but they fail to address Mulryne's doubts, nor do they link the incest motif to other elements in the play. The anthropological view of incest, emphasizing not sex relations but the maintenance of institutional forms, allows us to add to Leech's evidence, incorporate Mulryne's logic, and integrate Ferdinand's behavior with the otherwise all-embracing issue of social mobility.

My core hypothesis can be briefly stated. I read Ferdinand as a threatened aristocrat, frightened by the contamination of his supposedly ascriptive social rank, and obsessively preoccupied with its defense. When coupled with Leech's evidence, this account construes Ferdinand's incestuous inclination toward his sister as a *social posture*, of extreme and paranoid compensation – a desperate expression of the desire to evade degrading contamination by inferiors. …

The news of her liaison, a secret plucked out by his agent Bosola, brings the swollen social focus of the threat clearly into view. For Ferdinand instantly assumes massive disparagement of rank. He imagines 'some strong thigh'd bargeman; / Or one o'th'wood-yard, that can quoit the sledge, / Or toss the bar, or else some lovely squire / That carries coals up to her privy lodgings' [2.5.42–45]. …For Ferdinand, to think of invaders is to repel and degrade them: they need to be marked as base, as mere laborers, defiled as such (as workers); yet by that very fact, they are well-equipped with poles and bars, hot and potent threats of defilement. By coupling with the duchess they couple with him and contaminate him, taking his place.

Language

Hereward T Price, 1955

[The Modern Language Association of America: an extract from *The Function of Imagery in Webster* by Hereward T. Price published by PMLA 70, September 1955]

In his well-known article on the imagery of Webster, the American academic Hereward T Price here discusses Ferdinand's famous line in Act 4. (For William Archer see page 239.)

> The executioners strangle her and Ferdinand enters. Fate has given him what he demanded of her. Bosola points to the dead Duchess and says: 'She is what /

You'd have her' [4.2.255–256]. And now that Ferdinand has achieved what he has planned, he exclaims: 'Cover her face: mine eyes dazzle: she died young' [263]. I do not wish to rush in where angels fear to tread and endeavor to improve on this famous line. But I am obliged to point out that it is not 'merely' superb 'poetry'. It is strong because it is built into the construction of the play. Ferdinand has never known his sister, and only now, when he has murdered her, and she is lying dead at his feet, does reality strike him and he sees her for the first time. William Archer will have none of this line. He says: 'It is not difficult to hit upon sayings which shall pass for highly dramatic simply because they are unforeseen and unlikely.' It is curious that a famous critic who spent his life in writing about plays should know nothing about the construction of a play. Webster has taken infinite pains to lead us up to this line. He foresaw it and when it comes, we recognize it was inevitable that it should come. It is the climax of the play, the watershed, the dividing line.

Kathleen McLuskie, 1985

[Palgrave Macmillan: an extract from 'Drama and Sexual Politics: The Case of Webster's Duchess' published in *New Casebooks, The Duchess of Malfi: John Webster*, edited by Dympna Callaghan (2000)]

McLuskie is Professor of English at the University of Southampton. Her analysis of the language in this extract focuses on the play in the theatre.

Interspersed with these visual set pieces [such as the dumb show] which suggest one kind of interpretation for the play are the verbal set pieces, the long speeches, the meditations and sententiae which present another perspective on the action. In the pattern of Webster's dramaturgy they often provide the generalising explanation with which characters attempt to make sense of events. Taken out of context, they are often 'impressive', if conventional, expressions of received wisdom; but just as the visual set pieces can only present the bare dramatic event, so these speeches must be seen in relation to the dramatic structure of a particular scene. A long speech allows a character to dominate a scene or a situation and we find Webster using set speech to suggest a character's attempts to do this. For example, in [3.2] the commonplace sermonising of Ferdinand's speech on Reputation, Love and Death brings that hectic sequence to a more controlled close. ...Webster's dramatic method, with its constant comparison between what is said and what is shown, exposes the empty conventionality which informs Ferdinand's oppressive violence.

It is significant, as a result, that the Duchess almost never resorts to sententiae to explain or excuse her conduct. On the one occasion when she is given a formal set speech – the tale of the salmon and the dog-fish at the end of [3.5] – the dramatic function of the episode is as significant as the moral point of her little homily. She uses the speech to reassert her control over the hopeless situation; overcome by the physical strength of Bosola and his troop of armed soldiers, she asserts her psychological superiority by reminding both Bosola and the audience of her rank. Her clear insult to Bosola in implying that he is a mere dog-fish with temporary power over the more naturally aristocratic salmon –

herself and Antonio – is her last wry joke before the darkness of Act IV. It is also the beginning of that 'strange disdain' [4.1.12] with which she 'fortifies her melancholy' in Act IV and which so enrages Ferdinand.

This ability to convey the shifts of psychological dominance in a scene and to suggest a variety of points of view on the action gives Webster's dramaturgy its particular force and makes the formal devices of dumb show and set speech effective. The visual and verbal set pieces provide a firm structure for individual scenes and the play as a whole, carrying the plot and its ethical context. Around them Webster uses more flexible broken verse lines and passages of prose to suggest the dramatic tension which exists between different characters. The verbal sparring between Antonio and Bosola during their midnight encounter [2.3.10–51] is echoed most effectively in the uncompleted half lines. Webster gains a similar effect in the attempted seduction of Julia, the Cardinal's mistress in [2.4], while the opposite effect of complicity between two characters can be seen in the way the brothers complete one another's sentences [see 1.1.298–332] or in the verse of the 'loving palms' dialogue between Antonio and the Duchess [see 1.1.482–487].

These dramatic moments as much as their grand conclusions about the relations of man to the universe, make Webster's characters 'live' on the stage, make their relationships and their passions believable.

Performance

After the publication of the play in 1623 it remained popular and was reprinted three times by 1708. In 1635 it was one of the opening plays of the octagonal Cockpit-in-Court theatre in Whitehall Palace for Charles I. The stage was lit by twelve iron candelabra, with three others in the auditorium. After the reopening of the theatres in 1660, the first actress to play the Duchess was Mary Saunderson, who shortly afterwards married her Bosola: Thomas Betterton (he was acclaimed for his performance of Hamlet). She was also the first woman to play Lady Macbeth and Ophelia, and unlike most actresses of the time had a virtuous reputation. Samuel Pepys recorded in his Diary for 30 September 1662: 'To the Duke's playhouse, where we saw "The Duchess of Malfy" well performed, but Betterton and Ianthe [Mary Saunderson] to admiration. Strange to see how easily my mind do revert to its former practice of loving plays and wine.' The playhouse was in a converted indoor tennis court, with the innovation of movable perspective scenery.

The play was rarely performed in the eighteenth century, though there was an adaptation by the Shakespearean scholar Lewis Theobald at Covent Garden in 1733. He changed the title to *The Fatal Secret*, began the action after the marriage and 'improved' 4.2.263 to read: 'Cover her face; my eyes begin to dazzle.' Instead of killing the Duchess, Bosola substituted a wax effigy of her body to deceive Ferdinand. The Duchess, of course, is reunited with Antonio in the final scene! The next notable performance in London was over a hundred years later, with spectacular scenery and a text that was cut and made 'respectable'. In the 1850s to

Performance

1870s Mrs Emma Waller created a 'profound Sensation' as the Duchess on New York's Broadway and on tour, rising to heaven at the end of the play in 'a cloud of white muslin'.

After World War I there was a 'naturalistic' production at the Lyric Theatre, Hammersmith in 1919. A review in the *Spectator* commented:

> They left out the whole of the famous Dirge. They interrupted the rolling periods of the dying speeches made by each of the eight persons who are murdered on the stage, by realistic splutters and gurgles. They tried to individualize every 'item' in the massacre by each dying in a different attitude. Having exhausted every other possible posture, the Duke Ferdinand was reduced to expiring upside down, his head on the ground and his feet over the back of an armchair. All the actors, without exception, 'broke up' their lines till they were unrecognizable as blank verse.
>
> > *Duke Ferdinand (enters staggering, draws aside curtain, and sees corpse of Duchess).*
> > > Cover her face.
> > > (Bosola *does so with spare overcoat.* Duke *takes quick turn round stage.*)
> > > *Duke (to audience).* Mine eyes dazzle.
> > > (Duke *pulls up socks and tidies his hair.*)
> > > *Duke (to Bosola).* She died young –
>
> a rendering which annihilated one of the most wonderful blank-verse lines ever written. The fact is that it was a mistake to take the plot so seriously.

A particularly interesting aspect of the production is that the Duchess was played by the Irish actress Cathleen Nesbitt, who had been romantically involved with the poet Rupert Brooke – a pioneering critic of Webster – who had died four years before (see page 240).

In the twentieth century the play was revived more frequently than plays by any other of Shakespeare's contemporaries. Peggy Ashcroft, Judi Dench and Helen Mirren were notable Duchesses between 1945 and 1981, and today it is often the actress who is cast first. Several modern productions are discussed or referred to in this volume, and the following four interviews (by Monica Kendall) are with directors and actors who have worked on *The Duchess of Malfi* in London and on tour.

Interview with Philip Franks, Director, Greenwich/Wyndham's Theatres 1995, 24 April 2003

Duchess: Juliet Stevenson; Ferdinand: Simon Russell Beale; Bosola: Robert Glenister (see photographs on pages 20, 90 and 178)

How did you approach directing the play?

I wanted to see whether you could treat Webster not like a freak show; whether it was possible to find all that you would apply to Shakespeare or Chekhov in terms of naturalistic setting, background story, character depth. It was a way of scraping the candle wax off. The way Philip Prowse does Webster [e.g. National Theatre 1985: see photographs on pages 66 and 164] has set a precedent: it was all about darkness and skulls and high style demonstrating the corrupt world. That's fine if you are Philip Prowse because it's your idea, but in the same way that English poetry collapsed after Milton because everyone was trying to do Milton, I think that a lot of people doing Jacobeans have collapsed under the weight of Philip Prowse, because they try and do the same thing, and also because it feels fab to have white face make-up and a big black frock!

You can do it naturalistically up to a point – but then you've got Act 5.
Then it all comes apart, which is what we tried to do: the set took its initial frame of reference from long galleries in Jacobean houses, so there was a planked floor, a long wall of receding doors and on one side a huge billowing curtain that gave out to the sea, because I wanted Malfi to be a place of light and beauty – which you've never seen in a Webster. I'd only ever seen Webster in black and white and I wanted to see what impact colour would make. And also people wearing Jacobean clothes that looked like clothes not costumes, because a lot of the Jacobeans tend to get dressed as though they're carnival and I think that gives the game away, because yes they do tip into the city of dreadful night but they have to start from somewhere.

The Duchess at the beginning thinks she's going to get away with it. She thinks as soon as this horrible holiday is over – where my brothers are saying these dreadful things to me – they'll be gone and I can do what I damn well like. You've got to feel that could be true, and she has many happy years of marriage. I wanted the bedroom scene – where Ferdinand comes in and she is talking to herself in the mirror – to be an idyll disrupted rather than a charnel house from the word go. Her bedroom was gorgeous, they were all half naked in their night clothes, and then this door creaked open and there was Ferdinand in a black dressing gown – like pouring ink into a glass of water.

What happened in terms of the design was that the long wall of doors, as night fell on the play, split, broke up – it hinged forward to become the prison, so she was in a tiny prison cell which was all doors. And then in the final beat of the play, when it is all going horribly mad, the set just broke up into rather random chunks: bits of it leaned against the back wall, bits had fallen over, so it had no relation any more to the harmonious architectural principles of the beginning of the play – people came up through the floor, or slithered through windows, and it was lit almost entirely from floor level by the end – there were huge cast shadows. It became a mad world but it didn't start off as one.

Duchess and Antonio
The Duchess is lonely. She wants companionship, she wants love, and she finds it. Antonio is a fantastically interesting man with a very good notion of what political philosophy should be. When we meet Antonio, the first thing (it feels like an irrelevancy, which is why it's often cut) is Delio asking: 'How do you like the French court?', and Antonio says: I thought it was terrific because it's led well from the top, the French king has worked out a way of weeding out corruption, and so should everybody. – And maybe that is something, as well as being physically attractive,

that the Duchess finds interesting about this man – he's got a positive philosophical bent for improvement.

Cardinal and Ferdinand
The Cardinal is an entirely cynical, secular creature – until his wonderful moment of terror at the end: 'I see a thing armed with a rake...' [5.5.6–7]. It's lying heavily on his mind; like Lady Macbeth his mind is cracking under pressure. If Bosola hadn't killed him, the Cardinal would undoubtedly have gone mad because it runs in the family.

There's such sensuality in Ferdinand's horror: 'Happily with some strong-thighed bargeman' [2.5.42] – the whole frame of his language is profoundly sexual, and even when he's talking about other women it's all about controlling them in quasi-sexual ways [see 1.1.141–143]. Ferdinand has deep sexual problems. Webster is not shy about sex: the Duchess's sexual relationship with Antonio is wonderful, loving and warm, and they have a lot of children – they don't have children in Shakespeare. Heartbreakingly her last thoughts are of them – 'look thou giv'st my little boy / Some syrup for his cold...' [4.2.203–205] – I'd defy anyone to hear that without crying.

Is Bosola sincere about Antonio in 3.2?
No, he's playing the game and he's obsessed with finding out. He's like one of those compromised detectives in contemporary detective fiction – to find out is everything, whether or not you ought to, and what you're going to do with the information becomes irrelevant in the chase. This scene [3.2] is his big final throw: if he's wrong he could lose everything. But he turns out to be right, and he's *so* excited. What I wanted from Bosola was an intellectual laser beam who's twisted up on himself, and then later on he becomes an avenging angel, a revenge hero. But with this terrible pain that most of what he's trying to avenge he himself has caused.

When does Bosola change and when does he disguise himself?
'Off, my painted honour' [4.2.335] – that's the final change. I had Bosola in disguise from 'I am your adventure' [3.5.95]. He was hooded and dressed like a monk. But when the Duchess was about to die she pulled his hood back and looked him in the eye, basically saying: I know exactly who you are – which gave him the most terrible shock. He couldn't meet her gaze. It was like an insect being pinned on a board.

The madmen (4.2)
I gave the text to the madmen and asked each of them to find one bit and say it over and over again at the same time as the others. They were behind a grilled door, just reaching in – a bit like Glenda Jackson in *The Music Lovers* [Ken Russell film on Tchaikovsky, 1971]: it was just hands. The executioners were in black, with black fencing masks, and all the doors on the set slammed open – because 'death have ten thousand several doors / For men to take their exits' [4.2.218–219].

How did you direct Delio's final speech (5.5.109–121)?
Delio was clearly going to be the one in charge. It wasn't 'I will poison him when he reaches the age of 16', it was more like: Cometh the hour, cometh the man. – I had him saying the moral statement: 'Integrity of life is fame's best friend, / Which nobly, beyond death, shall crown the end' in a kind of – And that's what I think and I'm now the one that you must listen to – and then I had the ghost of the Duchess wandering

on, surveying the carnage with a hopelessness as though she is going to be forever by herself – that there is no neat joining up of things after death. So the final thing you were left with was a figure picking over the battlefield.

Interview with Phyllida Lloyd, Director, National Theatre 2003, 9 May 2003

Duchess: Janet McTeer; Ferdinand: Will Keen; Bosola: Lorcan Cranitch (see photographs on pages 1, 48, 92, 124, 134, 144, 170, 184 and 222)

What were the reasons for the modern dress and the non-specific setting?
I felt that little was to be gained by a minute reconstruction of the Jacobean world that Webster was writing in, and even less by a reconstruction of the period that these historical events took place in. I was conscious that this, to a Jacobean audience, was a real story. For them it would have been like watching an historical incident from a hundred years ago being performed in modern costume, and therefore would have felt very immediate. I didn't want to put barriers between the modern audience and a play that I saw as startlingly contemporary in its depiction of dynastic power battles. I read a book about the Gucci family, and the subtitle was: 'a tale of murder, madness, glamour and greed' – here was a modern semi-aristocratic Italian dynasty that was so desperate to keep power in the hands of the family that they were prepared to stop at nothing to achieve that.

Your production started with 'Who took the ring oft'nest' (1.1.90), and gave Delio Antonio's lines.
I knew that some might feel unsettled that the evening didn't begin with the line they thought it was going to. That's part of the disturbance that one's trying to create. The disturbance is there anyway for anyone who hasn't seen the play: it's the thrill of a new story; and for those who've seen it umpteen times there's a disturbance that it's not quite as you remembered it. We swapped Delio and Antonio for that first speech [1.1.1–4] because I felt it was helpful to the audience to believe that Antonio had been in the Duchess's household for some time before the play begins. If he literally has just got off a boat from a foreign country then what is the nature of their relationship? And it seemed that Delio was this more ambiguous outsider figure who kept coming back. We imagined he was some kind of journalist and built his whole persona on the fact that he was outside the action.

Delio is an ambiguous character – what is his tone at the end of the play?
We began with that final sequence [5.5.109–121] a lot more edgily, a lot more that somehow Delio was going to be the power behind the throne and he was going to force this child into this position, even though one assumes that Delio would know that Antonio's heartfelt wish was that his children fly the courts of princes. So surely Delio is going absolutely against Antonio's hopes for his child, and that doesn't seem to suggest a lot of integrity. Then you really look at the text and you feel that 'Integrity of life is fame's best friend' is such a powerful, potent line which suggests that some cleansing of the corrupt world is about to take place.

Performance

What was your approach to Bosola?

In some way he is the most interesting character in the play, which could quite easily be subtitled 'Bosola's redemption', though I don't know whether he is redeemed by the end of the play or not. What's difficult about taking the play out of the period and trying to build a world for it now is this whole culture of dependency that they are in: that unless you were attached to a great house you were literally in the gutter. It is like the Mafia: we did watch very closely all the *Godfather* films, one of which starts with Al Pacino telling his sister that she will not be marrying this man, and there's no question of her defying his wishes – and that's the twentieth century.

That scene in Act 3 scene 2 is fantastically ambiguous as to what he feels about Antonio. We've rehearsed it in many ways: as if he really believes what he's saying about Antonio, and then just saying it to try to soften up the Duchess. When we did that I think Janet just felt: I don't believe a word of this. So it seemed to release the scene more truly if Bosola is being gradually transformed by his contact with the Duchess and Antonio. Maybe that's why he takes so long to find out what's going on between them – because he doesn't want to find out.

There's a great sense of competition between Antonio and Bosola at the beginning: who's got promotion and who deserves it, who's getting above themselves. But it's important that something that Antonio and the Duchess are doing in creating this domestic harmony is like a light in the middle of this hellish, festering world of intrigue and disease. We deliberately set out not to paint Bosola as the villain of the piece, but more in the tradition of the hired killer in a western who is fundamentally a good person; the real corruption is in Ferdinand and the Cardinal; Bosola is very much a victim of their power.

What was the thinking behind the glass screen and steps?

What seemed fundamental was this sense of spying, eavesdropping, voyeurism, that people were listening to each other. The only moment when the characters aren't being spied upon is when we turn out all the lights [4.1]. So we had the screen, which was also a window, and the thing behind which everybody is listening. It's also used to project icons: it's portrait shaped, so that when you see the Cardinal, Ferdinand or the Duchess projected on to it [in 1.1 when Antonio describes each of them to Delio] you are looking at them like photographs. And the steps were there to further amplify this sense of being watched – the contrast between the public and private worlds of the play, which is so central to it – the Duchess has this public role to play, but her private world is very different, and yet even in the private scenes there are people sitting watching on the bleachers [steps], observing it.

Everyone who was killed stood up to say their last lines to the audience. How did that come about?

In rehearsal in Act 5 there was a point when everybody was lying on the ground groaning, like something out of *The Good, the Bad and the Ugly*! I wanted to find a way of hearing these lines. So I said: I can't solve this, we're going to do a workshop. You've got to separate your body and your soul. Your soul has got to end up on the bleachers, and your body can remain lying down here on the stage. In the workshop when the Cardinal died he suddenly stood up and became this Zen master – his whole body was free of any stress and pain, he had gone through some door into the next world. They were all looking at death as a release from this world. The Duchess stands up at the end of Act 4 and just looks up and says 'Mercy' – that was to establish that device. It was to allow those self-revelations at the point of death, to throw them into relief, so you could hear what people were thinking.

Ferdinand
From that very opening scene of Ferdinand and the court, there's clearly something unbalanced about him, maybe he is manic depressive, maybe he's had breakdowns – you get the feeling that when the letter comes [2.5] that isn't the first time the Cardinal's seen Ferdinand lose the plot. He says: Thou hast killed 'my dearest friend' [4.2.279] – he regards her as the most important thing in his life. After the bedroom scene he is clearly in a terrible state, and he's trying to close the gap between the two of them and put her in the same place as him, which I think is a very twin-like instinct – to not let the gap between them widen, so that by reducing her to madness, despair, they can become one entity.

Why did you replace the scene with the madmen (4.2) with a video of what was in the Duchess's mind?
I decided that I was not going to use the text because our relationship to insanity has changed so massively since the seventeenth century. The astrologer, the lawyer, the doctor – it just seemed so much local colour of 1613: local London loonies. I didn't see what it was going to achieve in this titanic battle the Duchess is having to hold on to herself. The company worked to develop their own 'mad person within themselves', and then after weeks of work we unleashed this group on Janet, but she was quite at ease with all these people on the edge of sanity. She felt that she had just seen her husband and child dead, there was little you could do to her that was going to be worse. And that's where the idea of the video came from, which was to explore what might be in her head. That video is a sensual assault in terms of loud noise and changes of gear. We were looking at what might be her fears – her nightmares of her brother assaulting her, incestuous feelings, fears for her other children – that's something that Webster doesn't help with – there are still two children alive, in prison.

I had always been very attracted by the Duchess. In some way she's the mirror for all the other characters. You could say that she is comparatively passive. She makes one step; she acts once. But she's the provocation; she's the thing that is aggravating, exciting, frightening everyone around her. There must be parallels with the role played by Diana, Princess of Wales. In some way that Ferdinand line: 'You were too much i'th'light' [4.1.41] always makes me think of Diana when I hear that – full of power and privilege, but in some way a victim of her fate.

Interview with Lorcan Cranitch, Bosola, National Theatre 2003, 21 May 2003

When does Bosola change?
The seeds of it are sown when the Duchess has been put into prison, and he sees the effect that this has on her. And that rather sick joke about Antonio and the son:

the stupidity of that, the abhorrence of what's happening, starts to sink in on him – this is not what he signed up to do. He's done the job. He's found out who her husband is. But he is under Ferdinand's thumb because of Ferdinand's power – he could just disappear but then he'd be back to square one again.

I don't think he really changes until the very end of 4.2 – when he lays the dead Duchess down and says: 'I'll bear thee hence / And execute thy last will' and 'somewhat I will speedily enact worth my dejection'. That's the point. I don't think it's any sooner than that. There's something that he can do because his own future is in such jeopardy: as far as Ferdinand is concerned the murder never took place – so what now, where does that leave him? Bosola has the guilt on his conscience of having killed these people, and Ferdinand then washes his hands of the whole thing and leaves Bosola to fend for himself. So Bosola really has very little to lose at that point.

He did seven years' hard labour, but we don't know the exact circumstance of it. Theoretically, for argument's sake, there was a murder. The Cardinal says, 'Don't worry, I'll sort you out', and it backfired and the result was that Bosola ended up doing seven years. The first thing I would want to do, if it had happened to me, would *not* be to go back to the person whose fault it was and say 'Give me another job' – it would be to get some kind of revenge for the seven years that they had taken away. But we see Bosola being reliant on these people and wonder why, and the only answer is – if you have no position in that society you're absolutely desperate.

Then the next question is, why does he initially refuse Ferdinand's offer of doing something which is basically detective work and which is not going to cost him an awful lot [1.1.269–272]? It certainly isn't going to get him into any trouble, in the way that murder is. It's only after he gets a position of the provisorship of the horse that he says, yes, I'll do it, albeit reluctantly. At the end of the play he says he was 'an actor in the main of all, / Much 'gainst mine own good nature' [5.5.85–86]. He didn't want to do any of this. Nevertheless he takes the job. And I've always got the impression that he'd much prefer to be doing something that he's good at, which is killing people. He's a professional assassin. – Ask me to kill somebody and I'll do it. Don't ask me to spy on anyone or sneak around like a thief in the night, that's a far more demeaning profession than mercenary killing.

In the bedroom scene [3.2], when the Duchess asks him about the officers who gave their opinions on Antonio, he says: 'these are rogues that, in's prosperity, / But to have waited on his fortune... / Would have... / Made their first born intelligencers'. So an intelligencer is the worst. And shortly afterwards he tells the audience about 'this base quality / Of intelligencer...every quality i'th'world / Prefers but gain or commendation'. He means: I have to tell Ferdinand all about this, and I'll tell you this much: every one of us in this room would do exactly the same thing given enough money.

In the bedroom scene (3.2), is Bosola being sincere or playing a game?

That is one of the trickiest areas. I think he's playing the long game. He goes to her bedroom and tells her that Ferdinand said, 'You were undone.' He is told that Antonio has basically stolen money from the coffers. And she says, 'Call up our officers.' And so, within minutes, they come back in – and Antonio is in the room! What the hell is Antonio doing in the room?! There's something afoot here. Then she in no uncertain terms throws Antonio out – and this is the man who had been 'chief man with the Duchess' for some years now. And she asks everybody else's opinion about Antonio. What does she need to hear? That she did the right thing? And if they all say you were dead right to get rid of him – good. She can slip off and nobody will smell a rat. But then she asks Bosola, 'What do you think of these?' And he backfires on the thing, but I think he deliberately does that. I'm not sure that he knows what's going to happen.

Does Bosola believe some of what he's saying in 3.2?
He does believe some of it. But what he says is such a glowing report, it is so over the top. He's no great friend of Antonio at this point. He's a sparring partner as far as their position at court is concerned. He knows him – they have had their locker-room banters – so he does have some opinion about him, but he certainly doesn't admire him as much as he says he does.

In 2.3 Antonio said: 'You gave the Duchess apricots today, / Pray heaven they were not poisoned' and he falsely accuses Bosola of stealing the jewels. The next time we see them on stage together is when Antonio is being sacked. So the last thing that Bosola says to Antonio is 'you're a false steward'; the next time we hear Bosola talk about Antonio is to the Duchess as being 'a trophy of a man, his breast was filled with all perfection'. So what is he really saying? This is where I think it's a gamble on Bosola's part to see what she says. What he really thinks of him and what he says of him are different things.

When he says to her 'Do I not dream? Can this ambitious age / Have so much goodness in't as to prefer / A man merely for worth, without these shadows / Of wealth and painted honours?' [3.2.273–276] – who is he talking about? I think that in some way he is talking about himself. Because what she says is – he's my husband. And in Bosola's head it's: Jackpot! And so his reply to her is not necessarily: What a wonderful thing you've done; in his own head he's thinking: Oh my God, I have just hit the jackpot! – Can this ambitious age that we're living in have so much goodness in it as to prefer a man merely for worth – which is *my* worth!

When Bosola is disguised varies in productions – you are not disguised until after you say 'Never in mine own shape' (4.1.130).
I think it's stretching credibility to a strange point in a modern production if he's disguised earlier. And it also helps if he has to look her straight in the eye and say: Yes, I'm the one. He says 'from the Lord Ferdinand...All love, and safety' [3.5.22–23] and there's a broken line – he can't continue because she looks at him; she says: You are the bastard who – 'Thou dost blanch mischief.' It's more helpful than to try and disguise him from her and not from the audience.

What happens to Bosola in Act 5?
Bosola has nothing to lose now; he has a motive and he has the passion to do it. In the first scene that Bosola has in Act 5 [5.2], the Cardinal feigns ignorance of the Duchess's death, which astonishes Bosola. And within ten seconds the Cardinal has employed him to kill Antonio [5.2.125–126]. But why does he then enlist the help of Julia to find out whether the Cardinal is telling the truth or not [5.2.201–203]? And when the Cardinal kills Julia under his nose, why doesn't Bosola take out a knife and

stab him then and there? It's like Hamlet – indecision. He does kill him ten minutes later, but what proof does he need?! Antonio wasn't his number one pal, but it's Antonio's death that says – I've had enough of this. But the person who killed Antonio was Bosola himself!

Perhaps Webster is saying: revenge tragedy is not neat?
No, it's not neat: 'We are merely the stars' tennis balls...' [5.4.54] is wonderful. There are so many contradictions. The director Max Stafford-Clark said: 'Play the contradictions'. All I've just said to you may be completely and utterly wrong but at the moment it's right for me. If it makes sense for other people then that's fine.

Interview with Will Keen, Ferdinand, National Theatre 2003, 16 June 2003

We imagined that the Duchess had been married to a man who's a lot older than her and who therefore wasn't in any way a sexual threat, so Ferdinand had never had to consider his sister as a sexual object. It was a thing I deliberated about a lot – but I didn't imagine him being conscious of sexual feelings towards his sister until he starts to become aware of it in the mandrake scene [2.5]. There's something about the power of the emotions that takes hold of him in that scene that frightens him. Then crucially in the bedroom scene [3.2] he finds out that she's actually married – she's having a sexual relationship which means something to her. Janet McTeer and I were keen to stress how incredibly close Ferdinand and the Duchess are at the beginning. The Cardinal is the cold, distant one, and in a way these two have to have a relationship which has been very close – they are twins, they have grown up together, and she's never had a man in her life who has threatened Ferdinand.

We tried the first scene [1.1] several different ways in rehearsal. He's allowed to hide behind the shield of his religious brother and I think that he's laughing at him, but he bonds with his sister, he makes jokes with her, he enjoys her humour and he says: Yes, be careful, because brother will get angry. So although he does end up revealing himself as pretty obsessive, he thinks that he's toeing his brother's line. For instance there's that odd bit where the Cardinal starts off with: 'We are to part from you, and your own discretion / Must now be your director' [1.1.298–299] in a rather formal, sermonising way. Ferdinand cuts in: 'You are a widow: / You know already what man is' – it's much more direct, much more jokey, much more affectionate. And they start interrupting each other and picking up each other's sentences, and I suspect when Ferdinand says: 'Marry? They are most luxurious / Will wed twice' he is again deflating the Cardinal's sermonising. And when the Cardinal says: 'O fie!' I think he's getting slightly irritated with Ferdinand.

Ferdinand doesn't want her to marry again, and it doesn't occur to him that she would. He takes out his father's dagger [1.1.335] purely as an example of something which belonged to their parents; and they're also bonded because I assume their parents are dead. But he's unaware that it's also a clear phallic symbol; that's something which the audience hears but he doesn't; he doesn't know what he's talking about.

What is he intending to do in the bedroom scene in Act 3?

He knows himself better at the end than he does at the beginning of the play. A lot of what he does until that point are instinctive, knee-jerk things, without knowing why he's doing them. On deep Freudian levels he wants to see her in her bedroom, he wants to be in the presence of her bed, where he assumes she's had sex. Although I don't think he's aware of that when he's planning to do it. Bosola says [3.1.82–83]: 'What do you intend to do?' He says: 'Can you guess?…Do not ask then.' He doesn't know. He's completely devoured by emotion. He's a child. He's unable to control his emotions and he's just impelled into the room, to busk it. But once he's in – if we put him on the spot he would probably say: I'm going to find out who the man is and kill him. There are so many inconsistencies in the play – not guessing that it's Antonio, and Bosola spending such a long time being such a bad spy! – which you have to forget, because what Webster's painting is an emotional picture; everything's filtered through an emotional lens. So what is his intention? He doesn't know what his intention is.

Suddenly he loses self-control on the bed and he's on top of her.

I said 'So you have some virgins / That are witches' [3.2.139–140], then I lost control. Ferdinand thinks this is the last time he'll see her. I went towards her with the gun and took her back on the bed, and rather than shooting her, kissed her and wanted to possess her – and then he realises it's a sexual thing, which sends him out with a stronger desire: 'I will never see thee more' [140] – 'thee' being more intimate than 'you'.

What do you think of the reputation speech (3.2.119–135)?

It's terribly truthful, though it sticks out like a sore thumb. It's no coincidence that he uses a story to her at the key moment and she uses a story to him – she sends a story back with Bosola [3.5]. I suspect it's to do with their childhood – that as twins they had games of telling each other stories so it's to do with specific vengeance, it's using the tool that you used as seven-year-olds together to punish, it's emotional manipulation and a real full stop to the whole of their relationship after that. The reputation speech is a punishment – Since you don't understand, I'll tell you a children's story. And I'll say this as simply as I possibly can because I need to regain control.

Why does he say before the bedroom scene 'I am to bespeak / A husband for you' (3.1.39–40)?

Phyllida [the director] was interested in the interplay between private and public, and here Ferdinand is forcing her to talk about marriage in a public place in front of a lot of people so that he can see how she reacts. On the other hand there could be just a very simple, practical thing, which is that since he knows she's had a child (because Bosola has told him) he could be saying: Right, we're going to marry you off. The Cardinal says at the beginning: You're never to marry anyone we haven't approved of. Ferdinand says: You're never to marry. [1.1.298–332] Crucial. But he now [3.1] is saying: Right, this is an embarrassment to the family – though not directly to her. I think he's definitely testing her to see how she reacts – whether she will panic and run, but she is well versed in the whole public/private thing. She plays it beautifully.

What is happening to Ferdinand in the mandrake scene (2.5)?

I suspect he's very drunk. He has this classic substance-abuser profile from the start, but having heard the bombshell that's been dropped on him he's probably gone to his room, smashed up the furniture and sat down with a bottle of whisky. I didn't play it like that but the equivalent is going on. It's one of those difficult parts since you see little of him as a normal man. I suspect as a normal man – such as in Act 1 – he's completely in control. He's very good at life – a winner, though he's one of those sexist, bullying winners who will never let the mask drop but in this play the one thing that would allow the mask to drop happens.

I got interested in the specific psychological state of lycanthropy – there's a good case study by Freud called The Wolf Man. At the end of Act 2 and beginning of Act 3 there are references to the fact that Ferdinand sleeps all the time. He's obsessed by it. It's a classic depressive thing – you just spend all the time exhausted by everything. So he's giving this impression of being completely awake but sleeping sixteen hours a night: it's weird to say at the end of that scene: 'I'll go sleep' [2.5.76]. There he is going off like a fire-cracker and he says: I know, I'll go and have a kip! And next time you see him it's: 'The Lord Ferdinand / Is going to bed' and he says: 'I'll instantly to bed, / For I am weary' [3.1.37–39] – having just arrived. It's a weird way to enter a scene!

What is he doing in Act 4 when he has put his sister in prison?

I don't think he knows. If you imagine her in an electric chair and him on a dial turning up the number of volts, the moments that he turns up the volts are the moments when Bosola gives him the information that she still loves Antonio, forcing Ferdinand to imagine their sexual relationship and her indifference to himself. When people talk about the madness of Ferdinand, it's *before* she's dead that he's at his maddest [in 4.1]; that's when he's lost control. And I think that after she's dead, the horror of realising what he's done – that he's killed his dearest friend and he's killed the thing that he loves, he's killed a bit of himself – that actually makes him saner than he's been for the last five years. But it's just too huge a thing to deal with.

And then he's the wolf and tries to throttle his shadow (5.2).

The shadow in 5.2 is him, or the shadow is Bosola, or the shadow's the Cardinal. I would change it night by night. In a way it's the Duchess because it's whatever is saying to him: you did it to me, or you made me do it. There are case studies of people who believe that they become animals, particularly in primitive cultures, and their animal side is an embodiment of their greatest fear – it's to do with having a fear so enormous within yourself that you have to externalise it into something. And it's so huge what Ferdinand's done that he needs to make a complete split. He can feel this thing inside him – that brilliant line the doctor says about having hairs on the inside [5.2.17–18] – it's an incredibly physical impression.

Act 5 is about Ferdinand fighting against that, not allowing the wolf to come out. If you take a mental leap that Ferdinand really believes there's a wolf inside him then the interesting thing about it is the extent to which he tries to fight, tries to push it down, that he doesn't want the shadow to follow him. So all of that scene [5.2] is about: Don't push me to a point where the wolf will come out. What he wants is patience – what he's always lacked – he wants to be able 'To drive six snails...to Moscow' without whip or goad [5.2.47–48], he just wants to be a normal person without this thing inside.

He knows that he has to kill Bosola, the Cardinal and himself – because it's to do with killing the wolf inside. I don't think that's just a moment of red rage [5.5.45 onwards], I think that's absolutely logical that he needs to kill Bosola as part of himself.

The Duchess of Malfi on video

A video recording of the 1995–6 Cheek by Jowl theatre production is in the National Video Archive at the Theatre Museum, Russell Street, London WC2. Appointments can be made by individuals or school groups to see the video at the Museum: 020 7943 4806 (educational groups) or 020 7943 4727 (individuals); website: http://theatremuseum.vam.ac.uk.

The plot of *The Duchess of Malfi*

The play begins at the court of the Duchy of Malfi, near Naples, in the early sixteenth century. The young Duchess has recently been widowed. Her twin brother Ferdinand, the Duke of Calabria, and their elder brother the Cardinal have been staying with her and are about to return to Rome. The new master of her household, Antonio, and his friend Delio watch as Bosola, the court 'malcontent', accosts the Cardinal. Bosola has served seven years in the galleys for a murder and is looking for a reward, but the Cardinal ignores him. Antonio describes to Delio the unsavoury characters of the brothers and his admiration for the Duchess. The Cardinal advises Ferdinand to employ Bosola as a spy in the Duchess's household, and Bosola is given the office of provisor of horse. The brothers warn the Duchess against marrying again, but, once they have gone, the Duchess ignores their threats and woos Antonio. They marry secretly, witnessed only by Cariola, her waiting woman.

In Act 2, about nine months later, Bosola suspects the Duchess is pregnant and tricks her into eating apricots, which cause her to give birth prematurely to a son. Bosola finds this out by accident and informs her brothers by letter. Ferdinand is insane with anger, but the brothers decide to wait until Bosola can find out who the father is. Meanwhile Julia, the wife of an old courtier at the Duchess's court, goes to Rome to be the Cardinal's mistress. Act 3 takes place a few years later. The Duchess has had two more children in secret and Bosola has still not discovered the identity of her lover. Ferdinand visits her court and confronts his sister in her bedroom. She tells him she is married. Furious, Ferdinand rides straight back to Rome. The Duchess fears for the safety of her family and pretends to dismiss Antonio from her service. Bosola praises Antonio, and the Duchess reveals to him that Antonio is her husband and that she is planning to flee Malfi to join him. Bosola advises her to pretend she is on a pilgrimage, but informs Ferdinand, who organises an ambush to capture her. Antonio and the elder boy, however, escape.

In Act 4 the Duchess, the two younger children and Cariola are in prison. Ferdinand mentally tortures her by displaying the supposed dead bodies of her husband and children. On Ferdinand's orders, Bosola has her strangled, along with the children and Cariola. Ferdinand shows signs of madness and gives Bosola a pardon for the murders instead of the reward he asks for. Bosola is filled with remorse and resolves to find Antonio in Milan. Act 5 is set in Milan, a short time later. Antonio, not knowing his wife is dead, plans to seek reconciliation with the brothers. Ferdinand is now fully deranged. The Cardinal pretends to Bosola that the Duchess is still alive and tells Bosola to find Antonio and kill him. Julia declares her love for Bosola and she agrees to find out what is troubling the Cardinal. The Cardinal confesses to Julia that he ordered the murder of his sister, and then poisons Julia, witnessed by Bosola. Antonio is on his way to confront the Cardinal when he hears an echo that seems to have his wife's voice. Bosola kills Antonio accidentally, then wounds the Cardinal. As they struggle, Ferdinand stabs both of them, and Bosola kills Ferdinand. Delio arrives with the eldest son of the Duchess and Antonio and sums up the moral of the play.

Themes

In order to establish Webster's themes in *The Duchess*, critics study the images and repeated words (e.g. animals, witches, storm and tempest, blood, fortune), the *sententiae*, the characters and their philosophic utterances, the action and structure, and compare the play to others. Critics, and directors, will have different opinions about the themes they see as important in *The Duchess*. For example, feminists may see the status of women as central. One editor of the play (Elizabeth Brennan in 1964) believed that the idea of confinement was dominant, and she also emphasised the play's contrasts between light and darkness; health and sickness; sanity and insanity. The critic Ralph Berry (1972) believed that the play's main concern was the resolution of the tension between human evil (including disease, appearance and reality, and 'great men') and the Law (including justice, revenge and reward). Other main ideas in the play that critics have commented on include: blood and virtue; power and religion; private and public life; and a struggle between scepticism and a religious conception of human life. The three themes below are what many recent critics have seen as Webster's main concerns.

True fame or worldly greatness
In death, the 'great' Cardinal ends in 'a little point, a kind of nothing' (5.5.79); the dying Antonio compares 'our quest of greatness' to a child blowing bubbles (5.4.64–66); when she is about to be killed, the great Duchess of Malfi is told she is merely 'a box of worm-seed' (4.2.122). In the face of death, the major debate of the play is: What is true greatness rather than simply worldly greatness? What will lead to true, everlasting fame? See, for example, 1.1.314; 1.1.463–465 and 468; 2.1.107–121; 3.2.119–135; 3.2.255–257; 3.2.277–295; 3.4.7–22; 3.5.113–137; 4.2.231–233; 5.1.72. The last speech of the play appears to sum up Webster's

message, that 'wretched eminent things' leave no fame behind them, whereas 'fame's best friend' is 'Integrity of life', but see the notes to 5.5.120–121.

Appearance and reality

'Appearances [in this play] deceive in many ways. They prevent us from seeing the good as well as the evil' (Hereward T Price, from his article 'The Function of Imagery in Webster', 1955). See, for example, 1.1.162–164; 1.1.177–178; 1.1.230–233; 2.5.62–63. People are said to pretend to sleep but are actually listening intently (1.1.182–183 and 288–291). Bosola's 'melancholy' is seen as an affectation (1.1.284–286; 2.1.95–98); he is accused of counterfeiting (3.5.97 and 114); but in Act 4 he deliberately puts on disguises. The Duchess is warned to avoid hypocrisy (1.1.312–321) but leaves 'the path / Of simple virtue' (1.1.450–451). Bosola misunderstands her (2.3.77–78) as does Ferdinand (3.2.71–72). Hereward T Price comments on lines 71–72: 'Webster twists the idea of appearance and reality to show that Ferdinand...cannot recognize virtue when it stands before him in its most beautiful form'; and he says about 3.3.63–65: 'Ferdinand sees her whiteness and imagines it is evil. He cannot see the reality and he misjudges the appearance.' But having lied about her marriage, the Duchess has to pretend to accuse Antonio of a 'feigned crime' (3.2.176–179) and feigns a pilgrimage (3.2.304), just as Julia the 'strumpet' does (2.4.3–5).

In 4.1 Ferdinand's hand turns out to be a dead man's hand, while the dead bodies of Antonio and the children turn out to be wax models. In Act 5 the Cardinal says he might pretend to 'feign myself in danger' (5.4.13–16), so when the danger is real, his followers do not believe his real cries for help (5.5.18–31). There are references to deceit by tradesmen and tyrants (1.1.436–438 and 447–448); by hiding the rotten body with rich clothes (2.1.65–67); spying or eavesdropping (e.g. 1.1.361–362); and 'poisoned pills' are disguised within 'gold and sugar' (4.1.19–20). There are images of painting to create a false appearance (3.2.276; 4.2.335; 5.2.294–295), which is like make-up (see note on the Old Lady, page 40); and glow-worms, like great people, don't actually give off heat or light (4.2.143–144). There are frequent references to masques and masks, visors and disguises (e.g. 2.3.77–78; 3.2.157–158), as well as acting and the theatre – some of which seem intended deliberately to jolt the audience into an awareness that they are watching a play: it's not real (e.g. 1.1.333–334; 3.1.8–11; 4.1.81–82; 4.2.287–289; 5.5.95–96).

Love and death

The critic Michael Neill (1997) argues that, at its core, Renaissance tragic drama is about 'the discovery of death'. He believes that plague threatened a breakdown in social order because it threatened to 'make nobody of everybody'. Webster added four more deaths to the story: Julia, Ferdinand, the Cardinal and Bosola; and he has the Duchess die twice. Poison, death and, above all, diseases are frequently referred to or used as images in the play, but what is particularly central to Webster's work is what the critic Charles Forker calls 'the ironic juxtaposition of love with death', for example in the wooing scene (e.g. see note to 1.1.380, 393); in Ferdinand's story of Reputation, Love and Death (3.2.122–135); the Duchess's execution written like a wedding masque (e.g. see note on Performance on page 144); and Julia's wooing of Bosola in Act 5, especially 5.2.161–162.

Further reading

The text of *The Duchess of Malfi* is available online courtesy of the University of Oregon at http://darkwing.uoregon.edu/%7Erbear/ren.htm. The latest scholarly edition (in old spelling) is a hardback, *The Works of John Webster*, vol. 1 (eds D Gunby, D Carnegie, A Hammond and D DelVecchio) (Cambridge University Press, 1995).

R V Holdsworth, ed., *Webster:* The White Devil *and* The Duchess of Malfi (Casebook series, Macmillan, 1975) has reviews of some productions 1919–71, and extracts by literary critics, including some quoted in this Longman book: Archer, Berry, Brooke, Calderwood, Frye, Lamb, Lucas, Theobald and Tynan.

J W Lever, *The Tragedy of State: A Study of Jacobean Drama* (Methuen, 1971) looks at the play against the background of political corruption and sees its main concern as one of power.

Jacqueline Pearson, *Tragedy and Tragicomedy in the Plays of John Webster* (Manchester University Press, 1980) argues that 'Webster's dramatic interests are in the incoherences of real life'.

There is a summary of Webster's life and cultural influences, and a perhaps 'old-fashioned' view of the Duchess, by Muriel Bradbrook: *John Webster: Citizen and Dramatist* (Weidenfeld and Nicolson, 1980).

Lee Bliss, *The World's Perspective: John Webster and the Jacobean Drama* (Rutgers University Press, 1983) has a useful chapter on *The Duchess*.

The main text on his life and works is: Charles R Forker, *Skull beneath the Skin: The Achievement of John Webster* (Southern Illinois University Press, 1986).

Martin Wiggins, *Journeymen in Murder: The Assassin in English Renaissance Drama* (Clarendon Press, 1991) has an interesting chapter on Webster's hired killers – including Bosola.

Michael Neill, *Issues of Death: Mortality and Identity in English Renaissance Tragedy* (Clarendon Press, 1997) is a fascinating book about death in the tragedies of Webster, Shakespeare and others, and about the different ways it was seen in this time of change, influenced by Protestantism and plague. Chapter 10 concentrates on '"Fame's best friend": The Endings of *The Duchess of Malfi*'.

Martin White, *Renaissance Drama in Action: An Introduction to Aspects of Theatre Practice and Performance* (Routledge, 1998) includes a fascinating account by Harriet Walter about playing the Duchess.

Dympna Callaghan, ed., *The Duchess of Malfi* (New Casebooks series, Macmillan, 2000) is a collection of essays, written 1985–93, which look at politics and sexuality in Jacobean society. This Longman book has quotations from the essays by Callaghan, Coddon, Desmet, Henderson, Jankowski, Rose, Wells, Whigham and White, who has a longer extract in the section on Criticism (above), as does McLuskie. Professor Whigham's longer extract in Criticism is a revised version of his essay in the Casebooks series.